Gender, Agency and

People's engagement with change is mediated by social and cultural factors that shape their experience and inform their identities. In this edited volume gender provides the main focus for exploring the processes through which the construction and performance of identity and agency take place. The chapters show that agency is complex, and is often expressed in contradictory ways, for example in strategies of accommodation and adaptation that can nevertheless generate new institutional arrangements. Alternatively, there may be an outright rejection of these processes while incorporating specific elements associated with them. The cases examined in this volume explore the ways in which different subjects engage in the reformulation of spaces, roles and identities, redefining the boundaries between, and the content of, the 'public' and the 'private'. The examples also provide an account of how gendered discourses are deployed to convey new meanings, a new sense of place and time, confirming or challenging ideas of 'tradition' and 'modernity'.

This collection will be of particular interest to students of anthropology and gender studies.

Victoria Ana Goddard was born in Argentina and trained as an anthropologist at University College, London. She is currently a lecturer in Anthropology at Goldsmiths College, London.

European Association of Social Anthropologists

Series facilitator: Jon P. Mitchell
University of Sussex

The European Association of Social Anthropologists (EASA) was inaugurated in January 1989, in response to a widely felt need for a professional association which would represent social anthropologists in Europe and foster cooperation and interchange in teaching and research. As Europe transforms itself in the 1990s, the EASA is dedicated to the renewal of the distinctive European tradition in social anthropology.

Gender, Agency and Change

Anthropological Perspectives

Edited by Victoria Ana Goddard

London and New York

First published 2000
by Routledge
11 New Fetter Lane, London EC4P 4EE

Simultaneously published in the USA and Canada
by Routledge
29 West 35th Street, New York, NY 10001

Routledge is an imprint of the Taylor & Francis Group

Typeset in Galliard and Gill Sans by
Exe Valley Dataset Ltd, Exeter, Devon
Printed and bound in Great Britain by
Biddles Ltd, Guildford and King's Lynn

British Library Cataloguing in Publication Data
A catalogue record for this book is availabe from the British Library

Library of Congress Cataloging in Publication Data
Gender, agency, and change: anthropological perspectives / edited by
Victoria Ana Goddard.
      p.   cm.
   Includes bibliographical references and index.
   1. Social change—Cross-cultural studies.   2. Sex role—Cross-cultural
   studies.   3. Globalization—Cross-cultural studies.   I. Goddard, Victoria A.

   GN358.G45   2000
   303.4—dc21   00–025487

ISBN 0–415–22827–1 (hbk)
ISBN 0–415–22828–X (pbk)

Contents

Figures

Tables

Contributors

Ben Campbell currently holds an award from the ESRC at the University of Manchester.

Gisela Geisler is Associate Professor of Anthropology at the University of Durban-Westville in South Africa and Research Fellow of the Chr. Michelsen Institute in Bergen, Norway.

Victoria Ana Goddard is a lecturer at the Department of Anthropology at Goldsmiths College, University of London.

Karen Tranberg Hansen is Professor of Anthropology at Northwestern University in the United States.

Gertrud Hüwelmeier is a social anthropologist and research fellow at the Humboldt University, Berlin, Institute of European Ethnology.

Siyka Kovatcheva is the organiser of a youth research network for Central and Eastern Europe and is a lecturer at Plovdiv University, Bulgaria.

Guy Massart is currently a doctoral student and a member of the Laboratoire d'Anthropologie de la Communication at the State University of Liège, Belgium.

Frances Pine teaches social anthropology at Cambridge University.

Nükhet Sirman is a social anthropologist at Boğaziçi University, Istanbul, working on the construction of gender in and through nationalist discourses.

Britt-Marie Thurén is Professor of Gender Studies at the Centre for Women's Studies, Umëa University, Sweden.

Preface

The present volume grew out of the Fourth Biennial Conference of the European Association of Social Anthropologists held in Barcelona in July 1996, on the theme of 'Culture and Economy: conflicting interests, divided loyalties'. I was invited to convene a workshop for the Conference, on gender, the remit of which was open-ended in order to attract a wide variety of analyses and participants. In fact the papers presented differed in their focus, methodology and perspective. These differences proved to be an asset and provided the basis for an exciting debate. The workshop was a success and we agreed to work towards publication of the papers. As convenor of the workshop I assumed the responsibility of editing a future volume which was also to include the contributions of those who had submitted papers for the workshop but had been unable to attend. The volume reflects many of the issues covered in the Conference, notably a concern with agency, identity and power in the context of profound global economic and political change. These issues are examined from the perspective of gender as a central axis of identity and agency and a structuring feature of social processes.

Three years have elapsed since then, during which we were able to maintain the relationship established at the Conference. I would like to thank the contributors for their perseverance and enthusiasm, and for their tolerance of my all too frequent incursions into their routines. I would also like to thank Jonathan Mitchell for his thoughtful comments and advice and, particularly towards the end of the process of preparation of this text, for his patience and flexibility. My thanks go too to Vicky Peters for her unswerving support and enthusiasm. Jenny Gault and Anna Whitworth have been a constant source of support and assistance. I thank them for all their help and their good humour, without which our working environment would have been all the poorer. I wish to thank and apologise to my son Joaquin and to all my colleagues and students at Goldsmiths College for any knock-on effects they may have suffered as a result of my concern to complete this volume. And last but not least, I am grateful to Joan Bestard Camps and the other organisers of the EASA Conference, for making it such a success.

Chapter 1

Introduction

Victoria Ana Goddard

A Southern Italian family sits around the lunch table watching a British sitcom. They are amused and comment on the exotic domestic arrangements of the characters on the screen. The discussion rapidly turns to their own lives and to the relative merits of life 'in the South' as opposed to life 'in the North'. At the very moment that representatives of the Mexican government signed the treaty linking their country to the USA and Canada under the North American Free Trade Agreement, the Zapatista rebellion exploded in the state of Chiapas. Reclaiming the mantle of the hero of the Mexican Revolution from the governing Institutional Revolutionary Party, the Zapatista movement has ably used the international media and the internet to publicise its cause. In a small town in France 242 workers in a Japanese hi-fi assembly factory lose their jobs when the company decides to relocate to Scotland because of its appealing profile of longer working hours, worker docility and lower rates of pay. Some of the women who will soon be unemployed predict that the company will move again, abandoning Scotland for more favourable conditions – probably in Asia – once the European Union subsidies run out. These randomly chosen and quite different situations all reflect aspects of the condition of 'being globalised' (Bauman 1998) that in one way or another affects us all. One of the more immediate effects of this condition is the experience of living through rapidly changing circumstances, largely beyond our control.

Change is a prominent, or perhaps the major, characteristic of modern times. Although social life cannot be reduced to change, it is a landmark in perceptions of social experience and in under- standing the social world 'as both promise and threat' (Smart 1992: 1; Touraine 1982). Increasingly, change is related to the spatial relations that govern the interaction of regions and localities. The technological revolution brought about by the dramatic expansion of new information technologies has promoted an acceleration and intensification of flows of goods, information and persons, giving rise to a new form of 'time–space compression' in the organisation of capitalism (Harvey 1989). The economic implications of this are well known, involving a new international division of labour and an emphasis on the flexibility of capital which necessarily demands the simultaneous limitation of freedom of movement and manoeuvrability of the producers themselves (Bauman 1998). While global relations of economic and political power, the material flows of goods, services and persons constitute the structure of a global system there is a simultaneous process of globalisation of cultural elements, entailing an awareness by individuals and groups of the global situation (Robertson 1992; Friedman 1994a).

The awareness of globality and the collapse or denial of space suggested by some observers (Jameson 1991) implies the emergence of a new and shared space: the global space and with it, a global culture. However this, like other spaces, is constructed and it is mediated by the relations of power and economic inequality that inhere in the global system. Evidence of growing gaps between regions and groups undermines proclamations of an increasingly homogenised world. Hoogvelt (1997) for one draws attention to the process of 'implosion' whereby the intensification of regional relations at one level is matched by the exclusion of other regions and groups. So globalisation has quite different implications if we are considering the process from the perspective of Northern Europe or of sub-Saharan Africa. Our position in the global space and our perception of it will differ if our location is Wall Street or the old mining towns of the Welsh valleys.

This volume explores the ways in which individual and collective actors experience and interpret processes of change. By taking the perspective of constructed localities, the chapters illustrate the fact that space is experienced differentially, both in relation to the global arena and to other actors within the locality. The global context does imply shifts at the level of localities: boundaries are redefined through work and migration, through consumption of global products, through changes in the constitution and character of the social arena. The chapters also illustrate the ways in which time and space are related conceptually, as actors weave together time and space in the process of making sense of change. 'Modern', 'western' or 'new' factors are valued positively or negatively in relation to 'traditional' cultural forms. References to a putative past, practices of a time imagined as prior to the modern and global present can either – or simultaneously – legitimate actions, appear as obstacles to the fulfilment and enjoyment of the opportunities offered by change or be deployed as a defence against its dangers.

The emphasis in this volume is on agency,[1] on the capacity and willingness of actors to take steps in relation to their social situation. The contributors approach these issues from a number of perspectives. What they share is a focus on gender, both because of a personal commitment to understanding how gender relations are constructed and negotiated and because gender provides a particularly useful focus to analyse the complexities of social, economic and political transformations. Gender analysis encourages the consideration of experience and agency. Because gender identities are integral to the construction of subjectivity and to the placing of individuals in their social world, they are central to broader issues of identity and inform discourses pertaining to the social universe, to change, community and nationhood. Gender categorisations cut across divisions in terms of class, ethnicity and community, and are located in the interstices of institutional and individual practices and ideologies. As such, a focus on gender affords a perspective from 'the dissonant, even dissident histories and voices' (Bhabha 1994: 5).

Claims that we are witnessing the 'end of history'[2] proclaim the victory of the West and the end of struggle and ideology, confirming western cultural and political values as the universal templates for social life. This is not apparent everywhere. In the first place, there is 'unfinished business' with the promises of modernity. The terms of reference may have changed, as have the global conditions, and the rhetoric and categories of high modernism may appear hollow. But there may yet be objectives in the project of modernity that have resonance and appeal. The claims of modernity may appear relevant, even urgent, and for many the struggle is still ongoing, whether to become 'modern', to achieve a nation-state or full citizenship within it, or to forge personal and collective identities that effectively engage with experience. These identities may differ from those associated with modernity and may require the invention of different sources of solidarity, but then the categories of modernity have never achieved universal validity or been fully encompassing, as anthropologists and feminists amongst others have pointed out. Liberal democracy does not signal the end of struggle or the achievement of goals. Its universality can be challenged. In many instances it is a transplant, a result of unequal global forces and its local characteristics reflect this fact. Nor does it accomplish a resolution of all contradictions, struggles and inequalities.

Furthermore, the drive towards 'westernisation' or, more broadly, homogeneity is constantly undermined as localities interpret, adapt and transform external influences just as readily as they might internalise them and make them their own. Given the relations that govern the global system and the dynamic and interactive nature of cultural processes worldwide, it is unsurprising that a diversity of local cultural strategies emerge. As Featherstone points out, we are confronted with 'global cultures in the plural' (Featherstone 1990: 10). In other words, the global context creates conditions that differentially affect the existence of actors and generates 'identity spaces' 'from which culturally specific institutional/representational forms are produced' (Friedman 1994a: 201).

Globalisation processes are important for our argument because they are an ever more significant source of new spaces, whether these are 'material' or 'imaginary' forms of space (Soja and Hooper 1993), that have implications for individual and collective identities. With these spaces come new challenges and opportunities for groups that meet these by realigning their boundaries and reconstituting the expression of their identities in a dynamic process of interpretation and response. But they are qualitatively different, they carry different weight, and have different implications. Globalisation encompasses but simultaneously creates margins, edges. These should be recognised not merely as sites of 'lack' and exclusion but also as sites of resistance (hooks 1991) which have direct implications for the system as a whole.

The chapters in this volume start from the premise that gender informs individual and collective identities. Questions of subjectivity, personhood and experience, not least as they relate to action, necessarily address issues of gendered identities. Contrary to what is depicted in the mainstream of anthropological and sociological research, persons are here conceptualised as invariably gendered. It follows that the construction of selfhood is necessarily a process of construction of gendered identities (Moore 1994; Howell and Melhuus 1993). It is this negotiation between the gendered self and the changing character of society that provides the focus for the chapters in this volume. The contributors explore the various and often contradictory ways in which men and women, young and old, understand, appropriate and/or reject elements available in the global space – frequently identified as 'traditional' or 'modern' – in their pursuit of individual and collective identities. Furthermore, the chapters explore the ways in which spaces are defined and redefined, boundaries are shifted or subverted and even the marginal spaces or the 'edges' can become locations of action, fulfilment and meaning for women and men.

Gender, identity and locality

The transformation of cultural and political boundaries and the weakening of entities such as the nation-state have given rise to opportunities for multiple sources of mobilising identities and an emphasis on flexible identities based on choice of life-styles in the current global context. But choice is constrained by the 'flexibility' of the world economic system that means that opportunities for production and work grow and wane, shifting continuously as some areas become recipients of investment while in others investments run dry. Work is no longer considered to be an inevitable and important part of individual identity and experience. Production is no longer identified as the prime mover of the system. It is therefore symptomatic of the current global system that so much recent work on globalisation has focused on consumption and redirected attention from 'productionist' approaches to a concern with reproduction and demand as a driving force in capital accumulation. (Friedman 1994a). Starting with the recognition of the culturally specific meanings and values attributed to goods and commodities (Appadurai 1986), recent work has analysed the specific forms of appropriation of goods in the construction and expression of identity (Friedman 1990, 1994a), stressing the dynamic and determinant role of consumption both in the global system and as a means of expression of human agency (Miller 1987). Although identity cannot be reduced to consumption, in these analyses consumption is inextricably linked to identity, so that 'consumption within the bounds of the world system is always a consumption of identity, canalized by a negotiation between self-definition and the array of possibilities offered by the capitalist market' (Friedman 1994a: 104).

The question of choice is linked to that of identity, recognising that the global context is experienced differentially and that local contexts condition the opportunities of different actors to exercise choice. Tranberg Hansen's chapter on Zambia illustrates these issues in her analysis of the selective appropriation of elements from the global arena by young men and women. Here used clothing made available through the global market provides opportunities for the expression of self-identity. Here, as elsewhere, clothing is used to express 'a sense of time or change' (Miller 1994: 73) and in particular draws out the different ways in which change is experienced by different generations and genders. The opportunities bring with them contestation regarding the meaning and value of different styles and items of clothing and variable interpretations of the possibilities offered and what they reflect in terms of personal status and the individual and the society's relationship to modernity. In the Zambian example young men and women choose their clothing strategies to express their sense of 'being in society'. This 'being' is also a claim to recognition that elicits responses that are in turn informed by the fact that the bodies of young men and women become the means of expressing desires and aspirations in a rapidly changing society and the focus for generalised reflections on modernity and tradition.

The Zambian example clearly demonstrates the point made elsewhere in this volume, that cultures do not have a single model of gender but display a multiplicity of discourses on gender (Moore 1994). The divergences in the self-representations of men and women and the expression of a range of gender discourses is also clear in the discussion of girls' initiation rites in Southern Africa offered by Geisler. This chapter explores the different perceptions of the rituals particularly between men and women on the one hand and young women and older women on the other. The different interpretations of what constitutes 'tradition' reflects the differential distribution of power amongst men and women as well as amongst the old and the young and between government and the urban elites and the ordinary men and women they intend to guide or control. Ambivalence towards 'outside' or 'western' influence is expressed in terms of a re-affirmation of the local through 'tradition', countering change through practices and ideas legitimised by reference to a constructed time and continuity of time-space in the locality. But the ambivalence encompasses a further dimension, where notions of gender and gendered relations and spaces articulate discourses of change and continuity.

Both examples remind us that the process of building identities occurs, at least in part, through appropriating items and ideas, but always within a context of power relations. The 'power-geometry' of globalisation (Massey 1993a) is evident both in the material conditions and inequalities between the constituents of the global arena, and in local configurations of status and influence. Globalisation can reinforce these broader and local relations or can provide the conditions for subverting them. In the cases discussed by Tranberg Hansen and Geisler the process has given rise to contestation, largely expressed in terms of morality or rather of competing moralities. Moralities that base their legitimacy on claims of 'tradition' represent a bid for safety and the protection of existing hierarchies and specific interests and values. On the contrary, claims for a rearrangement of the status quo and/or the prevailing power relations may be expressed through a critique of or a challenge to traditional practices. Explicit appeals to the modern might promote new practices or social arrangements while a reinvention of tradition provides legitimacy in changing situations. This means that 'tradition' is necessarily a pliable entity, inevitably subject to interpretation and contestation and a vehicle for claims and counter-claims regarding power and authority.

In fact, Geisler's chapter shows there is little consensus regarding what is recognised and accepted as traditional, and the disagreements map out the fault-lines of the relations between different social groups. For example, young women defend bride-wealth as a legitimate tradition whereas young men question its validity. On the other hand, men and older women support the continuation of the initiation of young girls and the transfer of some aspects of the ritual to the public domain, yet young girls express a great deal of anxiety regarding both of these practices. At the same time, these moral debates provide a context for actions and choices. In the Zambian case, young girls might reject certain items of clothing because these render them vulnerable within the terms of current moral discourses. There is also a concrete dimension to this vulnerability: some items of clothing provide greater protection from sexual assault. Young women must therefore pursue their identity strategies balancing self-expression and personal safety in a social context where violence against women is on the increase.

Pine's chapter on rural Poland also illustrates the uneven process of negotiating definitions of tradition, specifically in relation to the rejection and recovery of certain practices. Pine describes a shift from rituals expressing household fertility towards conspicuous consumption and the appropriation of styles and commodities from the outside. Whereas certain traditional practices are abandoned in favour of 'modern' ones, a recall of tradition becomes the nostalgic basis for expressions of anxieties regarding changes that escape the control of the locality or indeed transcend the boundaries of the nation-state. At the same time, the 'past' cannot be construed as unproblematic. The Górale, the people among whom Pine conducted her research, are at least as ambivalent about the past, i.e. the socialist era, as they are about the present. The common thread to Górale concerns is its relations with the outside, whether this is the socialist state, the post-socialist state or the global labour market. Perhaps against expectations, the centrality of the house and the community is not waning. The shifts in 'tradition' and the incorporation of 'global' commodities are not reflections of the decline of the house and the community, but rather represent the changing emphases in the relationship of Górale with the wider arena.

The nature of the wider arena has shifted dramatically and in the case of Poland especially so since 1989. In rural Poland, the political and economic changes have generated opportunities, such as migration. This migration is selective and it is women who tend to leave to work in urban centres throughout Europe. Whereas this represents a viable economic strategy for the Górale, there is growing public concern for the potential or actual loss of morality by women who, because of migration, have become detached from their social context. The 'consciousness of the global' (Robertson 1992; Friedman 1994a) here produces strategies as well as ambivalence and conflicting moral responses.

It is notable that in the cases outlined by Pine, Tranberg Hansen and Geisler 'public' anxieties concerning change are largely focused on sexuality and women, and particularly on young women. The appeal to tradition revolves around concerns for the vulnerability and corruptibility of women, as the 'moral panics' generated by economic and social change are expressed in terms of the morality or lack of it of young women. Both the promotion and the critiques of modernity focus on the bodies of women as maps of change and resistance. These examples contrast with the case described by Campbell where transnational strategies are also engaged in to contend with changes at home. In the area of rural Nepal where Campbell carried out his fieldwork, land availability has declined, causing significant shifts in the options open to men and women. Young women in particular are able to deal with these changed circumstances by working in Indian cities, often in the sex trade. Yet for the Tamang people the sexual autonomy of women does not represent a threat to the integrity or identity of the community. Their work in the cities does not arouse moral panics such as those encountered in Poland or Zambia. Campbell explains this in terms of the pre-existing kinship and exchange networks that attributed considerable ranges of agency to women as well as men. The chapter points to the skilful agency of Tamang women in securing continuing acceptance and support, as the women work at maintaining important networks. In other words, Tamang women actively 'produce respect' despite the exigencies of concubinage and sex work. The Tamang example is a reminder of the variability of gender systems and of the specificities of the local (see also Frances Pine's chapter in this volume). Clearly, the moral anxieties noted elsewhere surrounding women's increasing mobility and independence derive from specific conditions and 'traditional' moralities attached to gender roles and ideals. At the same time, Campbell raises as an issue the long-term effects of these transnational strategies embarked upon by women where their sexuality is involved in a context of the growing impact of the AIDS pandemic.

These examples illustrate the ways in which agents define themselves and devise identity or reproduction strategies within the constraints and possibilities of specific contexts. Furthermore, they illustrate the process whereby gender discourses and the material expression of gender ideologies that determine different positionalities inform the experience and perception of situations that are lived at a more general level. Gender discourses are central to the constitution of subjectivities, and as such they are productive of powerful symbols, the meanings and significance of which have widespread ramifications. Because of this, gendered discourses are deployed both by powerful collective actors and entities and by those in resistance or opposition to them, in order to instigate or to address social change.

What the moral panics described above are expressing is an implicit link between order and boundaries – gendered boundaries. The transgression of these boundaries is associated with the breakdown of social order, and the risk of chaos. The containment of these borders, expressed through the bodies of women, presents a viable remedy to such risks. On the other hand claims to change, whether they are articulated from above or from the grass-roots, may be expressed or even achieved through the transgression of boundaries, a deliberate redefinition of boundaries and a clear break with the past. Under socialism in Bulgaria, the claim to gender egalitarianism was central to the socialist project of a society of equals. During the socialist period, legitimisation of the government relied on gendered images that placed women within the public arena of the state and the economy. At the same time, in Bulgaria as elsewhere the reshaping of gender stereotypes was used to express opposition to the regime and, as Kovatcheva illustrates in her chapter, the gendered nature of political discourse persists since the collapse of socialism after 1989, though it has assumed various and contradictory forms. Similarly, generational differences both in relation to the socialist past and the market-dominated present are also captured by these symbolically potent images.

The state and social change

The deployment of gendered symbols in the construction of collective identities, in particular of national entities and the legitimisation of states, is an important though still under-researched issue. Yuval-Davis and Anthias (1989) have argued convincingly that gender models are central to the construction of the boundaries of state and nationhood. In their study of Latin American national identities Radcliffe and Westwood (1996) explore the articulation of race, class and gender in what they refer to as the 'externalities', that is icons, histories, governments and the 'internalities' or the subjective experience of the nation (see also McClintock 1993; Kandiyoti 1991). These are embedded in notions and experiences of class, race and gender so that collective identities and individual subjectivity are correlated, linked through complex exchanges and flows. As they explain, 'subjects are constituted through the discursive practices and power effects of gender, sexuality, "race" and class, simultaneously as the investments in nation-building impinge upon their subjectivity' (Radcliffe and Westwood 1996: 166).

Individuals and groups are involved in a creative and ongoing process of interpretation and relocation of 'official' versions of nationhood, according to their varying and changing positionality (in terms of race, class, gender and place). This ongoing positioning and expression of identity takes place at a number of different levels of 'locality' but nevertheless within the context of the global. The very notion of the nation-state is intrinsic to the modernist project with which Latin America, to take one example, has a long history of engagement. In the nineteenth century the state was a prime agent of modernisation. The struggle for a particular form of state, generally though not necessarily accurately defined as the nation-state, was the basis for anti-imperialist movements such as the Risorgimento in Italy, or the wars of independence in the Americas. This struggle for independence was to continue into the twentieth century, always relying on some variant of the nation-state model (Anderson 1983). A priority of the emerging states was to bring about the process of modernisation and the benefits that were assumed to accrue automatically from such a strategy. In the end, the emergence of autonomous states and the collapse of imperial structures confirmed the commitment to modernisation, a goal that would only be extensively questioned at the end of the twentieth century, when the mechanisms of neo-colonialism became more widely understood.

In fact, until the 1970s the 'nation-state' continued to be the principal actor promoting change. 'Development' was an objective tackled by governments in both the developed and the developing countries. This often involved the adoption of policies intended to change the structure of the labour market and the institutions of civil society with the aim of achieving greater economic output. Such policies often challenged prevailing customs, in particular with regard to gender relations and family systems and values, either as a corollary of economic and political changes or as a deliberate intervention in the realm of the private and domestic in order to align morality and values more closely with 'modern' orientations.

However, since the 1980s there has been a shift towards globally determined policies that promote a withdrawal of the state from direct intervention in the economy and stress the importance of the free operation of the market. The growing influence of transnational corporations, the international debt and structural adjustment programmes are amongst the most important factors in the internationalisation of the state and the erosion of its sovereignty in particular with regard to 'the market'. In fact, governments are increasingly constrained to define policies in relation to the global market, abandoning a social welfare orientation in favour of measures that will privilege the market and enhance competitiveness (Alonso 1997: 6). The combination of the withdrawal of state welfare policies and the processes unleashed by globalisation give rise to new, more complex bodies of citizenship which tend towards structural inequality (Alonso 1997: 5). At the same time, and in contrast to these structural features, international bodies promoting and supporting global policies, such as the International Monetary Fund and the World Bank, have increasingly stressed political democratisation as a condition for continuing participation in circuits of trade and aid.

The shifts in the remit and autonomy of the state clearly have implications for individuals and groups both in their relations to the state and their relations to each other. More generally, observers point to the erosion or outright loss of a basis for effective oppositional movements. Zygmunt Bauman considers that:

One of the most seminal consequences of the new global freedom of movement is that it becomes increasingly difficult, perhaps altogether impossible, to re-forge social issues into effective collective action.

(Bauman 1998: 69)

It is easy to share Bauman's pessimism. Yet anthropologists and others concerned with studying the local are well aware of the various forms of resistance embarked upon by local communities. It is undoubtedly the case that collective action is inadequate to tackle or control global material flows and power relations. But steps, some small and some more ambitious, are taken by individuals and collectivities to make sense of their world and to act upon it and leave their imprint upon it. Modes of action change and reflect the ways in which locally and globally generated transformations impact upon the spaces of political action. The local space and in particular the ways in which the public arena – and necessarily the private arena as well – are bounded, defined and given content therefore become important objects of reflection (Alvarez *et al.* 1998; Scott *et al.* 1997), as does the redefinition of what constitutes 'political' action. These reflections coincide with long-standing debates regarding the relationship of women to the political, whether in relation to issues of political action or the gendered nature of democracy and citizenship.

The mirage of democracy and the question of citizenship

Democracy has largely supplanted economic development as the key concept that is intended to shape the major objectives of national and international entities. Democracy has become a symbolic intention for many, a mobilising ideal capable of generating ties of solidarity across identities and national boundaries. However, as the cases described in this volume show, the attainment of a democratic system is neither straightforward nor does it entail in itself an automatic solution to the problems of marginalisation, subordination or exclusion.

In spite of the constraints on governments to implement social policies and control the economy and even to allow for legitimate spaces for political participation, democratic government does provide new sets of referents and new parameters for actors and it does generate new and/or different spaces for agency. Democratic government produces opportunities for new groups and movements while others that might have had purpose during periods of authoritarian rule may become obsolete. It raises issues of legitimisation and participation and provides a new focus for local relations, conflicts and alliances.

The post-socialist countries exemplify the contradictory trends occurring during the 1990s and in particular the shift to democratic politics. Here a rapid and dramatic collapse of the structures of support of the socialist state and an equally dramatic and rapid introduction into the world market and the shift to democracy have brought about profound changes, as discussed here in relation to Poland and Bulgaria. Considering the process of democratisation from a gendered perspective raises important questions about assumptions inherent in the model of modernity such as the absolute gains that accrue from democratisation. Feminist activists and academics concerned with or involved in the transition in Eastern European countries have drawn attention to the emergence of a 'masculine democracy' (Watson 1997). In Bulgaria for example women have lost ground in both the economic and political arenas. In spite of their higher qualifications, women in post-socialist Bulgaria are far more likely than men to be unemployed, and are markedly under-represented in elected government posts. The student movement studied by Kovatcheva also reflected and reproduced these patterns. Comparing young women's involvement in differerent types of organisations within the universities, Kovatcheva notes that more women held higher positions in the organisations promoted by the university, where women were appointed to these positions. This leads her to suggest that the implementation of a quota system may be strategically necessary to ensure adequate representation of women in political bodies. Democracy did not in itself resolve deep and long-standing assumptions about gender difference, in spite of half a century of official sexual egalitarianism. If anything, the 'opening up' of the political arena in Eastern European countries resulted in a reaction that marginalised women from the political arena, as gendered oppositions between public and private spheres were re-established.

At an earlier date, and in a markedly different economic and political context, Spain underwent a political transformation from authoritarian rule to democracy. In 1977 democratic elections officially ended a period of forty years of authoritarian government and initiated a long and self-conscious process of democratisation. This process has entailed changes not only at the institutional level but has also had implications for the evolution of grass-roots organisations such as the neighbourhood movement. These were fomented during the Franco regime as a substitute for participatory democracy, though they rapidly became a vehicle for the expression of opposition to the regime, as described in Thurén's chapter. Here, as elsewhere, democratisation shifted the content and direction of political groups and altered the boundaries of public space, affecting the form and degree of participation of men and women. The Spanish case also highlights the question of local context: Thurén's multi-sited research shows how the characteristics of the localities she studied informed the character of the local neighbourhood organisations and the form and extent of participation of men and women in them.

In Cape Verde the transition from one-party rule to a democratic government was initially met with great enthusiasm, later replaced by misgivings and feelings of disillusionment. Massart's chapter in this volume illustrates the ways in which young men experienced the opportunities and contradictions opened up by electoral politics. Democratic politics requires individual decision-making and choice and therefore enhances individuality (Jaquette and Wolchik 1998). This has implications for the relationship of actors to the state and to their community. In the Cape Verde example the most significant reference group for young men is the peer group. This provides the context for the performance of individual identity, now stressing the responsibilities and potential of exercising choice. Massart's study of the interactions between young men demonstrates the centrality of gendered selfhood in the practice of political agency. Significantly, the young Cape Verdeans perceive their selfhood, their reputations and their relations to others as a continuum, whereby their private selves and strategies and their relations, particularly with female partners, are comparable to their public selves and their relations, to the governing strata. At the same time, the continuities expressed by men have serious implications for women, for as the democratic system fails to incorporate young working-class men, they must rely on their domination over women in the private sphere to express their self-worth and minimise their powerlessness.

In other instances, such as in the case of grass-roots movements in Argentina, actors might operate through multiple sites. A case in point is the Mothers of the Plaza de Mayo who along with other human rights activists effectively used the global media to exert pressure on recalcitrant governments. Undoubtedly globalisation has facilitated and reinforced inequality and political repression. We need only recall the clientelistic alliances that resulted in training military and other repressive personnel, the supply of arms and official and less official alliances such as 'operation Condor' to recognise that repression is also a globally organised phenomenon. At the same time, the global context and in particular the global media offer opportunities for action that internationalise political strategies and extend and redefine the 'public arena', cutting across national boundaries and challenging the remit of the nation-state to determine the rights and duties of individual citizens.[3] The spaces carved out by individuals and groups, generated or suppressed by the global context, raise the issue of the potentialities for agency and the issue of public and private personae as actors negotiate different spaces of action. Several questions suggest themselves. What is the meaning and value attributed to different spaces? How are boundaries 'used'? Under what circumstances does a space become private or public and how does this affect the agents concerned?

The Public and the private revisited

Anthropologists who eschewed biological explanations of women's subordination identified the source of women's secondary social status as being in their relationship to the public sphere. The distinction of public and private and the relegation of women to the latter, excluding them from full participation in the public arena, became central themes in the explanation of gender status (Rosaldo 1974). The public and private distinction was seen both as the explanation for women's subordination and as a crucial factor in the construction and reaffirmation of gender inequality (Davidoff 1998). At the same time, the recognition of the public as separate from the state,[4] like the concept of 'civil society', offered the possibility of conceptualising social action as effective – and political – in a variety of contexts and considering the content and boundaries of spheres of action as shifting and subject to re-definition and reinterpretation. Amongst other things, it was compatible with the recognition of multiple forms and sources of power beyond those defined within a strictly 'political' field.

In its original formulation the dichotomy of public and private was intended to explain the emergence of hierarchy and ultimately of the state while accounting for the dynamics of social reproduction in particular as they affected men and women differentially. Applied to historical and ethnographic studies, the approach stressed the constructed and contingent character of gender relations and their connections to broader relations of inequality (Leacock and Lee 1982). However, more recently the public/private framework has been criticised by a number of feminist theorists, not least in anthropology. One of the most widespread criticisms of the use of dichotomies including the public and private is that they are ethnocentric constructs and 'should be understood as features of anthropological discourse rather than as features of other cultural discourses' (Moore 1993: 194; Collier and Yanagisako 1987).

A further concern is that dichotomies such as the public and the private contain – and therefore produce – a relation of inequality. Jay (1981) compares the opposition of contraries such as A/B that are not logical contradictories and allow for continuity between them, and are therefore capable of transformation and change and oppositions that are envisaged as logical contradictories in the A/not-A mode. These do not allow for continuities and no third term or alternative is possible. Furthermore, only one term has positive reality, its opposite being defined purely as the negation of the first. Because of this negative definition, i.e. it is only and everything that the other is not, the not-A is associated with infinitation and, therefore, disorder and chaos. In fact, anxieties surrounding the integrity of boundaries and the protection of order relies on maintaining the rigid either/or distinction. This kind of opposition is inherently conservative, resistant to change and, by imputing different values and properties to its two terms, reproduces inequality. Jay points to the 'susceptibility of gender distinction to A/not-A phrasing' (1981: 54) where woman is associated with not-A. Through logical extension, other gendered oppositions, such as nature/culture or private/public are similarly imbued with the implications of negative value and infinitation. These distinctions are sometimes obvious but are usually concealed and taken for granted. They are dangerous in that they represent modes of constructing difference in ways that work to the advantage of specific groups (Jay 1981; Massey 1993b). Struggles for change, particularly in revolutionary movements, may well abandon rigid gender dichotomies, as occurred during the English, French and Chinese revolutions. The latter example represents the most extreme case of reduction of gender distinctions, which Jay explains in terms of the dominance of the A/not-A principle that governed pre-revolutionary Chinese society largely through the exogamous patrilineal clan system. This produced men clan members and women as non-clan members in the sense that their destiny was to be married out of the clan they were born into (Jay 1981: 53).

The 'danger' represented by these apparently innocuous distinctions (Jay 1981) forces us to take them on board, to analyse, deconstruct and ultimately redefine them. Informed by the implications of the theoretical critiques and the accumulation of empirical studies, we need to abandon rigid conceptualisations of the private and the public and instead understand these terms as ideological constructs that define spaces, activities and persons in differing ways. The meaning and significance of actions and spaces need to be contextualised and we should not underestimate the capacity of *agents* to redefine and/or undermine such boundaries and distinctions. If today we retain the use of the dichotomy we must recognise not only the cultural and historical variability in the form and empirical relevance of such a theoretical device but also the implications of the global context. This is because increasingly globalisation and global material processes affect the context within which actors operate, in that they may promote changes in the division of labour, in the distribution of objects and persons, in the perception of opportunities, and in the content and availability of spaces.

And then, as suggested in Jay's argument, these dichotomies are deployed within specific social, economic and political processes and become concrete through bids to construct spaces, positions and statuses that result in the unequal distribution of access to material and non-material objects. In the context of capitalist society, the distinction between public and private is an important ideological tool, and in relation to this we should also consider the economy. Whereas some analyses would be inclined to locate the economy within the realm of the public, the economy is increasingly represented as standing outside of society, autonomous and subject to its own 'natural' laws. The logic of the economy is understood to be impermeable to political or ideological interference. Inversely, the effects of the economy, such as unemployment or inequality, are seen as consequences of the natural unfolding of that logic and therefore inevitable. On the other hand, issues, practices or persons associated with the domestic or private arena are depoliticised also because they are naturalised, but here it is through association with the personal and the familiar (Fraser 1989: 168). This is because the private sphere is represented as 'natural' and, therefore, as standing for what is universal in human activity. It is the space for actions, sentiments and practices embedded in the biological, in the process of human reproduction. The private sphere, seen as timeless, natural and unchanging, contrasts with the culturally constructed sphere of work and polity. This is the sphere of agency and change, the space of struggle *par excellence*, and is the arena where the potential of human freedom can be realised. It is also, significantly, associated with a specific mentality, a rational-instrumental attitude, and with male actors who are seen as most likely to embody this mentality (see Benhabib 1998; Honig 1998; Dietz 1991; Arendt 1958).

This volume outlines concrete examples of different constructions and interpretations of this conceptual division of spaces, actions and people. Pine's chapter draws attention to the contrasts between general conceptions of the private–public division and the Polish case where the house is associated with both men and women and was especially highly valued over the public sphere during the socialist period. Pine also indicates the existence of a divide between 'official' versions of categories such as the state, work or the family and local understandings of these in the area of her fieldwork.

Under socialism, the aim of the state was to erase the distinction between the state and society, between the public and the private. In the pursuit of equality difference was negated and all, regardless of ethnic or gender identity, were to be subsumed under the category of 'worker'. The non-existence or 'irrelevance' of political rights reinforced the role of work as the means to and the arena for achieving equality. This was especially clear in the case of women for whom entry into production would provide the key to equality with men. This in turn resulted in the 'irrelevance' of gender distinctions or the de-gendering of spaces (Gal 1997: 35). For the Górale the house was and is opposed to the outside, represented by the state and more recently the market. In this case such an opposition can be interpreted as a local claim to and defence of the integrity of the private space versus the state. Here the private space works as a safe place for men and women, both of whom are identified with it, albeit carrying out different – though largely interchangeable – roles and tasks. As the socialist regime defined men and women as 'workers', so does work constitute a fundamental aspect of identity for both men and women of the Górale today. Interestingly, a marked distinction is made between work for the house, which is highly valued, and work for the 'outside'.

The centrality of the house is one of the main themes to emerge from Hüwelmeier's village study in Germany. Here it is the house that constitutes the core of individual identities. The naming system of houses in the German case creates a specific topography of identity that could be seen as a kind of 'counterpublic' space. This emerged with the changes that have taken place since the Industrial Revolution and in response to external pressures on the village economy, the most important of which are perhaps the pressures forcing men into long- and short-term migration. This left women with sole responsibility for the household economy and encouraged the emergence of specific networks of relationships and solidarities within the village. A complex superimposition of systems of classification of space and persons has developed alongside the changes in the economic and social structure of the village. So today, the official classification of persons and households according to the criteria defined by the state bureaucracy is matched by a parallel system based on descent from the women who founded the 'houses'. Full participation and 'belonging' in the village derive from the positioning offered by the houses system rather than by the official bureaucratic system of classification. The primacy and the persistence of notions of gender, kinship and descent through a radically modernising process in an advanced industrial country is evident here, as is the capacity of actors to respond creatively, carving out spaces of action and autonomy from the hegemonic claims of the state and the economy.

Yet another, and quite different, perspective is offered when we consider the political from the perspective of young men. Guy Massart's discussion of the discourses of non-elite young men in Cape Verde examines the ways in which they blur the distinctions between their private and their public personas. They express continuities in their identities, as in the ways in which they talk about their relationships to politics (and politicians) and their relationships with women. In expressing their identities as young men, they draw on and evaluate or demonstrate their worth in relation to both areas of experience. Distinctions between public and private behaviour appear irrelevant in this example. Nevertheless, it is precisely the capacity of these young men to draw on their experience in the private sphere, where they define themselves as in control of and superior to women, that allows them to bolster their self-worth in the context of their relatively weak and subordinate position *vis-à-vis* elite men.

Where spaces are recognised and experienced as differentiated and gendered so that men are associated with the public sphere and women with the private sphere, crossing the boundaries can be daunting and redefining space might be too great a challenge. Both Thurén and Kovatcheva raise this issue, pointing to the reluctance of women to participate in 'the political' sphere. But both also show ways in which women can gain a sense of belonging in such spaces. The literature offers many examples of women in grass-roots movements or other groups that fall outside the defined remit of formal politics and where women participate or even assume positions of leadership (Afshar 1996; Radcliffe and Westwood 1993; Jaquette 1990). Being outside of the official sphere of politics, these movements frequently resort to different kinds of tactics and organisation. Goals are generally defined in terms of issues or concrete concerns rather than absolute bids for power (Escobar and Alvarez 1992). Thurén's discussion of the character-istics of the neighbourhood movement in Spain addresses precisely the issue of what motivates women to participate and what forms that participation can take. The movement has its origins in the Franco regime, when it was intended as a depoliticised space for collective action and identity. However, as the only legitimate channel for the expression of discontent, it became – amongst other things – a base for opposition politics. Democratisation signalled the opening up of the public arena and the creation of spaces for citizenship and the movement lost many of its members (mainly men) and some of its objectives. This in fact made the local associations of the movement more attractive to women, who have joined the movement in large numbers. Thurén emphasises the fact that the movement is based on the neighbourhood, a space that for a number of practical and ideological reasons is considered appropriate for women as well as for men. As an intermediary space between the domestic and the public, the neighbourhood is a semi-public and a semi-political space. This suggests that localised and 'layered' forms of democracy may provide a number of suitable spaces for the participation of different groups, particularly those that are rendered vulnerable, or are otherwise 'de-politicised'.

The feminisation of the political

The metaphor of space, prominent in much of this volume, has also been implicated in efforts to reconstitute political struggle. The decline of what have historically been key forms of interpellation such as class, and the growing recognition of multiple voices, has encouraged the search for new perspectives to define forms of struggle and possibilities of solidarity and alliance. For hooks, as a black American woman, academic and activist, the nature of radical opposition is achieved through the transgression of space, by moving 'out of one's place' 'pushing against oppressive boundaries set by race, sex and class domination' (hooks 1991: 145). What she refers to as the 'politics of location' requires an identification of spaces from 'where we begin the process of re-vision'.

The chapters in this volume support the claims that spaces are not neutral.[5] The examples illustrate their gendered nature and analyse them as expressions of power and sites of struggle. The chapters draw attention especially to the negotiation of boundaries and the ways in which agents use them, shift or undermine them or redefine the meaning and value of the spaces they are intended to keep apart. The implications of spaces are therefore contextual. For example, in the rhetoric of governments and the response of individuals the domestic sphere or the family is set apart from the public as a place of sentiment, intimacy and safety. The role of the family, or more broadly of the domestic, as a refuge becomes acute in situations of economic and political stress. This is the situation described by Kovatcheva and Pine for Bulgaria and Poland respectively where individuals sought respite from the exigencies of the economy and the limitations of the political system.

Governments may have a vested interest in promoting the family as a sacred, separate space, in a drive to depoliticise at least certain sectors of the population. However, the very values attributed to the family, its very depoliticised character, can become the basis of a strong and convincing critique of the status quo, as occurred during – and since – the repressive regimes of Chile and Argentina as discussed in Goddard's chapter. The family can become the site not merely of withdrawal but of the elaboration of parallel or counter-strategies, as a counterpublic space.

The differentiation of spheres and the differential allocation of men and women to them gives rise to varying interpretations of the political. In terms of a political project for the future, Arendt considered that the point of departure for such a project had to be the public sphere, as the domain of human freedom and the realm of citizenship (Dietz 1991). On the other hand, at least one strand of feminist thinking on the political proposes that the democratisation of the polity can only take place through a feminisation of the public sphere. This entails not only the greater and fuller participation of women in the public arena but also the transfer to the public domain of values associated with the private sphere (Gilligan 1982). In particular, the values associated with mothering are seen to constitute a basis for the construction of a new politics, an alternative to the 'male' values that have historically shaped the political arena (Elshtain 1981, 1997; Ruddick 1989). Others reject the possibility and the desirability of transferring 'maternal' values to the public sphere as a basis for a new politics, arguing instead that the promotion of democratic practices can only be achieved by the performance of women as citizens (Dietz 1991; Mouffe 1992). It is not through the language or ideology of kinship, of motherhood or of private loyalties that we can achieve an equal and just society. In Dietz' words, 'only the language of freedom and equality, citizenship and justice, will challenge non-democratic and oppressive political institutions' (Dietz 1991: 60).

That the very concept of citizenship is gendered[6] and that this has implications for the capacity of different actors to exercise agency is illustrated in several of the chapters in this volume. An objective indication of this are the difficulties and struggles involved in achieving women's suffrage in democracies in the core as well as the periphery as raised by Kovatcheva regarding the Bulgarian case and discussed in some detail in Goddard's chapter on Argentina. In this example the populist government of Perón granted the vote in what many felt was a political ploy to increase his support base. The Peronist government was dependent on mass mobilisation and as Radcliffe and Westwood (1996) point out, it was concerned to mobilise the people as gendered citizens. This did in fact result in greater inclusion of women in the public arena, as women's political participation became a key element of the regime. Eva Perón, the President's wife, played a central role in the mobilisation of men and women and promoted a political discourse of gender while carefully avoiding challenging women's primary role as domestic carers and as reproducers and the specific qualities that were considered appropriate to that role. On the contrary, these qualities and responsibilities were highlighted in her speeches as central to the political project of Peronism. Resorting to the language of the private sphere, expressing her most intimate feelings, whether of love or hatred, Eva's political discourse broke with the traditional discourses of the public arena where a rational-instrumental use of language prevailed. In this way, Eva Perón embodied many aspects of the modern project yet did so through the language of intimacy and sentiment. She challenged the oligarchic social order by rallying men and very importantly women into the political arena yet preserved the values of a so-called traditional female role.

Thirty years earlier than the Peronist regime in Argentina, Turkish modernisers also placed the issue of women's political rights at the centre of the nation-building process. Sirman's chapter considers the careful re-drawing of public and private spheres during the Republican period in Turkey as justice and equality were pursued through a conception of citizenship that was linked to new modes of conjugality, with important implications for gender identities. Sirman approaches the issues that emerged during this period of marked deliberate change in the public and the private sectors through the writings of Halide Edip Adıvar. Her focus is on Edip's exploration of forms of love as the key to change in both the political and intimate fields of experience of Turkish men and women. The contradictions of her position as a woman, a nationalist and a feminist are reflected in her struggle to follow through these ideas in her novels.

These historical examples have a direct bearing on current debates regarding the feminisation of the political. In the case of Turkey and Argentina emotions were deployed in the public arena (in the cultural–literary field in the case of Turkey, in the space of political rhetoric and practice in the case of Argentina). In both cases profound social changes were underway, which involved the undermining of long-standing interests and traditions where the issues of legitimisation of current government and of subversion of existing institutions are taking place concurrently. In both instances the incorporation of the mass of the population was important to the success of the political project. And in both the recognition of women as political agents was central to the project of political and economic modernisation, even though in Turkey this involved a radical transformation of the domestic sphere and of gender ideals, whereas in Argentina the attempt was to keep these intact.

From very different positions and perspectives, Halide Edip Adıvar and Eva Perón claimed there was specificity to women's understanding, drawn from the experience of motherhood. Motherhood granted women a different perspective and different values from those of men. Superficially Eva Perón's rhetoric regarding the contribution of women to the political shows some resemblance to the 'maternal thinking' and the 'ethics of care' proposed by some feminist thinkers (see Gilligan 1982; Ruddick 1989). The qualities – the morality perhaps – that women could bring into the political arena were, potentially, profoundly subversive and transformative, conducive to a better society. Although the similarities are superficial, the example does show that without a radical transformation of the domestic sphere, the limits of 'maternal thinking' become evident in the public arena. In the absence of change in the private arena the appropriation of sentiments and images from the domestic sphere remains susceptible to what are ultimately conservative and hierarchical objectives. What Jordanova describes as the huge rhetorical potential of the public–private dichotomy can be deployed in very different types of discourse. This supports the proposals of feminists such as Mouffe or Dietz that a more just and free society can only be achieved through a restructuring of the public arena itself and a re-elaboration of notions of citizenship that are simultaneously heterogeneous and egalitarian. This would entail a challenge to the boundaries between public and private and with it a reinvention of the domestic and the recognition of the gendered nature of economic, political and cultural phenomena.

Conclusions

The question of heterogeneity is central to this collection. The cases examined in the volume show there can be no simple formula to encompass the needs of all men and all women. This has implications not only for the sociological categories we might employ but also for the political proposals and strategies we might support. In the examples of Turkey and Argentina, it is clear that feminists recruited from the educated elite failed to engage the women from the working classes and the rural areas. In the Spanish example, there was reluctance among neighbourhood activists to become too closely associated with feminist goals for fear of antagonising local women as well as men. Other examples reveal the deep schisms between women of different generations, and men and women of different classes. The issue of heterogeneity is pertinent to current debates concerning the dangers of univers-alism, whether in relation to citizenship and rights or to our use of the category of women that also demands deconstruction, as we have seen. This in turn constitutes a warning against approaches that focus exclusively on gender to the exclusion of other forms of difference, as eloquently stated in the challenge to western feminism launched by third world and black feminists (see Mohanty 1993; hooks 1982, 1984).

Whether we are discussing the impact of change on concepts of sexuality, the body or rather specific bodies, on the defence or attack of traditions, or on the political behaviour of young men and women in new democratic situations, what the examples in this volume show is the centrality of gender to the construction of identity and agency and its relevance to complex contemporary processes. As has been stressed earlier, this is not to the exclusion of other forms of difference and distinction or indeed of unity and solidarity. Instead gender is articulated through multiple and changing configurations that cannot be defined a priori and must be derived from the local context in which they are realised and expressed. The local context is changing, its boundaries are continuously redefined. Globalisation and its' implicit claim to inevitable and progressive homogeneity makes more pressing the need to record and understand the ways in which collective and individual actors seize opportunities and give meaning to themselves and their lives. A focus on gender encourages us to bridge the conceptual gaps between processes of change, public scenarios and the everyday lives of men and women.

Global processes are themselves gendered, for example typically selecting young girls for assembly work, but local relations too are more or less empowering for different categories of agents. The Tamang example comes to mind as it provides a positive example where the social context enables women to negotiate, strategise and build relationships of support. Interestingly, for the Tamang the family does not constitute a place of safety, a refuge. Here the crucial reference group is constituted through broader sets of relations through kin and affines. This suggests that restriction of women to bounded groups and spaces, such as the family, as opposed to having access to wider sets of relations of support, may be a factor in the unequal capacity of men and women to consolidate strong social positions. The Tamang case, along with the other ethnographic examples in the volume, alerts us to the importance of detailed studies of localities that can start to unravel the complexities of local social and cultural processes. The importance of such work is more pressing in the current phase of globalisation, both in relation to the dangers of economic, political and cultural homogenisation as a consequence of global processes, and as a means to inform the ongoing construction of a global civil society, the definition of universal human rights and truly and effectively representative democracies.

The chapters approach gender as constructed and contested. Agency takes many shapes and forms. The examples illustrate the creation of alternatives and the emergence of counterpublic spaces. Gender is integral to processes of change, to the construction of community and nationhood and to the concept of citizen. But do women, specifically, bring something new into the political, as many feminists claim? The answer would have to be affirmative. Not because of any essential qualities that women might be thought to possess but because they derive their (various) perspectives from alternative spaces, from places that are outside the political, and even from the margins, which for hooks constitute sites of resistance and change. However, without challenging the relations and the ideals that characterise the private, the domestic sphere, that contribution can equally support hegemonic claims as well as counter-hegemonic ones, its implications can be conservative or subversive. The aim then should not be the transposition of the values from one sphere to another, but to reconsider one in the light of the other. Or more to the point, to work on the boundaries, and break down the distinctions. This is not an argument in favour of homogeneity, but rather for the recognition and acceptance of difference and of the necessity for material, cultural and emotional equality in all areas of social life, including the most intimate and private.

Notes

1 By agency I refer to the capacity of individuals or groups to embark on processes of autonomous self-realisation. The approach is one that considers agency as 'located in a dialectic relationship with social structures' and 'embedded in social relations'. (Lister 1997: 37).
2 See F. Fukuyama 1992 and the critical collection by T. Burns (1994).
3 For an analysis of globalised political strategies see the chapters by Alvarez, Yúdice, Slater and Ribeiro in S. Alvarez *et al.* 1998.
4 Feminist debate on this issue has often found the work of Habermas useful. For a feminist evaluation of Habermas' contribution to the conceptual framework of public and private see Benhabib 1998 and Fraser 1991.
5 See D. Massey (1993b) and E. Soja and B. Hooper (1993).
6 As feminist critics of the concept of citizenship have pointed out, the universalist definition of citizenship (and of 'rights') is in fact constructed as male, white, heterosexual. In fact, in both the liberal and the republican conceptions of citizenship, the exclusion of women to the domestic or private sphere is a condition for the active participation of male citizens in the public arena (see Lister 1997; Fraser and Gordon 1994; Young 1989).

Bibliography

Afshar, H. (ed.) (1996) *Women and Politics in the Third World*, London: Routledge.
Alonso, L.E. (1997) 'Globalización y vulnerabilidad social', in V. Maquieira and M.J. Vara (eds) *Género, Clase y Etnia en los Nuevos*

Procesos de Globalización, Madrid: Instituto Universitario de Estudios de la Mujer, Ediciones de la Universidad Autonóma de Madrid.

Alvarez, S.E. (1998) 'Latin American feminisms "go global": trends of the 1990s and challenges for the new millennium', in S.E. Alvarez *et al.* (op.cit.)

Alvarez, S.E., Dagnino, E. and Escobar, A. (eds) (1998) *Cultures of Politics Politics of Cultures. Re-visioning Latin American Social Movements*, Boulder, Colorado: Westview Press.

Anderson, B. (1983) *Imagined Communities. Reflections on the Origin and Spread of Nationalism*, London: Verso.

Appadurai, A. (1986) *Modernity at Large. Cultural Dimensions of Globalisation*, Minneapolis and London: University of Minnesota Press.

Arendt, H. (1958) *The Human Condition*, Chicago: Chicago University Press.

Bauman, Z. (1998) *Globalisation: The Human Consequences*, New York: Columbia University Press.

Benhabib, S. (1998) 'Models of public space: Hannah Arendt, the liberal tradition and Jurgen Habermas', in J.B. Landes (ed.) *Feminism, the Public and the Private*, Oxford: Oxford University Press.

Bhabha, H. (1994) *The Location of Culture*, London: Routledge.

Burns, T. (ed.) (1994) *After History? Francis Fukuyama and His Critics*, Boston and London: Rowman and Littlefield.

Collier, J. and Yanagisako, S. (1987) 'Gender and kinship: essays towards a unified analysis', in J. Collier and S. Yanagisako (eds) *Gender and Kinship*, Stanford: Stanford University Press.

Davidoff, L. (1998) 'Regarding some "old husbands' tales": public and private in feminist theory', in J.B. Landes (ed.) *Feminism, the Public and the Private*, Oxford: Oxford University Press.

Del Valle, T. (1993) *Gendered Anthropology*, London and New York: Routledge.

Dietz, M.G. (1991) 'Hannah Arendt and feminist politics', in M. Lyndon Shanley and C. Pateman (eds) *Feminist Interpretations and Political Theory*, Oxford: Polity Press.

—— (1998) 'Citizenship with a feminist face: the problem with maternal thinking', in J.B. Landes (ed.) *Feminism, the Public and the Private*, Oxford: Oxford University Press.

Elshtain, J. Bethke (1981) *Public Man, Private Woman*, Princeton N.J.: Princeton University Press.

—— (1997) *Real Politics. At the Center of Everyday Life*, Baltimore and London: The Johns Hopkins University Press.

Escobar, A. and Alvarez, S.E. (1992) *The Making of Social Movements in Latin America: Identity, Strategy and Democracy*, Boulder, Colorado: Westview.

Featherstone, M. (ed.) (1990) *Global Culture. Nationalism, Globalisation and Modernity*, London: Sage.

Fraser, N. (1989) *Unruly Practices: Power, Discourse and Gender in Contemporary Social Theory*, Cambridge: Polity Press.
—— (1991) 'What's critical about critical theory? The case of Habermas and gender', in J.B. Landes (ed.) *Feminism, the Public and the Private*, Oxford: Oxford University Press.
Fraser, N. and Gordon, L. (1994) 'Civil citizenship against social citizenship?', in B. van Steenbergen (ed.) *The Condition of Citizenship*, London: Sage.
Friedman, J. (1990) 'Being in the world: globalization and localization', in M. Featherstone (ed.) *Global Culture. Nationalism, Globalization and Modernity*, London: Sage.
Friedman, J. (1994a) *Cultural Identity and Global Process*, London: Sage Publications.
Friedman, J. (ed.) (1994b) *Consumption and Identity*, Chur, Switzerland: Harwood Academic.
Fukuyama, F. (1992) *The End of History and the Last Man*, London: Hamish Hamilton.
Gal, S. (1997) 'Feminism and civil society', in J.W. Scott, C. Kaplan and D. Keates (eds) *Transitions, Environments, Translations. Feminisms in International Politics*, New York and London: Routledge.
Gilligan, C. (1982) *In a Different Voice: Psychological Theory and Women's Development*, Cambridge, Mass.: Harvard University Press.
Harvey, D. (1989) *The Condition of Postmodernity*, Oxford: Basil Blackwell.
Honig, B. (1998) 'Toward an agonistic feminism: Hannah Arendt and the politics of identity', in J.B. Landes (ed.) *Feminism. The Public and the Private*, Oxford: Oxford University Press.
Hoogvelt, A. (1997) *Globalisation and the Postcolonial World: The New Political Economy of Development*, Basingstoke: Macmillan.
hooks, bell (1982) *Ain't I a Woman: Black Women and Feminism*, London: Pluto
—— (1984) *Feminist Theory from Margin to Center*, Boston: South End Press.
—— (1991) 'Choosing the margin as a space of radical openness', in *Yearning: Race, Gender and Cultural Politics*, London: Turnaround.
Howell, S. and Melhuus, M. (1993) 'The study of kinship; the study of person; a study of gender?' in T. del Valle (ed.) *Gendered Anthropology*, London: Routledge.
Jaquette, J.S. (1990) *The Women's Movement in Latin America: Feminism and the Transition to Democracy*, Boulder, Colorado: Westview Press.
Jaquette, J.S. and Wolchik, S.L. (eds) (1998) *Women and Democracy. Latin America and Central and Eastern Europe*, Baltimore and London: The Johns Hopkins University Press.
Jameson, F. (1991) *Postmodernism, or, the Cultural Logic of Late Capitalism*, London: Verso.

Jay, N. (1981) 'Gender and dichotomies'. *Feminist Studies*, 7(1): 38–56.

Kandiyoti, D. (1991) 'Identity and its discontents: women and the nation', *Millenium: Journal of International Studies*, 20(3): 429–43.

Leacock, E. and Lee, R. (1982) *Politics and History in Band Societies*, Cambridge: Cambridge University Press.

Lister, R. (1997) *Citizenship. A Feminist Perspective*, London: Macmillan.

McClintock, A. (1993) 'Family feuds: gender, nationalism and the family', *Feminist Review* 44: 61–80.

Massey, D. (1993a) 'Power geometry and a progressive sense of place', in J. Bird, B. Curtis, T. Putnam, G. Robertson and L. Tickner (eds) *Mapping the Futures*, London: Routledge.

—— (1993b) 'Politics and space/time', in M. Keith and S. Pile (eds) *Place and the Politics of Identity*, London and New York: Routledge.

Miller, D. (1987) *Material Culture and Mass Consumption*, Oxford: Basil Blackwell.

—— (1994) 'Style and ontology', in J. Friedman (ed.) (1994) *Consumption and Identity*, Chur, Switzerland: Harwood Academic Publishers.

Mohanty, C. (1993) 'Cartographies of struggle: third world women and the politics of feminism', in C. Mohanty, A. Russo and L. Torres (eds) *Third World Women and the Politics of Feminism*, Bloomington: Indiana University Press.

Moore, H. (1993) 'The differences within and the differences between', in T. del Valle (ed.) *Gendered Anthropology*, London: Routledge.

Moore, H. (1994) *A Passion for Difference: Essays in Anthropology and Gender*, Oxford: Polity Press.

Mouffe, C. (1992) 'Feminism, citizenship and radical democratic politics', in J. Butler and J.W. Scott (eds) *Feminists Theorize the Political* , London & New York: Boutledge.

Radcliffe, S. and Westwood, S. (eds) (1993) *Viva: Women and Popular Protest in Latin America*, London: Routledge.

—— (1996) *Remaking the Nation. Place, Identity and Politics in Latin America*, London and New York: Routledge.

Ribeiro, G.L. (1998) 'Cybercultural politics: political activism at a distance in a transnational world', in S.E. Alvarez *et al. Cultures of Politics, Politics of Cultures*, Boulder, Colorado: Westview Press.

Robertson, R. (1990) 'Mapping the global condition: globalization as the central concept', in M. Feathersone (ed.) *Global Culture. Nationalism, Globalization and Modernity*, London: Sage.

Robertson, R. (1992) *Globalization: Social Theory and Global Culture*, London: Sage.

Rosaldo, M. (1974) 'Woman, culture and society: a theoretical overview', in M. Rosaldo and L. Lamphere (eds) *Woman, Culture and Society*, Stanford: Stanford University Press.

Ruddick, S. (1989) 'Maternal Thinking'. *Feminist Studies*, 6(2): 342–67.

Scott, J.W., Kaplan, C. and Keates, D. (eds) (1997) *Transitions, Environments, Translations. Feminisms in International Politics*, London and New York: Routledge.

Slater, D. (1998) 'Rethinking the spatialities of social movements: questions of (b)orders, culture, and politics in global times', in S.E. Alvarez *et al.* (eds) *Cultures of Politics, Politics of Culture*, Boulder, Colorado: Westview Press.

Smart, B. (1992) *Modern Conditions, Postmodern Controversies*, London and New York: Routledge.

Soja, E. and Hooper, B. (1993) 'The spaces that difference makes: some notes on the geographical margins of the new cultural politics', in M. Keith and S. Pile (eds) *Place and the Politics of Identity*, London and New York: Routledge.

Touraine, A. (1982) 'Triumph or downfall of civil society', *Humanities in Review*, Cambridge: Cambridge University Press.

Watson, P. (1997) 'Civil society and the politics of difference in Eastern Europe', in J.W. Scott, C. Kaplan and D. Keates (eds) *Transitions, Environments, Translations. Feminisms in International Politics*, London and New York: Routledge.

Young, I.M. (1989) 'Polity and group difference: a critique of the ideal of universal citizenship'. *Ethics*, 99: 250–74.

Yudice, G. (1998) 'The globalisation of culture and the new civil society', in S.E. Alvarez *et al.* (eds) *Cultures of Politics, Politics of Cultures*, Boulder, Colorado: Westview Press.

Yuval-Davis, N. and Anthias, F. (eds) (1989) *Woman–Nation–State*, Basingstoke: Macmillan.

Chapter 2

Gender and Difference

Youth, bodies and clothing in Zambia

Karen Tranberg Hansen

Like all bodies, Zambian bodies are not only physical and material, but they are also socially constituted and managed. This chapter explores how we may view clothing consumption practices of young adults of both sexes in Zambia as a form of bodily praxis that tells us something about 'being-in-the-world' on Zambian terms (Friedman 1994: 112–6; Miller 1990). The link between body and knowledge suggested here derives from Bourdieu (Moore 1994: 78). The bodily praxis discussed here refers to young women's and men's understanding of social distinctions through their bodies and recognising that their particular position within social relations is based on that knowledge. In an essay on clothing consumption in his family Benard, a grade-twelve student in Mansa, acknowledged how Zambian society 'traditionally' has constructed embodiment. He explained:

> I'm of a family of five boys and four girls. Boys are supposed to wear trousers starting from their adolescence: this is due to our traditional dressing. For girls, they are not allowed to wear trousers because it's against our culture and it is part of family rules. Because if they start wearing trousers, they will show no respect to our parents who bought our clothes. Therefore girls in our family are only allowed to wear dresses with *vitenge* material (Bemba for printed cloth) covering the bottom part of their dress.

What is most noticeable about Benard's version of Zambia's clothing 'history' is his close attention to how the everyday social interaction through which gender is embodied differs for women and men. In effect, he describes how young women are taught to be much more concerned about the proper way to dress than young men. The respect expressed for seniors by young women whose bodies are covered properly through dress also signals their socially constrained and controlled sexuality. Clearly, Benard's statement has implications about male domination and female subordination in a society that overwhelmingly constructs gender in heterosexual terms.

If the 'tradition' of western-style clothing in Zambia is a recent one, its gender embodiments have roots in the region's local societies. Far from being static and reducible to biological essentialism, the cultural presuppositions that help to construe bodies through clothing are expressed differently in time and space. In fact, they develop distinct edges or sharpness that are influenced by the changing cultural politics in society at large. But while long-standing presuppositions about embodiment inform young people's clothing practices, they do not contain their desires. For clothing is central not only to how young people see themselves but also to how they imagine change and social transformation. That much of this clothing is second-hand does not diminish its role in mediating and constituting change in cultural terms. Last but not least, because dressing the body requires the wearer's intervention, the field of consumption provides an excellent site for exploring agency and subjectivity.

There is a rich literature on youth culture in the West in which the visual mass media is given pride of place in shaping self-identity and understanding of the world one inhabits (Hebdige 1979; McRobbie 1991). Media exposure in our late twentieth-century world has introduced western youth to a worldwide variety and quality of clothing (Hollander 1994: 198) that their grandparents hardly could have imagined. But when it comes to negotiating identity in a developing country like Zambia in the mid-1990s, most young persons (except the very rich) engage less with visual images on television, video, film, and the glossy print media than their western peers. This is in part because of unequal access and unequal exposure to the products and ideas emanating from the west's mass communication industries, plus a host of other inequities in the historical relationship between a country like Zambia and the West. But it is also, and perhaps more significantly for the purpose of this paper, because Zambian youth pay little attention to, or are not interested in, particular clothing practices that they consider too strange or, plainly, too weird, and not conforming with local cultural conventions of acceptable dress. In 1995 for example, such practices included ripped, torn, and cut-off jeans, and clothes with decorative patches sewn onto them. To be sure, in Zambia as in the West, fashion trickles both up and down (Craik 1994: 13, 217). What is of particular interest in this interaction is how the local and the West influence each other and especially how the difference between them is expressed and experienced (Carrier 1992).

Youth identities and desires in Zambia are shaped in complex ways in interaction with people, commodities, and ideas that stem from the world beyond home. Still, local cultural notions are in a position of dominance in influencing what is acceptable dress or not. This introduces special entanglements in the construction of space and time in relationship to clothing consumption practices as Zambian youth so very obviously are contending with the products of the world from beyond home. The twists and turns have revealed themselves particularly strikingly since the late 1980s when the commercial import of second-hand clothes from the West began to grow rapidly. But while the ready availability of second-hand clothing has redrawn the world map of clothing, opening access to it for the masses, consumers of this commodity are not particularly concerned about the provenance of the previously owned garments that they buy. Unlike the *sapeurs* in the Congo who showcase upscale brand-name clothing acquired in Paris during club displays in Kinshasa (Gandalou 1989), Zambian consumers have as yet paid scant attention to label-worthy garments. What they care about are affordable clothes that will fit Zambian bodies (Hansen 1994).

My ongoing study of how people in Zambia deal with second-hand clothing imported from the West places analysis of clothing consumption – both new and second-hand for of course they implicate one another – in the details of everyday life and in the realities of Zambia's postcolonial economy. Like most Zambian consumers of second-hand clothes, I do not privilege 'the West' over other influences when accounting for the meanings used garments acquire as they become part of new social dramas in Zambia (Hansen 1995), although I am concerned to unpack the many meanings 'the West' assumes in the context of clothing consumption. This paper represents a small segment of that larger study and is concerned in particular with the local cultural pre-suppositions about sex and gender that influence clothing practices of young adults. The argument I develop draws mainly but not exclusively on observations from what we might call clothing autobiographies. These are essays on clothing consumption written in 1995 by twelfth-grade students of both sexes in English composition classes in Lusaka, Zambia's capital, and two small towns, Mansa and Kawambwa, in the Luapula Province. From these essays I try to draw out how we may consider Zambian clothing practices on their own terms, that is in local terms, rather than as western derivations. I shall be arguing that those terms are very much to do with structures of difference, involving sex, gender and age, but also class, which inform but do not always contain clothing practices in Zambia's strained economy.

Because I focus specifically on student representations of clothing practices through written essays, I shall have little to say about the global processes that embroil my research subject. And it goes without saying that the voices of the young people to whom I turn shortly do not in themselves constitute transparent pieces of evidence. Rather their statements are products of other discourses that emerge in youth interaction in different areas of social life (McRobbie 1994). As such, what these young adults say is expressed in terms Zambian society has made available to them. Because these terms construe female and male bodies as essentially different, they subject women's dressed bodies to considerably more control than men's. In turn, young women reckon with societal morality and their own vulnerability by careful managing of their sexed bodies through dress. The paper begins with a brief discussion of postcolonial Zambian economy and society, sug-gesting that changes in major institutions like the family, education and the labour market are affecting young people's experiences. Then I consider clothing and discuss the importance we may attribute to it and why, in the topography of desire in economic and identity terms in Zambia. Before turning to the students' contributions, I discuss the essay as an ethnographic genre and describe the circumstances under which this particular essay was written. The core of the paper consists of two sections, a discussion of young men's clothing practices, followed by one about how young women put themselves together with clothes. In the con-clusion, I raise questions about the persistence of cultural presuppositions that shape youth clothing practices in postcolonial

Zambia, suggesting that political and economic changes in major institutions have important roles to play in unsettling deeply entrenched ideas about women's and men's gendered bodies and places in society.

Postcolonial Zambia: economy, society and youth

Zambia attracted international attention in 1991 as one of the first countries in sub-Saharan Africa to introduce a multi-party political system through peaceful elections. Prior to that was the not too distant legacy of close to twenty years of a one-party political reign, the Second Republic (1972–91), during which Zambia's economy experienced a sustained, rapid and substantial decline that adversely affected all sectors of life, including health and education (Kalumba and Freund 1989), and changed the country's ranking in the World Bank's categorisation from a high-income to a low-income country. With the winds of change during the first half of the 1990s, the new president gained widespread approval within the international donor community as he set the economy on a fast-paced structural adjustment programme. The Third Republic was to prosper as a market-driven economy. Some previously state-owned companies were privatised, the construction industry experienced a boom, and there were traders everywhere, selling all kinds of goods not manufactured in Zambia.

The image of bustling economic activity was deceptive. While the country's first stock exchange opened, major banks went bankrupt. The manufacturing sector had all but collapsed, including most of the textile and garment industry. Retrenchment in the public and private sector and wage freezes have been accompanied by a decline in the provision of health and education. The gap between poverty and wealth has increased while rural–urban disparities in standard of living have narrowed. The human and social costs that this progressive decline has helped to set into motion include rising unemployment, illness because of poor health services and inadequate nutrition, epidemics like cholera and AIDS, and troubles on the family front such as premarital pregnancies, marriage instability, and a growing incidence of female-headed households.

While there is depressing documentation of the frightening range of adverse effects of Zambia's economic decline (Bates and Collier

1993), development scholarship has had little to say about the cultural side of this process, specifically about how the ongoing decline is experienced by people who are actually living through it (Geisler and Hansen 1994; Roeber 1994). These processes form part of the backdrop against which young adults of both sexes project their sense of themselves. Most of the country's grade-twelve cohort, that is youth between approximately 17 and 22 years of age, is growing into adulthood facing poverty, political insecurity and public squalor. Confronting growing unemployment, this group of youth encounters a landscape of opportunity that differs from that of their parents and their older siblings in several respects.

Many parents still hope that education might help their children to progress in society even though the quality of education has deteriorated so badly and the economy is in such straits that a completed high-school education provides little job guarantee (Kelly 1991). As parents know only too well, real wages have eroded so much that being employed does not mean earning a living wage. Crowded living conditions at home prompt many young people to seek leisure and pleasure elsewhere, thus giving rise to parents' or guardians' complaints over the difficulty of controlling them, especially young women. Everyone knows that premarital pregnancy has serious consequences for young women because it results in expulsion from school. But young boys and girls who 'sit' at home do not face the same circumstances. If parents have the means, they are most likely to encourage young boys to continue schooling or special training. Many households experience tensions because of the different expectations their members have about appropriate behaviour between the generations and the sexes. Because of the depressed economy and a gender ideology that encourages male initiative and female dependency, today's young women are caught in a bind. Wanting to have it all on the terms Zambian society has made available to them, young women secondary-school students are particularly careful about how they put themselves together with clothing.

Clothing and topographies of desire

Zambians fashion their identities and lives from a variety of resources within the political and economic circumstances available to them, drawing inspiration from the past and the present as well

as from individual desires. Clothing – new and used – is an important cultural resource that goes to the heart of widespread Zambian
understandings of socio-economic well being. According to
McCracken (1990: 61), clothing not only reflects 'changing
historical circumstances but also [serves] as a device which creates
and constitutes this change in cultural terms'. Clothes are important in conveying class, gender and generational aspirations. This is
why clothes and fashion are highly relevant to experiences of social
change. It is also the reason why African preoccupations with
western-styled dress made clothing a powerful medium for debate
during the colonial era in Zambia. The ability of clothing to
provoke debate derives from its centrality to the project of
modernity, in particular to new notions of propriety, wealth and
development. The literature on colonial Zambia offers rich
examples of this.[1]

Aside from fulfilling basic needs, clothing – new and used –
constitutes a site where social identities are both constructed and
contested. Thus dressing, and dressing up, is both an end in itself
and a means that may entail a certain liberating potential (Wilson
1985). For clothes are not worn passively but require people's
active collaboration. The result is considerable devotion of time and
effort by people set on expressing identity through clothes and
attracting appreciation of it by others. As Hollander has suggested
for western clothes (1978), the presentational form (Miller 1987:
87) or the 'look' that emerges from this management process in
Zambia has reference to visual images, to a spectrum of desirable
ways of looking at any given time that has obvious western traces.
Yet such images are also tied up with local Zambian notions of the
body and sexuality, with distinctions drawn by gender and generation, and they are also affected by the economic imperatives of
everyday living and the relative power of the state. The youth
clothing practices which I describe shortly reflect individual and
peer values regarding dress practices that are informed by, but not
always contained within, local norms about social etiquette and
sexual decorum. The emergent clothing system is always in process,
its meanings generated in particular contexts.

Some articles of clothing are more powerful than others in
negotiating identity. This observation is particularly relevant to
school-going youth whose scope for dealing with clothing is
constrained by their need to wear school uniforms and by the
disposable incomes of their parents or guardians. How youth

dresses when away from school also depends, especially for young women, on the religious orientation of their household. Christianity played an important role in the homes of many of the young essay writers of both sexes, helping to influence the organisation of clothing practices in both space and time. Some young women from Christian homes who were regular churchgoers wrote of wearing long skirts and tops with sleeves when attending service. Anastasia lamented: 'I do want to wear trousers but my father is too religious and says that trousers are meant for men and not women as far as the bible is concerned.' Regardless of church orientation, most of the young people organised their dress practices across space and time by distinguishing between clothes they would wear at home when working or enjoying leisure, and clothes they would put on when leaving home, either for shopping, strolling or being part of group interaction. The presence of different 'others' like peers, friends of the opposite sex, the general public or seniors also influenced how young people dressed.

Student essays: clothing autobiographies

The written essay as a genre of oral narrative adds valuable insights to ethnographic information collected through other conventions of scholarship. The use of the essay form in making ethnographic observations in this region dates back to Hortence Powdermaker's research into African experiences of modernisation on the Copperbelt during the first half of the 1950s (1956; 1962). Her use of the written essay as a means to learning about the aspirations of young people was extended in social psychological research conducted from the University of Zambia during the late 1960s, about half a decade after independence. Leonard Bloom who had secondary-school and beginning university students write spontaneous autobiographies noted their desire for independence (1972: 296). Where Powdermaker emphasised that students experienced growing into adulthood in a changing society as a conflict between tradition and modernity, Bloom found his essay writers stressing the liberating dimension of socio-economic change (1972: 297). He suggested that '"tradition" and "modernity" [were] likely to achieve a significant and stable accommodation' in the future (1972: 300).

Tradition and modernity co-exist, but uneasily so, in the essays secondary-school students wrote for me about clothing practices in their families in 1995. In fact, there was more tension between the tropes tradition and modernity in the young girls' essays than in the young men's. I constructed these essays to invite young adult women and men to describe clothing practices in their homes, discussing as well how they really like to dress and what they hate to wear and why. Given the nature of my larger study, I was also concerned about where their clothes were bought, how often, and by whom.[2]

A total of 173 grade-twelve students wrote this essay. They were 49 young women in Kabulonga Secondary School for Girls and 57 young men in Kabulonga Secondary School for Boys, both in Lusaka, and 38 young women in St Mary's Secondary School in Kawambwa and 29 young men at St Clement's Secondary School in Mansa, both small administrative centres in Luapula Province. The Lusaka schools are day schools, whereas the schools in Luapula enrol both day students and boarders. Although none of these schools are elite schools, and their students come from across the country, representing a wide range of socio-economic backgrounds save the top and the bottom, the student essay writers are more privileged than their out-of-school age cohort. For unlike many of their peers, these particular students had passed their secondary-school entrance exams after grade seven. And being close to completing secondary school, they had managed not to drop out. For the young women essay writers in particular, avoiding pregnancy and expulsion from school was a real achievement.

Some of the essays were written with an immediacy and directness that draws the reader into the student's household. We can almost see Moses's father, an employee of a parastatal company in Lusaka whom Moses describes as a 'thin birdlike man pushing forty who always wears rimless glasses'. In his spare time he sews clothes and is, according to Moses, 'one of the best tailors in Zambia'. He continued:

> Usually on weekends he would sew from mornings till evenings; his face placid at the sewing machine with a thin whistling from his lips. In the backyard at lunchtime he would sit behind the desk attending to his clients on a bench.

Other essays compel attention by making a world of imagery come true. When describing how everyone in her family liked to dress,

Rachel, whose father is a businessman, explained that she liked all sorts of clothes as long as they fit her nicely and her 'African figure is comfortable in it'. She seeks her grandmother's advice when she is uncertain about how to dress. Turning to her young sister, she explained that she

> is the one who lives in dreamland because she always wants to look the best, that's why we all at home call her Alexis (Joan Collins). She likes looking expensive, by which I mean she doesn't like cheap clothes. She is 14 years old now.

Young men's clothing practices

Second-hand clothes imported commercially into Zambia do not arrive with ready-made meanings attached to them. Rather, they are conceptually and materially reworked in processes inspired both by societal shifts and western influences. The resulting constructions are adjusted to local dress conventions, but not without struggles, as I have hinted. The chief differentiating factors in these processes are class, gender and age distinctions. I provide a few examples from young men's clothing universe.

In the second-hand tie market, 'New Culture' silk ties with floral designs were much sought after in 1995. 'New Culture' is also a term used by the press for the liberalised economic regime and political opening-up under President Chiluba and the new set of values supposedly ushered in by political and economic reforms. Some of the 'new' men in power dress Chiluba style: in double-breasted suits with floral ties and matching handkerchiefs. This dress convention has created considerable work for tailors who are busy, closing up vents and altering oversized single-breasted jackets into double-breasted ones. They also take in large-sized men's trousers, adding pleats and loops at the waist, one back pocket, and cuffs at the legs.

Suits in this style were the preferred wear of male white-collar workers in 1995. In today's popular discourse in Zambia, wage labour is coming close to meaning white-collar work. In fact, such employment tends popularly to be referred to as 'work' (in contrast to 'business' or 'trade'), and its jobholders as 'officers', 'workers' or simply 'working class'. The implication of this social categorisation is clear. White-collar work is one of the few wage labour opportunities to which young adults can aspire in Zambia's declining formal sector. Dressing in this way conveys something important about educational background, respectability and responsibility. In short, it implies that the wearer is a man in charge.

Many young adult urban men aspire to this dress ideal and the responsibility and social respectability that follows from holding a steady monthly-paid job and thus being a man in charge. 'I want to be wearing clothes like those that people who work wear, because I want to be looking like a man rather than a boy,' wrote Arnold, a twelfth-grade student in Lusaka. 'Suits are the clothes I like most,' explained Simon, 'because they make me look decent and soon I will be joining the society of workers.' Morgan, one of their classmates, described a present of a pair of trousers and a jacket he recently had received: 'I was full of joy . . . I like these clothes because a lot of people say that I look like a general manager and not only that, they also say that I look like a rich man.' Other classmates liked jeans, particularly because they are durable, but also because 'they are in style now'. Lubasi put it this way: 'I try by all means to be in line with style because when I am watching video music tapes like those recorded on MTV, I have noticed that most of the singers wear jeans.'

But wearing jeans has a flip side. In the view of many of these young urban men, jeans too readily call forth the image of rough guys and street vendors. Simon whose preference for suits we just heard about said that he didn't like jeans 'because they make me look like a "call boy"'. Call boys are young men at the mini-bus ranks who call out the destination of the bus, rough up passengers, and collect fares. According to Moses: 'I hate jeans because people may fail to distinguish between cigarette sellers and myself.' Martin also hated wearing jeans 'because they make me look like one of the naughty boys and thieves who hang around the corridors in town'. Lusaka's downtown streets are full of young male traders. They put much effort into being seen and many of them dress in a striking manner: in oversized jeans, high-top unlaced sneakers, and flashy T-shirts; a baseball cap is almost *de rigueur*; and the most daring wear bandannas as headgear. Since domestically manu-factured garments of this type are not readily available, most of these clothes are imported, either new or second-hand. Regardless of their source, such garments look costly.

There are at least two issues at stake in the young men's com-mentaries on the street vendors' get-up. First, because they are close to completing secondary school, they have higher economic aspirations for themselves. To be sure, young male secondary students do not want to be mistaken for the school-drop-outs turned loafers who are viewed as a threat to society's stability and security. And secondly, the apparent expense of the street vendors' outfit readily implies that the clothes have been acquired by illicit means, thus the association with thieves. Such extravagant display of wealth raises suspicion and, in fact, 'gangster' is a term residents of medium- and high-income areas use frequently to describe the street vendor clothing style.

Thus suits and jeans frame young urban adult men's desires for a better life. Young adult men in rural areas have similar desires, but they appear more circumscribed by the conditions in which they live. Some twelve-graders in a secondary school in Mansa expressed this clearly. Joshua explained:

> Of all the clothes, I like strong ones which can serve me longer such as jeans. I like them because it is not easy for me to buy soap, and most of the time I do manual work in order to earn my living.

The suit figures in the desires of these young rural men mostly by its absence. According to Cepas:

> I dislike these types of clothes because they are very expensive and only meant for working class people. Since we do not work or get paid and only lead our lives by subsistence farming, I cannot go for this type of clothes.

Nicholas used fairly similar language to describe why the suit combination did not fit his situation: 'Such clothes can easily be torn and I think they are for office working people, so they don't suit me.' Yet he added as an afterthought: 'If I had a choice, I would really like to wear suits.'

The term 'New Culture' may well have conveyed the initial optimism Zambians expressed about better opportunity and more access in their new multi-party state in the early 1990s. While the expectations of the wearers of new culture ties and second-hand suits have certainly faded, Zambians from most walks of life continue to rummage the piles of used clothing, putting their lives together as best they can. Depending on location in class and regional terms, and on gender and age, Zambians themselves read highly ambiguous meanings about freedom from wants and normative constraints into clothing consumption. I illustrate this point with reference to young women's dress practices below.

Clothing competence and embodied femininity

The world of second-hand clothing consumption is not one of cultural fragmentation in which anything goes. Zambian consumers do not put together their clothing universe at random, but in ways that implicate cultural presuppositions. Normative ideas about gender and authority are among the dominant cultural representations through which they interpret clothing practices.

The dominant cultural discourse in Zambia is one that strongly privileges men over women at all levels of society. For an example, I turn to an interview conducted in 1995, during my survey of clothing consumption practices, with an air traffic controller in one of Lusaka's low-density areas. It was late morning, he had just completed a night shift and was relaxing at home, wearing shorts, a T-shirt and sandals. At one point I asked him what he thought of the clothes of the young male street vendors. 'It is all right,' he said. 'Even though our parents didn't like it at all, my generation loved jeans and we insisted on wearing them.' When I asked him how he viewed miniskirts for young women, his tune shifted markedly. 'I can't allow that,' he said vehemently, 'not even for my own daughters. Young women are not supposed to show their legs in the presence of their father.' This remark, with its unequal scope for male and female dress practice, was echoed again and again, voiced by women of all ages and men in both urban and rural areas. The chief exception to this was *apamwamba* (Nyanja, meaning those at the top) households in which some women within the age category of 20–35 years readily admitted wearing miniskirts, especially if they had the body to go with them.

The remarks of the air controller turn on the miniskirt and pertain to tight and revealing clothing in general. Young women's clothing competence is a product of early socialisation. It hinges on what young adult women describe as body structures and private parts, as well as on comportment and presentation. When young women speak of body structures, they refer to whether they are thin or fat (mostly the former), including observations about thin arms and legs, and the relative size of their breasts. When they use the term private parts, they refer to vaginas and thighs. As Benard explained at the outset of the paper, young girls are taught to dress decently and respectfully; as adolescents they are taught to wrap a *chitenge* (Nyanja for printed cloth) around their waist when working at home, and to wear loose and not revealing dresses and skirts reaching below the knee when in public. When sitting, their legs should neither be apart nor exposed. And their clothes must, of course, be clean and well ironed.

While these presuppositions inform young women's clothing practices, they do not contain their desires. Some young urban women who want to 'move with fashion' do wear miniskirts in public while others put them on when their parents are out. Yet most are apprehensive about exposing the body. While this concern arises from the need to show respect for elders, it also pertains to the issue of decency and the implications raised by miniskirts about loose morals. But above all, this concern expresses young women's fear of sexual violence. As Abigal, a grade-twelve student in Lusaka, explained:

The clothes I like least are short (mini) and tight clothes; and I like them least because here in Zambia when you dress in such kinds of clothes, people may start having ideas about you, because some people think that if you dress in mini skirts or dresses, you are a prostitute because they think prostitutes dress like that. I can give you one example,' she went on. 'Here in Zambia, if you put on mini and tight clothes, men can easily rip your clothes and you might be raped at the same time. And some people think you are of an unrespectable family if you dress in such kinds of clothes.

Abigal's remarks touch on a highly charged issue which pre-occupied at least one third of her Lusaka classmates who made direct associations between miniskirts and rape. The specific backdrop for this close association was the public stripping of a woman wearing a miniskirt by street vendors at Lusaka's Kulima Tower (a major bus stop) on 18 March, 1994. It was widely discussed in the press and prompted demonstrations by women's groups. (At least two issues were raised at these events. Firstly, women's freedom to dress and secondly, violence against women.) But this particular event was not the only one of its kind. According to Jessie:

> Here in Zambia when you go to town the street vendors tear your dress or whatever you are wearing because it is very short. And they call you all sorts of names, for instance *hule* (prostitute) and they can rape you.

Cleopatra was more explicit:

> In Zambia there is no freedom of dressing. If you wore mini skirts, bicycle shorts or leggings and decided to go shopping in town, you would be stripped naked . . . this kind of dressing arouses men's emotions.

Young men enjoy considerably more freedom to dress than young women whom society blames for provoking men's uncontrollable desires when they wear short or tight clothes. Perhaps this understanding of dress is involved in many young women's liking for jeans; the preferred style in 1995 was a loose cut, giving a slightly baggy silhouette. 'The reason why I like jeans', explained Habenzu, 'is that when I wear jeans, I feel comfortable when I am sitting with boys because I can sit the way I want.' And according to Sameta:

> If I am on a journey or taking a stroll with friends I wear jeans. I walk without being worried. Secondly, when I am in a minibus or where most of those grown up people are, I don't have to worry about how I am supposed to sit.

Hlupekile brought home the point about jeans:

> The clothes I like best is office wear, that is, skirt and blouse, or suit skirt and jacket . . . I like these clothes because in our country Zambia there are lots of rape cases. When you put on a mini skirt, you cannot go around town without being attacked by street boys or even raped. I prefer jeans because when you are surrounded by these kinds of people, it will take time for them to undress you. You can scream and at least people might be able to hear your screaming and come over.

The miniskirt is not the only item of clothing that gives rise to conformity in some areas of life and dissent in others. Trousers for women do so too, depending on context. In general, the association between miniskirts and rape was less explicit in rural female grade-twelve students' dress practices. The young women at St Mary's Secondary School at Kawambwa expressed less concern about the body-exposing issue in relationship to notions of decency, respectability and sexual violence than their urban peers. Many liked dress and suit combinations and quite a few liked to wear jeans. Yet jeans were not acceptable everywhere. Astridah graphically related the following incident:

> When I visited my aunt last month I wore jeans. Immediately she saw me, she started shouting. Is this the way you dress as a daughter of Lupupa? Our clan or family does not allow a woman to put on male clothes. I am telling you Astridah, in our family with your father, we don't allow such a way of dressing. Astridah added: I was so shocked. She even complained that we learned this type of dressing from my mother which is not true.

Women's dressed bodies receive considerable critical scrutiny. The constraints on their dress practices are far more pronounced than on men who can create the smooth, continuous line, enveloping their bodies to perfection from the combination of suit and tie (Hollander 1994).[3] Yet there is one clothing platform where women take safe clothing conventions in their own hands and develop them to the fullest. This is the two-piece *chitenge* outfit, the postcolonial creation of a 'national dress' tradition that continues to take on new shapes, influenced in particular by Zairian and West African clothing trends. Today *chitenge* outfits are worn to work by office workers and teachers and put on for special occasions especially by mature women who have the body to support them. But young adult women do not agree on whether or not they like *chitenge* fashions. Those who do not wear them usually explain that they are too thin to look good in *chitenge* outfits. Ambiguous about the challenges and burdens of adult womanhood, and concerned about the ramifications of revealing body structures and private parts, their preferred dress style in 1995 was the two-piece suit that covers their bodies loosely, consisting of a hip-length top and straight skirt, reaching below the knee.

Bodies and clothing: power, control, and desire

The student essays clearly demonstrate that young women work harder on the social management of bodies and sexuality through clothing than do young men. In fact, the young women expressed more acute awareness, or anxiety, about approaching sexual maturity than the young men. There were three reactions to approaching adulthood among the young women writers. A small group said that people called them tomboys and that they preferred to wear jeans and casual clothes. Then there were several young women who looked forward to wearing suits and dresses. They included Sameta whose mother had given her a long skirt with a slit at the back and matching blouse for Christmas. Sameta explained:

> I was very happy . . . I liked myself that day and I looked like I was a working class even though I am still schooling. Sometimes when I wear office wear I feel comfortable and it makes me feel that one day I will become a grown-up woman.

Finally, there were quite a few young women who were approaching sexual maturity with unease and who saw dresses as an icon of this. As 18-year-old Tanera put it: 'Clothes like dresses really make me feel uncomfortable . . . I feel as if I look married or like a mother . . .' Carolyn didn't like dresses because they made her look old fashioned; what is worse, 'when you wear such clothes people will not even talk to you because they will think that you are running a home or you are somebody's grandmother'.

Young men by contrast said far less in their essays about clothing in reference to the opposite sex and their own physical and social bodies. There were exceptions of course. The main reason Justin gave for liking jeans was to 'please the cute girls so that I can be of attraction to them . . . cute girls never bother to say hi to you when you are putting on clothes that are rather old fashioned'. Moses, the young man whose father tailors on weekends, was very body conscious. Describing his delight over a double-breasted jacket his father recently had sewn for him, he elaborated:

After wearing it I surveyed myself in the mirror. I looked like a film actor . . . it was really a nice jacket. I like jackets because they suit me like a second skin. I have plenty of beef and muscles around my shoulders which forms a good round shape if I wear one [a jacket].

The reverse applied to Norman who felt physically awkward. He complained:

Whenever I am wearing a suit, I am always thinking that everybody is looking at me . . . My physical structure does not earn me the prestige of wearing suits. I am slightly short and very thin. So whenever I put on a suit, it does not accord me the beauty of appearing best in clothes.

Above all, the essays express the discomfort many young women experience as objects of the male gaze. After having complained about her religious father that 'not only does he not permit me to wear trousers but also what they call miniskirts which leave the thighs to the open or outside,' Anastasia went on: 'I personally don't like miniskirts despite his not wanting me to wear them.

They are an exposure to men and if one gets raped, who will be to blame [but yourself] because rape cases have increased.' Anastasia's remarks are not surprising. Zambian society does not allow women to have sexual desires but rather warns them to keep their sexuality within bounds through clothing. By contrast, Zambian society takes men's sexual urges for granted: perhaps this makes young men worry less than young women about how their clothing expresses sexuality.

In sum, the major distinctions these essays reveal between young women's and men's dealings with clothes are to do with the social construction and organisation of sexuality, the sexualisation of the female body, and the discomfort young women experience through being made the object of the male gaze. These problems arise not only or even mainly in the representation of sexuality in these student essays but are above all products of actual sexual behaviour within the broader context of social and economic life in Zambia. Their reality helps to account for the very high profile the women students gave to the miniskirt in their essays. While there have been controversies over miniskirts before, and not only in Zambia (Wipper 1972), the 1994 event differs from previous ones, for example in the early 1970s, when cultural nationalism was at issue. But the 1994 event has a much sharper edge, as it took place in the time of the AIDS epidemic when violence against women appeared to be on the increase (Phiri 1993). The high prevalence of AIDS in Zambia in the mid-1990s has not re-mapped sexual boundaries but affected the terms of sexual exchange to women's disadvantage.[4] This means that common-sense thought in Zambia continues to accept men's uncontrollable sexual urges yet blames women for passing on the disease. Clearly, the dressed body is more than a site of representation. As Holland *et al.* have noted in work on AIDS in the West: 'Women have to live with the physicality of bodily encounters, and often with physical violence, in ways in which Foucault did not examine' (1994: 22). It is not surprising that these young women feel under pressure to construct their physical bodies into a particular model of femininity through dress.

Conclusion

Much scholarship on youth in the West has explored the anxieties and pleasures of growing into adulthood through analysis of the visual media. In a developing country like Zambia with far less media exposure, clothing consumption constitutes a particularly rich site from which to examine how young women and men are experiencing the possibilities and constraints of growing into adulthood. This paper has argued that it is through young people's dealings with clothing that they make sense of postcolonial Zambian society and their own place within it and in the world at large. In effect, youth preoccupations with clothes comprise a politics of consumption that tells us something about 'being-in-the-world' on Zambian terms.

In making sense of their own place in the late twentieth-century, several differences are intruding on shaping the particular experience of young Zambians. One of these differences is class which in structural terms positions most of these youths as disadvantaged relative to their cohort in the West. The unprecedented vitality of the international commercial export of second-hand clothes to a country like Zambia is due to no small degree to the accessibility and crossover appeal of clothes to poor consumers. And poverty is one reason why the majority of Zambian youth gets unequal exposure to the products of the West's mass media industries. But second-hand clothing has brought the world within reach and with it imagined communities that may differ from those based on the printed word and the visual media.[5] Although they derive from the West, second-hand clothes are interpreted through representations locally available, their meanings informed in important ways by the structure of social relations and dominant cultural presuppositions in Zambia. And it is these relations and presuppositions that make practices involving western-styled clothing local.

Clothing consumption practices in Zambia are marked through with structures of difference at several levels, not only those already mentioned based on class but also on age and gender. These structures of difference comprise the local cultural notions or cultural presuppositions which I described at the outset as holding positions of dominance in influencing what is acceptable dress or not. These presuppositions are both contested and redefined and so they leave space for the social actor; and they vary both contextually and biographically as we have seen through the examples I have given involving youth versus seniors (Astridah and her aunt) and street, or work versus home. We saw this with regard to the young adult fairly well-educated men's interpretation of the street vendors' clothes and the suit.

What young people's dealings with clothes in Zambia show most dramatically is that the cultural presuppositions that influence people's actions are not equal. Some carry much more social leverage and reward than others do and some are negatively sanctioned. Thus the young women I have introduced here do not slip easily into the gender role of adult woman that Zambian society assigns to them. Rather, they do so in bits and pieces, gradually reining in – as they say themselves – body structures and private parts, constructing through clothing the material and symbolic referents of a particular body image.

This is to say that the meanings of clothes do not inhere in the garments themselves, but are attributed to them by acting social beings. Through the associations young women have learned to make between specific articles of clothing and behaviour, they construct an understanding of their world and of how the female body inhabits it. According to the dominant cultural construction of embodiment in Zambia, because women's bodies are open to invasion, they need managing and constraining through clothing, whereas men's bodies follow second nature, dressed in that social skin that envelops their sexed bodies to perfection: the suit.

Changing this habitus of gender relations in Zambia will depend in part on destabilising its most powerful icons: the suit and the dress and behaviours associated with them within the organisation of everyday life and in the wider setting. And this depends on institutional practices and the importance that changes in schooling, employment and family life may have on shaping the opportunities for young people, providing them with new terms with which to express a differently gendered landscape from that in which they are growing up.

Acknowledgements: This paper draws on research conducted in Zambia and Europe between January and December 1995, supported by grants from the Social Science Research Council (US) and the Wenner Gren Foundation for Anthropological Research. For facilitating the student essay-writing exercise, I owe special thanks to Mary Lungu of the curriculum department in the Ministry of Education and Violet Chuula, head of English at the Kabulanga Secondary School for Girls in Lusaka.

Notes

1 I am referring to observations made by Godfrey Wilson, J. Clyde Mitchell, and Audrey Richards, among others, and the simplistic criticism by Magubane (1971) of the complex place of western-style clothing consumption in African everyday life. For a recent commentary on this, see Vaughan (1994: 15–19).

2 I received permission to undertake this exercise from the provincial education officer in Lusaka and the district education officer in Luapula province. Secondary-school principals or department heads allowed me to contact English teachers who in turn administered the essay after I explained the reasons for my interest in the subject matter to them. They introduced my interests to the students.

   The essay was worded as follows: How do you dress in your family? Describe who buys the clothes for your family and where most of your clothes are bought (from the shop, tailor, *salaula* [second-hand], or any other source). When was the last time that you were bought or received clothes and what kind of clothes were they? What kind of clothes do you like best and why? And what kind of clothes do you like least and why? Please indicate where you live, the size of your family, and what your parents or guardians are doing (farming, fishing, work, business, trade, etc.).

3 Although Hollander's work is about the place of clothes in western art depictions, I find several of her arguments resonating with the history of clothing consumption in Zambia. For example, her most recent book emphasises the enduring appeal of the suit in creating the perfect man (1994: 92). She also suggests that female dress always makes a strong, almost theatrical visual claim, but that male tailored costume sets the real standard (1994: 8). Adult Zambian women's commentaries on the differences between male and female clothing practice are very similar to Hollander's suggestion.

4 With HIV/AIDS adult prevalence rates estimated at between 22 and 25 per cent for urban areas (and 10 and 13 per cent for rural areas), young urban adolescent women are particularly vulnerable (GRZ and UN 1996: 56). Rates of infection among adolescents are reported to be seven times higher for women between the ages of 15 and 19 than for men of the same age (Webb 1996: 2).

5 I have elsewhere (Hansen 1995: 142) referred to Hannerz's suggestion that expressions of symbolic modes carried by distinct technologies (e.g., writing and print, television, media, and music) distribute themselves differently in their local reception. Arguing that what is initially alien may be interpreted through representations locally available, he suggests the possibility of finding alternative imagined communities to those posited by the work of McLuhan and Anderson.

Bibliography

Bates, R.H. and Collier, P. (1993) 'The politics and economics of policy reform in Zambia', in R.H. Bates and A.O. Kruger (eds) *Political and*

Economic Interactions in Economic Policy Reform: Evidence From Eight Countries, London: Blackwell.

Bloom, L. (1972) 'Some values and attitudes of young Zambians, studied through spontaneous autobiographies', *African Social Research*, 14: 288–300.

Carrier, J. (1992) 'Occidentalism: the world turned upside-down', *American Ethnologist*, 19, 2: 195–212.

Craik, J. (1994) *The Face of Fashion*, London: Routledge.

Friedman, J. (1994) *Cultural Identity and Global Process*, Thousand Oaks, CA: Sage Publications.

Gandalou, J.D. (1989) *Dandies à Bakongo: Le Culte de l'Élégance dans la Societe Congolaise Contemporaine,* Paris: L'Harmattan.

Geisler, G. and Hansen, K. Tranberg (1994) 'Structural adjustment, the rural-urban interface, and gender relations in Zambia', in S. Pressman, N. Aslanbeigui and G. Sommerfield (eds), *Women in the Age of Economic Transformation: Gender Impacts of Reform in Post-Socialist and Developing Countries*, London: Routledge.

Government of the Republic of Zambia and the United Nations System in Zambia (GRZ and UN) (1996) *Prospects for Sustainable Development in Zambia: More Choices for our People,* Lusaka: Pilcher Graphics.

Hannerz, U. (1993) 'The withering away of the nation? An Afterword', *Ethnos,* 3–4: 377–91.

Hansen, K. Tranberg (1994) 'Dealing with used clothing: *Salaula* and the construction of identity in Zambia's Third Republic', *Public Culture*, 6: 3: 503–23.

——— (1995) 'Transnational biographies and local meanings: used clothing practices in Lusaka', *Journal of Southern African Studies*, 21, 1: 131–45.

Hebdige, D. (1979) *Subculture: The Meaning of Style*, London: Methuen.

Holland, J., Ramazanoglu, C., Sharpe, S. and Thomson, R. (1994) 'Power and desire: the embodiment of female sexuality', *Feminist Review*, 46: 21–38.

Hollander, A. (1978) *Seeing Through Clothes*, New York: Penguin Viking.

——— (1994) *Sex and Suits: The Evolution of Modern Dress*, New York: Alfred A. Knopf.

Kalumba, K. and Freund, P. (1989) 'The eclipse of idealism: health planning in Zambia', *Health Polity and Planning*, 4, 3: 219–28.

Kelly, M.J. (1991) *Education in a Declining Economy: The Case of Zambia, 1875–1985*, EDI Development Policy Case Series, Analytical Case Studies, No. 8. Washington, D.C.: The World Bank.

Magubane, B. (1971) 'A critical look at indices used in the study of social change in colonial Africa', *Current Anthropology*, 12: 419–31.

McCracken, G. (1988) *Culture and Consumption*, Bloomington: Indiana University Press.

McRobbie, A. (1991) *Feminism and Youth Culture: From 'Jackie' to 'Just Seventeen'*, London: Macmillan.

—— (1994) 'Different, youthful, subjectivities: towards a cultural sociology of youth', in A. McRobbie (ed.) *Postmodernism and Popular Culture*, London: Routledge.

Miller, D. (1987) *Material Culture and Mass Consumption*, London: Blackwell.

—— (1990) 'Fashion and ontology in Trinidad', *Culture and History*, 7: 49–77.

Moore, H.L. (1994) *A Passion for Difference*, Bloomington: Indiana University Press.

Phiri, E.C. (1993) 'Violence against women in Zambia', Lusaka: YWCA Council of Zambia.

Powdermaker, H. (1956) 'Social change through imagery and values of teen-age Africans in Northern Rhodesia', *American Anthropologist*, 58: 783–813.

—— (1962) *Coppertown: Changing Africa. The Human Situation of the Rhodesian Copperbelt*, New York: Harper and Row.

Roeber, C.A. (1994) 'Moneylending, trust, and the culture of commerce in Kabwe, Zambia', *Research in Economic Anthropology*, 15: 39–61.

Vaughan, M. (1994) 'Colonial discourse theory and African history, or has postmodernism passed us by?', *Social Dynamics*, 20, 2: 1–23.

Webb, D. (1996) 'The socio-economic impact of HIV/AIDS in Zambia', *SafAIDS News*, 4: 2–10.

Wilson, E. (1985) *Adorned in Dreams: Fashion and Modernity*, Berkeley: University of California Press.

Wipper, A. (1972) 'African women, fashion, and scapegoating', *Canadian Journal of African Studies*, 6, 2: 329–49.

Chapter 3

Women are women or how to please your husband

Initiation ceremonies and the politics of 'tradition' in Southern Africa

Gisela Geisler

In April 1995 two South African magazines reported the revival of the centuries-old custom of testing girls for virginity in KwaZulu not far from Durban. According to the reports young girls dressed in 'traditional' clothing flocked to the virginity inspections where they were asked 'to lie on their backs on grass mats with their knees bent, baring their genitals', in order to obtain one of the highly prized virginity certificates. *Ukuhlolwa*, the Zulu term for virginity testing, is said to be 'the only solution to teenage pregnancy', since as one of the inspectors explained, 'girls cannot indulge in sex if they know they will be checked regularly'.[1] This evocation of a 'tradition' of women's chastity happens in a country with one of the highest rape figures in the world, and in a province where 15 per cent of all rapes reported to the police alone happen on average every 84 seconds (Leclerc-Madlala: 1995: 16). This 'old tradition' is revived at a time when 'jackrolling', a 'new tradition' of abducting young women at gunpoint from the sides of their boy-friends and raping, mistreating and sometimes killing them is on the rise in South Africa's townships.[2]

The intricacies of claims as to what is 'tradition' and what is not, or which 'tradition' is useful and which obsolete, are complex and contradictory. Anthropology students at the University of Durban–Westville in an essay discussing the future of the customs of bride-wealth (*lobola*) and polygamy exemplified this eclectic and arbitrary evocation of 'tradition'. The majority of women students considered *lobola* a 'real tradition' which must not be interfered with, but rejected polygamy either as outdated and repulsive or as 'not our tradition', just as the majority of male students thought *lobola* was obsolete but polygamy worthy enough to merit recognition as a 'tradition'.[3] *Lobola*, the practice requiring the groom to pay large sums of money to the parents of the bride, which some believe make women the property of men, is also acceptable for prominent members of the South African government which constitutionally guarantees gender equality. Under the title 'Madiba's daughters say yes to *lobolo*. It does not degrade women. It's part of our culture', *Drum* magazine ran in August 1995 an article which revealed that Nelson Mandela's daughter Zinzi was married off for '25 bulls worth at least R2000 each' and that she and her sisters believe that 'far from being degrading to women it is actually a sign of respect' and that therefore '*lobolo* should be maintained as an important part of African culture'.[4]

South Africa is not a singular case where disputation about 'tradition' is and has been happening. In Zambia, Zimbabwe and Mozambique, as elsewhere, 'tradition' has never been static, and it has been an important arena of social and political struggles. Colonialism and the introduction of the British legal system which codified fluid African 'customary laws' has been shown to have resulted in a period of claims and counter-claims for and against 'tradition' and 'custom', a period marked by alliances and divisions between ruler and ruled, rural elders and urbanised young men. As Chanock has aptly pointed out, the notion of 'tradition' has also been 'a crucial ingredient in cultural nationalism' (Chanock 1985: 4) and as such it has remained an important arena of contestation in modern African states.

The competition over what is and should be 'tradition', whether invented, modified or reinforced, has largely been the prerogative of men, who have used it to ensure their control over women and to circumscribe the scope of women's action. 'Tradition' and 'custom' are therefore often seen as the linchpin of African women's subordinated status and the single most important obstacle to their emancipation. But, as the example of discussions about *lobola* in South Africa shows, African women have sometimes appeared as the custodians of 'tradition' and thus the agents of their own subordination.

This chapter considers African women's agency in the making and remaking of 'traditions' and unravels some of the factors involved in explaining the salience of 'traditions' interpreted both as women's 'culture' *and* as women's oppression. The chapter concentrates on what is often identified as the most important women's 'tradition', girls' initiation ceremonies marking the transition from girlhood to adulthood. It considers the actions and reactions of women's organisations and groups toward initiation ceremonies, and the political contexts in which they have occurred. It focuses on Zambia, where discourse on women's initiation ceremonies has revolved on perceptions of a breakdown of women's morality among urbanites under the influence of 'westernised', 'un-African' notions of womanhood. The discourse on women's morality or the lack thereof has, since the 1980s, been actively promoted by a government whose economic performance has declined drastically and which has always tended to scapegoat young professional urban women for both moral and economic decay. In post-independence Mozambique, by contrast, the Marxist-Leninist government of Samora Machel led a campaign against what it considered to be 'traditions' detrimental to women's emancipation and degrading to women's dignity. Besides polygamy and *lobola* the government of the Front for the Liberation of Mozambique (Frelimo) and its women's wing, the Organisation of Mozambican Women (OMM), targeted women's initiation ceremonies. Government policy was resisted and detested by women in the matrilineal North, for whom it constituted undue interference in their affairs, and a further indication of their declining social and economic status. The chapter raises questions about the nature of what is described by the initiation leaders – and sometimes by anthropologists – as important expressions of women's culture, identity and solidarity, worthy of the status of a 'good tradition'.

Initiation ceremonies

Initiation ceremonies vary between areas and between those for men or women, but they share certain basic features. Common to all such ceremonies is the seclusion of the initiate, the physical and social removal from society followed by a 'coming out', a renewal and reintegration into society as a new changed social being (Van Gennep 1977). At times physical changes may be induced to mark the transition such as circumcision of the penis, the cutting off of fingers, the filing down or knocking out of teeth for boys, the removal of the clitoris and vaginal lips, the elongation of vaginal lips or ornamental scarring for girls. More commonly, however, girls' initiations in Southern Africa seem less concerned with painful operations that test endurance and physically mark the adult than with inculcating psychological change, preparing the girl for the rigours of marriage and life as a social and legal minor. By contrast boys' initiations confer onto the initiate the status of a respected member of society. They represent 'the road and the gate to independence [*ukuzimela*: literally, standing for oneself] in all spheres of life' (Pauw 1962: 93), as one Xhosa initiate put it in the 1960s. Initiation ceremonies thus transfer onto boys the public and private authority of men, also over women. These differences have led researchers to suggest that girls' and boys' initiations differ because boys have to be made into men via complex cultural processes, whereas girls are simply prepared for marriage, growing into women more 'naturally', as it were (Lutkehaus 1995: 18).

Initiations can happen in age groups, in groups that are not age bound, and singly. For girls they are typically associated with physical maturity, that is the first menses; for boys the age of initiation varies. Some societies initiate only boys or only girls, others initiate both sexes.[5] Initiations are associated with secrecy, both in that the initiates are not allowed to divulge to others what has happened during the seclusion, and in that they are brought in contact with so-called secret knowledge, such as songs and poetry, sometimes in what is described as secret language, the meanings of which might not be explained to the initiates. Audrey Richards reported in 1956 from the *chisungu*, the girls' initiation of the Bemba in what was then Northern Rhodesia, that 'I have never heard of any part of the ceremony explained and that if any information was given the candidates themselves would be the last people to have a chance of acquiring it' (Richards 1982: 126). And Jean La Fontaine, in her introduction to Richards' book suggests that '*chisungu* neither gives additional knowledge nor the right to use it' (La Fontaine 1982: xxii). In 1981 girls initiated in the south of Zambia were not taught the meaning of initiation songs (Geisler 1990: 181). In 1996 a young Pedi initiate from South Africa admitted that she did not learn anything new and the songs she had to learn by heart made no sense at all, some of them being incomprehensible mixtures of Sotho, Afrikaans and English.[6]

That some kind of 'ritual drama' (La Fontaine 1985) is happening during initiation ceremonies there is no doubt. The secrecy shrouding initiation ceremonies render them mysterious to the non-initiated, thus preserving the attraction of participating. The coercion of public opinion or real force might work for those who are not taken in by the mystery. It is the experience of the ritual itself that marks the initiation. In many cases aspects of initiation ceremonies are in fact known to initiates before they enter into it, and the seclusion represents merely the finishing touch to a socialisation process that lasts throughout the life of the initiate. But it is surviving the initiation that constitutes a secret which one cannot possess without undergoing the ritual (Jeannerat 1995: 15).

In Northern Mozambique, as elsewhere in Southern Africa, the elongation of the small vaginal lips that used to make or break a girl's initiation was started when the girl was eight or nine years old (Arnfred 1989: 3). Venda girls in South Africa learn the special greeting towards elders (*u losha*) by prostrating themselves on the ground well before initiation (Jeannerat 1995: 5). Among the Toka of Zambia in the 1980s, all girls and women were obliged to participate in parts of the ceremony. Moreover, the supposedly secret dances of the girls' initiation, which imitate desirable sexual movements, were known even to small children who playfully practised them in full view of annoyed adults.

Other than the desirable movements during sexual intercourse, girls are instructed in socially acceptable behaviour towards adults and particularly husbands. Bemba, Toka and Venda girls are told just like girls in Northern Mozambique to respect their husband, warm his washing water in the evening, cook for him and his relatives, never refuse sexual intercourse except during menstruation, to wash or wipe the husband's penis after sexual intercourse, and they are informed about the use of certain medicines and practices, as well as ornamental scars and cicatrices, to keep the husband 'hot' and in the house. It is probably instruction on the latter issues that are new or secret to the initiate, what Richards' Bemba informants in the 1950s called 'the secret language of marriage' or 'the intimacy that surrounds the physical relation of husband and wife, described as the secret things of the house' (Richards 1982: 127) which are taboo to children and need to be talked about in code, if at all. What concerns the formal activities of a wife, mother and housewife would have been learned during their youth. It is, explains Richards, not the activities as such but the socially approved attitude towards them that are transmitted (ibid: 128). According to Arnfred's informants in Mozambique girls learned 'a series of rules for normal, decent, subservient, respectful female behaviour', which apart from those already mentioned included that a wife 'must not talk' and must show 'shyness and modesty with other men', lest she be considered of indecent character (Arnfred n.d. 1: 17–20).

Initiation ceremonies are often described by the actors as a moral school for women, making girls grow into women, thus teaching them the codes of 'proper wifehood'. Richards believed that 'the women in charge of this ceremony were convinced that they were causing supernatural changes to take place in the girls under their care, as well as marking those changes' (Richards 1982: 125). For La Fontaine, initiation ceremonies mark a division of the sexes, 'which also produces the justification for male domination in society, even in societies where descent is reckoned through women and only women are initiated' (La Fontaine 1985: 118). Other interpreters are inclined to suggest that girls' initiation rites are 'an important focus for the reinforcement and celebration of shared female identity and for the strength as women, collectively, *vis-à-vis* men' (Arnfred n.d. 5: 9–10). All writers, the last included, do, however, agree that initiation rites for girls have a lot to do with the subordination and humiliation of young women.

From women, for or against women?

'We go to initiation camps because the old women want to have some fun,' remarked the already quoted Pedi initiate, not without sarcasm.[7] Older women do indeed run the girls' initiations and their fun consists in mocking, teasing and humiliating the young initiates. Clearly noting the oppression of the younger women Arnfred suggests that in Northern Mozambique initiations 'also provided a kind of free space where the women could get together on their own without the interference of men. This was the place where women had fun and games amongst themselves' (Arnfred 1989: 5).

The 'fun' of older women started when they instructed smaller girls how to pull their vaginal lips, mocking them if they did not pull enough. Girls were, moreover, not told about menstruation, so that at the first showing they were 'bewildered and afraid'. Instead of telling the girls then, the older women would 'fetch men to give the girls a thrashing' if they were not able to indicate where the blood was coming from. They were then told about the polluting effect of menstrual blood, which they said could kill a man. During the actual initiation the punishment of 'ill-mannered girls' was common. The girls were beaten, forced to carry burning embers in their bare hands for hours on end, insulted that their vaginal lips were not long enough and forced to run gauntlets between two rows of women beating them with sticks (Arnfred n.d. 1: 12–14).

In the 1930s Lovedu girls in South Africa's Northern Province, who also had to pull their vaginal lips and had cuts made on their clitoris, were severely beaten and forced to hop on one leg and pick up stones, and to eat fresh cow dung (Krige 1966: 104–5). In the same period Bemba girls were made to cry during initiation: 'If they cry we know that they have understood.' Richards observed girls being 'pulled about and tormented', 'rolled on the ground' and 'swung to and fro by fingers hooked inside their mouths'. They had 'their heads bound with grass above the eyes so that the eyeballs stood out'. She reported the girls to be 'strained and taut, under constant fire of criticism, and apparently simply concentrated on following blindly the commands shouted at them' (Richards 1982: 79). The humiliation of public crying, even without apparent reason, was also expected of Mozambican and Pedi girls. The former were refused food until they had filled a pot with tears, the latter were forced to cry when entering the initiation camp for the simple reason that the old women ordered them to do so. They were also forced to whisper throughout the three months they spent in the initiation camp and to kneel and clap in the presence of those already initiated. Pedi girls were also forced to attempt the impossible, such as picking up with their mouths small sticks placed close to a fire or to make a fire in the river. This would be followed by severe punishment and ridicule such as being stripped naked and made to dance in front of the elders. Towards the end of the seclusion the girls were marked on the cheek with the red-hot circular end of a whistle, causing in some cases severe swellings and infections.[8] In Mozambique and in South Africa the elders also avenged disrespect and lack of submission of girls prior to the initiation by subjecting the culprits to particularly harsh ill treatment (Arnfred n.d. 1: 13).

In the early 1980s during initiation ceremonies in Southern Zambia the initiate sat demurely in the centre of a circle of women and girls of all ages. Every female in the village had to attend, and the initiated girl, with all other young uninitiated girls in the circle, could be ordered by the old women to do the almost impossible. There were the more usual tasks of 'dancing in bed', often with one of the old women pretending to be the male, the constant deferential clapping and lowering of eyes, the order to cry, roll in the dirt, etc. The old women carried sticks and beat the initiate if she did not perform well enough. The young girls in the audience were also forced into the circle, and those too embarrassed to comply would run screeching into the darkness, followed by the old women with their sticks. More embarrassing still were the dances the old women performed, grabbing each other's genitalia, baring their bottoms and pointing them in the faces of the initiate and the younger women in the audience. Their demeanour became more and more obscene as the night wore on when they started to imitate men. They bunched their *chitenge* between their legs to represent an erect penis and they would attack the initiate, who had to resist but then subject herself to the penis-brandishing old woman, shocking and embarrassing the younger audience (Geisler 1990: 189). Young Mozambican women had to undergo ritual defloration by the initiating old women, with a clay penis, a practice that was discontinued after one of them broke inside a girl's vagina (Arnfred n.d. 1: 15).

'The women find all of this great fun,' Arnfred informs us, and she points out that 'to them it is a kind of revenge for the self control they have to maintain in their daily lives, their coexistence with men and from respect for custom'. It all happens, she admits, on the back of the poor initiates but then women run women's matters and men have very little to do with the female initiation rites. It is therefore an expression of a 'shared gender identity' which is 'marvellous but not emancipatory' because 'it is very clear that who are the oppressors here are not men but older women' who follow their own agenda, rather than running 'errands for the men'. She also interestingly suggests that the old women are both beating submission into the girls *and* teaching them sexual pride (Arnfred n.d. 2: 9–11).

Such interpretations are at the core of a broader understanding of the political economy of girls' initiation ceremonies and they might explain why they have been both very pervasive and an important terrain of gender struggles.

For women's or men's glory?

Girls' initiation ceremonies are indeed gender-exclusive affairs, at least during the period of seclusion. They are occasions where women get together on their own, where they are able to exclude men, and where some women, those with the status of being seasoned teachers, and with the added advantage of being past child-bearing and therefore almost honorary men, can let go. But their 'revenge' in Arnfred's terminology comes precisely after a lifetime of constraint and self-control in their relationships to men and to senior women. It is, moreover, a 'revenge' that is directed neither towards the men nor the older women, but against the most vulnerable members of society, young women who are in limbo between being child and adult and have no status at all. Girls might be allowed certain liberties, though few, because they are after all children, but the initiation makes them women, who, until they themselves have older children, have to submit to the authority of guardians, husbands, grandmothers, and mothers-in-law. They are, even in matrilineal societies, subjected to authority on all sides and, noted Richards, forced 'to calmly accept the fact that their husbands will beat them "when they are young and their hearts get hot quickly"' (Richards 1982: 50).

Who then directs and decides what happens during a girl's initiation? Do the old women really create what Arnfred interprets as a 'special unity' or 'sisterhood'? Who and what is their reference point when they humiliate and subordinate their younger 'sisters'? Who, one wonders, desires the elongation of vaginal lips, a practice described as painful until you get used to it? Arnfred's OMM material about the discussions held with men and women about the future of initiation ceremonies in the early 1980s supplies answers that do not support her own interpretations.

Older women supported the elongation of vaginal lips because they held that 'women without extended lips would not be called women' and that men would despise such a woman because 'she does not give pleasure' and that 'the man will feel next to nothing when having sex with her'. Moreover, according to the women the elongated lips 'help men with a small penis' and they make 'men get stiff /have an erection sooner'. And one man thought that 'initiation teaches women better movements for the man'. We also hear that extended vaginal lips apparently keep vaginas dry, the way men like them for more pleasure, just as women learn to use medicines that constrict the vagina. Furthermore, in areas where extended vaginal lips are *en vogue,* not having them might be reason for divorce or, worse still for the women concerned, not getting a husband at all (Arnfred n.d. 3: 2–13).

Arnfred's quaint picture of young girls sitting in the bush pulling their genitals which, she suggests, is an issue of 'boasting and competition' and of female pride in and control over their sexuality (ibid: 13) could indeed indicate the opposite. In 1980 Isaacman and Stephen, for example, suggested that Mozambican initiation ceremonies instructed girls in 'ways to give their husbands sexual satisfaction with no thought to their own sexual pleasure' (Isaacman and Stephen 1980: 8–9). That women controlled neither their sexuality nor the content and the practices during initiation ceremonies was not only obvious by the very fact that they were required to 'go to bed with the husband whenever he wants to' (Arnfred n.d. 1: 19). It seems that the practice declined in areas where men's interest in elongated vaginal lips declined. While in the North initiation ceremonies were defended because men wanted their women 'to be prepared' they were rejected in the central and southern regions of Mozambique because men tended to prefer their women without extended vaginal lips. There they caused men to leave their wives who were thus prepared, in search of younger women that had *not* been prepared (Arnfred n.d. 3: 16–17). The reference point both for and against the initiation practices is thus the preferences of men, and the need of women to please their husbands so that they first marry and then not divorce them.

In Southern Zambia as elsewhere the 'coming out' ceremony is the high point of the initiation, when the initiated girl is to demonstrate to the public eye, and particularly to the men, that she has learned her lessons and that she is ready to be married. The climax of the 'coming out' is the public demonstration of her skills at 'dancing in bed'. Sparsely dressed and decorated with beads that are draped crosswise over her bare breasts, the girl is required to demonstrate her ability to 'wriggle her waist' and thereby to indicate that she is able to sexually satisfy her future husband. The songs sung during the 'coming out' ceremony do not hide the fact that the girl's readiness for men is a main concern:

> The virgin is to be taken to the boys,
> the virgin is taken to the boys to be used
> Let us lift her and take her to the boys to be used.
>
> (Geisler 1990: 186)

Originally the initiated girl married immediately after the ceremony and passed over to her husband's authority. But already in the 1940s Colson reported that amongst the Plateau Tonga in what was then Northern Rhodesia, girls married considerably later (Colson 1958:

283). Yet the preparation of girls in Southern Zambia, Mozambique in the 1980s and amongst the Venda in the 1990s was and is directed towards marriage and acceptable behaviour within marriage. Girls learn to endure pain and behave demurely, and above all to listen, and suffer in silence. 'Listening', writes Jeannerat of the *Vhusha* ceremony of the Venda, 'means deferring control over oneself to other people . . . by whom one is dominated and controlled and whose authority one has to accept. In this manner young women are taught that it is part of female nature to be silent.' This is particularly important during marriage (Jeannerat 1995: 23). 'Be quiet and suffer' is how Southern Zambian women described their lot in marriage. It is as if the individual who is subjected to pain and fear loses her identity and becomes de-individualised.[9] Girls are turned into women that are mere vessels, lacking their own opinions: 'When the man is talking the woman cannot answer. When the man gets angry, the woman must keep quiet', explained an old woman in Cabo Delgado (Arnfred n.d. 4: 6).

Initiation ceremonies may be constitutive of a women's culture in the sense that it is a ritual that is run by women with women, but both content and outcome of the ceremonies reaffirm gender inequality. Their ultimate objective is the perpetuation of men's domination and women's subordination. At best they might create a sisterhood of suffering, but even that is doubtful, since ultimately the initiation ceremonies separate women and lock their experiences of subordination and ill treatment by husbands and other men into silence. Young women are certainly not keen to participate in initiation ceremonies and they have been known to rebel against certain aspects of ritual, while others try to avoid or delay participation. Many feel uncomfortable about it, such as a Zambian Lozi woman who in the 1970s reported: 'It made me sick, it was so disgusting. I used to cry thinking about it.' For a while, she and others were afraid of sexual activity altogether (Schuster 1979: 44 and 45). Elizabeth Colson has reported Tonga girls' rebellion against puberty ceremonies as early as the 1940s (Colson 1958: 282).

In 1981 young Toka girls were awed by the prospect of their initiation. They feared being beaten by the old women, and they all confessed to feeling shy when it came to the 'coming out' ceremony, when they are required to dance sexually suggestive initiation dances in front of all the village, particularly the men, who are excluded during the seclusion. Questions about the content of the initiation ceremony met with a stony silence or embarrassed giggles, and vague information about learning how to stay with a husband. The only consolation for the embarrassment of publicly dancing 'like in bed' was that during the dance people would donate money, and some would be used to buy the initiated girl new clothing. Many were afraid not to live up to expectations and to be ridiculed or even sent back into seclusion. Some tried to hide the fact that they had started menstruating, not an easy task under the watchful eyes of the old women, who claimed to see the onset of menstruation in the small of the back and the back of the knees. They were said to follow girls to where they wash and inspect their clothing and blankets for traces of blood. Eventually all girls were found out and forced to submit to the rigours of seclusion, softened by the doubtful hope of gaining the little status that comes with being an adult woman (Geisler 1990: 187).

Similarly, in the 1990s Venda girls complained that initiation rites were cruel and that the pain they had to endure was senseless. They also said that the sexual education they had received was inadequate in that it did not inform them about the consequences of 'playing with boys'. It did not help them with their future lives in any way (Jeannerat 1995: 16).

Girls' initiation ceremonies with their code of secrecy and their message of women's silence have created an effective way of dividing women. Young women who have been initiated are not at liberty to speak about their experiences with the younger uninitiated ones. They are also unable to exchange notes with other initiated girls, particularly if initiation is, as among the Toka, done individually. In all the examples presented here, moreover, mothers have very little to do with the sexual education of their daughters. They are not involved in teaching their daughters during seclusion. Venda, Pedi and Toka girls are not encouraged to discuss their sexuality or the 'affairs of the house', matters that concern the more private aspects of the relationship between husband and wife, with their mothers. After initiation they are no longer allowed to enter their parents' bedroom even when they themselves have grown old. Pedi girls and girls in Northern Mozambique are not told about the onset of menstruation, and if they do hear about it, it will not be from their mothers. Their reference point for such issues is the generation of the old women. Speaking in general terms, La Fontaine has pointed out that 'initiation rites separate [the girl] from her mother and establish her adult identity. Initiation rites thus separate between the generations' (La Fontaine 1985: 108).

In the last decade, even Toka girls of the same age did not feel free to discuss any of the information they had received during initiation. While the initiation dances were known to all, knowledge about how to please and keep a husband were carefully guarded, even though such knowledge might well have been very uniform. The young women said that they feared to talk about the 'affairs of the house' to their friends, lest they be ridiculed for doing something wrong, or for fear of revealing secrets that might make them the laughing stock of their friends. They also claimed to trust nobody with these private matters, since they might be advised wrongly, in a way that alienates the husband, or that might make him like other women more. But communicating over these issues with the generation of the grandmothers might also bring little joy (Geisler 1990: 198–202).

Toka grandmothers have a special relationship to a newly wed couple, *ikwamba zitondwa*, or a joking relationship. It indicates that they are part of the couple's house – a grandmother and the husband of her granddaughter call each other 'husband' and 'wife', and thus they are able to share the 'affairs of the house'. It is a relationship that is established during the marriage ceremony when bride and groom receive a stone from the grandmother which they first have to bite and then press to their hearts. This is said to ritually indicate that the 'affairs of the house' must stay a secret between the couple and the grandmother. But if husband and grandmother have indeed things to joke about, the relationship of the granddaughter to her grandmother is ruled by the authority/ subordination that was established during the initiation. Far from being an understanding confidant, the grandmother is the guardian of her granddaughter's good behaviour, because it is she, as representative of her generation, who is held responsible for the young wife's appropriately subordinate behaviour. If the latter does not show the right respect for her husband or displays disagreement with male behaviour, the grandmother will be held responsible. And since such complaints imply a loss of status the old woman is at pains to keep her female charge in line. The confidants of women are therefore by definition staunch supporters of male value systems, and they are great assets for husbands to enforce subordination on their wives. Women therefore have little chance of gaining support from other women against their husbands; they have little hope of communicating the trauma of their sub-ordination to other women, remaining isolated in their personal experiences with men (ibid.)

Similarly Jeannerat shows Venda women achieve status as mothers-in-law, via the submission of their daughters-in-law, incul-cated during the initiation ceremony. A mother-in-law has a vested interest in the docile behaviour and selfless nature of her daughter-in-law. This explains the importance of the effective subordination of the initiates because if the latter 'learns this submissive behaviour properly, the status of the mother-in-law for the older women will be insured' (Jeannerat 1995: 16). The contents of the initiation teachings are determined by the needs of men, and old women can only achieve high status if they reinforce the subordination of other, younger women. A Toka initiation teacher, who personally held radical views about the status of women, admitted that none of these could ever transpire in her teachings since it would render her a *persona non grata*.[10]

Such considerations were also on the minds of the women in Cabo Delgado when they complained that without initiation ceremonies the young women would lose all respect and they would lose all control over them: 'We all have lots of problems with our children, with their disrespect, they do not listen because they are not threatened in the initiation rites' (Arnfred n.d: 4).

Initiation ceremonies therefore seem to be antithetically opposed to women's emancipation, in that they isolate women and establish a tight web of control over young and old women alike, a web which makes the old the agents of suppression of the young within a male-defined ideological framework. Whatever the liberating or emancipatory elements of such rites, they remain partial and peripheral, such as when old women past child-bearing are for once allowed to mock and imitate men, and to sing songs like the Toka song that praises 'the leopard in the mountains, how he roars!'. The leopard symbolises the lover and his passion as compared to the lion, the husband, and the work that sex with him represents, might well roar in the minds of the old women, as they roar their own frustrations about life with men at the initiates. But such evocation of the other is not for the young women to emulate just yet (Geisler 1990: 192). They are instead reminded in many other songs about the fickleness of lovers, who like the bird Kanga Nyungwee are very wise, because 'he eats all the millet, and when he is finished, he goes to sit on a hill. Then he flies away'.

The politics of initiation ceremonies: official banning

At the opening of the first OMM conference in 1973, Samora Machel, the leader of FRELIMO in exile in Tanzania, declared that 'the antagonistic contradiction is not between women and men, but between women and the social order, between all exploited people, both women and men, and the social order'. He talked about the revolution as 'freeing the initiative of women, integrating them in society as responsible members and involving them in decision making' (Isaacman and Stephen 1980: 17), and he stressed that 'the emancipation of women was not an act of charity' but a necessity (Urdang 1989: 22). The constitution adopted in 1975, after Mozambique gained independence, granted women and men equal rights. In order to facilitate this aim, FRELIMO started a political campaign against 'certain backward practices' which were considered debasing for women, particularly *lobola*, polygamy, child marriages and initiation ceremonies.

At the third OMM conference in 1984, which was to discuss social aspects of women's emancipation and for which information had been collected across the country, Samora Machel attacked aspects of initiation rites that 'do psychological violence to women, treating them as mere objects of pleasure'. He went on to say that such negative traits 'should be clearly distinguished from any genuinely educational aspects of initiation ceremonies'. He did apparently not specify further which aspects he was referring to (Mozambique Information Office 1984: 2). On the same occasion he stressed that the family is the basic unit of society and harmony should start in the family. Such harmony, he declared, was disturbed in the cities, where a crisis of values had led to promiscuity, immorality and delinquency.

On the same occasion OMM presented a document on the social situation of Mozambican women which stated that these rites induce 'concepts and behaviours of submission and inferiority of women in front of men' (Arnfred 1989: 31). It therefore held initiation rites as largely responsible for the difficulties women have in entering productive activities outside the family, and it characterised them as 'wrapped in a mystical atmosphere, full of superstition and obscurantism'. It therefore suggested that 'political campaigns should be waged in areas where initiation rites are still deep rooted' so that people will 'understand that abandoning obsolete traditions

does not affect our personality as Africans' (Mozambique Information Office 1984: 3).

The condemnation of initiation ceremonies as being detrimental
to women's equality with men followed consultation and research
that showed that these practices were still popular in the North of
the country. Some five years later, Isabel Casimiro criticised this
dismissal as superficial and ill-informed which 'led society to react,
and to reinforce these practices' (Casimiro 1989: 9). According to
Arnfred in 1982 the older women of Cabo Delgado were very
upset about the FRELIMO ban on initiation ceremonies, complaining that they liked the party and independence but that 'our
big problem is the initiation rites. The drum is our only possibility
for playing. How is it really that FRELIMO is loving us'. They
pleaded 'we want *unhango* [initiation] because our children do not
respect us'. And one woman threatened that 'today the men are
growing old very early and they are getting weak because they have
sexual relations with menstruating women' (Arnfred n.d. 4: 3),
intimating that young women no longer respected either themselves, their husbands or the old women's tales about the deadly
effect of menstrual blood.

Interestingly, initiation ceremonies were not officially condemned wholesale. 'Genuinely educational aspects' of the ceremony
were to be preserved. These, one can but presume, must have
related to the concerns expressed by Machel in his OMM conference speech about 'a new generation without roots – without
what was positive in the values of the past' (Mozambique Information Office 1984: 3). They probably referred to a general decline
in morality, such as the prostitution he explicitly mentioned. For
Arnfred this is not astonishing, since she believes that FRELIMO
policy was strongly influenced by Protestantism and its dislike of
sexuality and 'immorality' (Arnfred n.d. 4: 3).

On the surface, such concerns seemed to have a lot in common
with those expressed by the old women, the leaders of the
embattled initiation rites, since they too talked about a lack of
respect among youth. But beyond that they seemed more
concerned about not being able to openly enact the ritual aspects
of the initiations. What they missed most were not the educational
but those other aspects that the party perceived as demeaning
women, the dancing, teasing and beating. Just telling girls about
respect and how to behave in marriage was considered 'an
undesirable form' of performance, which was 'not enjoyable any

more' because 'the teaching is incomplete'.[11] Rather than being concerned with the curtailing of women's self-determined sexuality by the party, as Arnfred would have it, the old women were concerned with the curtailing of the privileges of mature woman-hood: the right to exert power over the younger women. And such power, as pointed out with regard to Toka grandmothers and Venda mothers-in-law, might indeed have repercussions well beyond the actual event of the initiation. On the other hand, FRELIMO did not seem to object to all sexual aspects of the initiations entirely.

According to the OMM survey in 1982 girls' initiation dances were in fact still officially performed, albeit in quite different social circumstances: as official contributions to national holidays. One woman in Cabo Delgado explained:

> We have stopped performing the initiation rites, but still more frequently we will be called to dance with no gain for us, and not knowing why. We are going off to the District Headquarters dancing on the 25th of September and on the 3rd of February, but we do not know the significance of those dances. In the old days we were beating our drums. It was in order to educate our children. It had an important meaning for us. . . . One day we could refuse. . . . The Party prevents us from dancing when we need to, and at the same time we have to dance at any occasion without any meaning for us'.
>
> (Arnfred n.d. 4: 6)

What clearly upset the speaker was the transformation of initiation dances from 'fun and games' for older women to party propaganda. While the dances had not substantially changed their content, as displaying the sexual maturity of the female dancers to the male onlookers, they might have still brought benefit to the men in the actual watching and in bed, but they no longer conferred any benefits on the old women. They were still dances for the glory of men including even the most Protestant party bosses, but they were no longer dances for the glory of old women. There was, moreover, little doubt that the male party machinery proudly called these remnants of the banned initiation 'our tradition'. In Zambia such contradictions were more openly expressed.

The politics of initiation ceremonies: official praising

In 1996 a grade-seven Zambian schoolgirl who went through five weeks of seclusion during the school period admitted to feeling ashamed of returning to school after dancing in front of the cheering crowd with her breasts uncovered. She was worried that the boys would point at her and mock her. She had difficulties concentrating and lost hope of taking her final exams later that year. Referring to such cases the chairperson of the National Women's Lobby Group, Gladys Mutukwa, was reported to have said that 'there are a lot of traditional values that need to be eradicated ' (Cheushi 1995: 19).

Twenty-four years earlier, in 1972, the women's wing of the United National Independence Party (UNIP) had called for the introduction of cultural committees 'to hold initiation ceremonies', as the answer to what in public discussion was called the break-down of morality in towns exemplified by teenage pregnancies, illegal abortions, and against the call from more progressive quarters for the liberalisation of contraceptives (Schuster 1979: 163–4). Since then girls' initiation ceremonies and discussions of what are desirable or undesirable elements have exercised the minds of Zambia's urban populations, political parties, or at least their women's wings, and more recently the women's movement.

Unlike Mozambique, debates on girls' initiation ceremonies in Zambia were never the result of a political ban, nor did they involve rural populations. On the contrary, the debates were and still are led by urban traditionalists in their opposition against young professional urban women. The most vociferous were members of the UNIP Women's League. Most of its members were conservative older townswomen, who cast themselves as the custodians of 'traditional' values which defined women as mothers and dependent and subservient wives. Their role within the party was restricted to women's issues, and even in that field they had little power over policy formulation. Instead they applied male-informed ideas about proper womanhood, to ensure, as one male politician put it, 'that girls are fully educated traditionally for them to make the grade in future marriages' (Schuster 1979: 160–70; Geisler 1987 43–66).

It was particularly young, professional women who were blamed for what was perceived as immorality and moral decay. They were easy victims because they were readily identifiable by their life-style and appearance. These 'modern' women no longer considered mother- and wifehood as the only purposes in life. They were the new generation of single women, and they were cast in the role of the enemy of the more 'traditional' women, out to change dutiful husbands into 'sugar-daddies' who spent their salaries on girlfriends rather than on the family. Men, thus absolved of blame, happily joined in the chorus about immoral single women.

In 1972 Chibesa Kankassa started to wage a war against mini dresses, urging women to wear more respectable attire, something more 'traditional'.[12] Years later miniskirts were joined by 'see-throughs', 'make-ups' (sic!), 'wetlooks', 'perms', 'slits' and 'other flamboyant fads' which were blamed as the cause of moral decay.[13] In 1985 Fitzpatrik Mukonde complained in a letter to the editor of a local newspaper about the 'shameful slits': 'When they start walking bare thighs are seen!' and he called on 'the people responsible for cultural values' to do something about 'this way of dressing'.[14] Two years later another letter to the editor suggested that women should be fined for damaging Lusaka's pavements since 'the fashionable women who wear high heeled shoes with metal tips' were responsible for the deterioration of the inner city.[15]

That dress styles were not the real issue was evident to those thus attacked. Responding to the Women's League ban on miniskirts in the 1970s one woman reader suggested that the debate was more about the position of women in society, and the talk about women having to wear 'traditional' dress meant that women should assume a 'traditional' role, because after all in 'traditional society women wore almost nothing!'.[16] The writer also pointed to the double standard involved in the attack on independent women, which allocated 'traditional' society to women, exempting men. 'I have yet to find a man who preaches the values of ancient traditions and culture who, if he could afford it, would not prefer to drive a modern car to 'footing' in an attempt to hold on to traditional values', elaborated another woman more than ten years later.[17]

Traditionalists mixed dress style, 'tradition', and the well-being of the nation into a single issue of female immorality. Isaac Mkandawire believed that 'especially the Zambian woman thinks and believes that anything Western is good; this is why we have a lot of terrible things happening'.[18] The Women's League had prepared the ground for such statements, as for example in 1982, when the Copperbelt provincial chairperson of the organisation 'castigated some working women for moral decay in society'. She was reported to have said that 'it was common knowledge that these young women could have as many as three sugar daddies, one to pay the rent, another to buy a fridge and another one to buy clothes'. Women's greedy passions were to blame, not men's desire for young girlfriends.[19]

Traditionalism also dictated, according to Bishop Mumba, that 'contraceptives are un-Zambian' and that 'pregnancies amongst teenagers were common because the nation had lost its traditional values'. Only women were apparently responsible since he suggested that 'the time has come to revive *insaka* [initiation] where young girls could be taught morals by custodians of traditional values'.[20] In the same spirit President Kaunda when commenting on the 'epidemic' divorce rate urged parents to readopt 'wise traditions which sustained marriages in the olden days' namely 'the custom of initiating young girls into the mysteries of marriage and parenthood'. These were after all 'very simple customs that our ancestors found suitable for preparing the good mothers of tomorrow'.[21] Nonetheless, not all traditions were good by any means. Three years after calling for the 'wise traditions of yesterday', Kenneth Kaunda was reported to have slammed 'archaic, obsolete, and retrogressive customs', such as – astonishingly – the fact that some people 'do not see the role of women beyond that of a kitchen attendant'.[22]

The value of the praised initiation ceremonies for girls was thus by no means clear-cut. There were, in particular, two aspects of the ceremonies that upset the more conservative women of the Women's League and some men: the public display of so-called 'waist-wriggling' that is part of the girls' initiation, and the 'kitchen party', an urban hybrid of a western bridal shower and the African initiation ceremony. Both institutions have, through the latter half of the 1980s and beyond, been criticised within the discourse on immorality. If the revival of initiation ceremonies was advocated as the answer to immorality amongst women, they were also seen as its cause.

In 1984 the Lusaka Urban and Provincial Women's League conferences called for a ban on the public performance of initiation dances, in which the dancers 'wriggle their waists'. Agness Lupupa, who acted as chairperson of one conference, was dismayed at these public performances and said that such cultural dances were not for the public, and the other conference concluded that such dances should not be screened by television, nor should they be performed at the international airport when welcoming visitors.[23] One year later the same body repeated its call for 'banning of waist wriggling dances at public gatherings' because they 'were not portraying any of Zambia's cultural values'.[24] Some men obviously supported the Women's League. In a local newspaper in 1994 Watson Hicks Lwiindi expressed the opinion that the dances of a group of local entertainers, the Masiye Band, were 'down to earth erotic, provocative and suggestive', so much so that they could 'also easily corrupt the morals of our youths if allowed to go on unchecked'.[25] Not all men, however, toed that line.

In February 1995 the *Times of Zambia* reported that the speaker of the National Assembly, Dr Robinson Nabulyato, had rebuked a female Member of Parliament, Matilda Kolala, 'for discouraging traditional dances' after she had suggested that 'she did not like the way traditional dances were performed at various ceremonies, especially wriggling of the waist by women which was not only exaggerated but embarrassing'. Ben Kakoma, then Minister of Youth and Sport, consequently questioned if she was 'in order to protest against the wriggling of waists when this was part of traditional dances'. Eventually the Speaker cut short the discussion by describing Mrs Kolala 'as a conservative woman who did not accept change'. The issue did, however, continue to exercise the mind of the Women's League. In 1987, the Kabwe Urban Women's League was reported to have appealed to the government to 'ban "dancing queens" in all drinking places alleging they were a source of immorality'. Rather than wriggle their waists in bars women should 'form cultural groups'.[26] Directly commenting on the League's concerns, the director of the Department of Cultural Services, Winner Simposya, was quoted as explaining that the government did not interfere with what patrons of bars liked watching, even if it was girls performing 'sexually exaggerated dances' intended for special occasions. He further commented that 'not all wriggling is bad wriggling' singling out 'wriggling that suggests sex that is in bad taste'. He pointed out that traditional dances had been modified 'to make them more appealing', and that such cultural changes were after all natural in any society (Kachikoti 1987).

The contradictions inherent in the initiation dance debate were complex. Officially the government supported conservative women in the Women's League in their call for a revival of initiation ceremonies in urban areas, apparently to curb immorality amongst young women. But while Women's League members idealised a rural-based 'tradition' as enforcing moral behaviour they also condemned certain parts of it as immoral. Their argument that the sexually suggestive dances of the initiation were not meant for public consumption was, moreover, illogical. Initiation dances are learnt to be performed for the future husband in the privacy of the bedroom, but they are also performed publicly in front of other men. The very *raison d'être* of the 'coming out' ceremony is the public display of young women's sexual maturity in front of men. No wonder then that many men claimed their 'traditional' right to view such displays, calling the older women who wanted that right curtailed 'conservative', a term that is in itself contradictory in this context. The older women on the other hand wanted to restrict and restrain the younger women rather than place their sexual qualities further into the limelight by taking them to market, as it were.

That the interpretation of what is 'tradition' could cause conflict between male and female UNIP supporters also became clear in another, albeit earlier, incident. In 1971 in protest against a new political party, the United People's Party (UPP), UNIP women demonstrated in the streets, stripped to the waist, and, ululating, they expressed their emotion 'traditionally'. President Kaunda felt moved by the spectacle until some days later he changed his mind about such a display of 'tradition' and expressed concern about the women creating a crisis. In his wake the local press mocked the 'half naked women' who needed to be packed 'on lorries for breast competitions' (quoted in Schuster 1979: 164). Good 'tradition' had in the space of days turned from being emotionally moving to embarrassing and bad.

When Ilsa Schuster commented on the Women's League's call for the revival of girls' initiations in 1979 she considered Kankassa's plan to form cultural committees to organise the initiations ludicrous, since 'who then would take the blame for the social problems that resulted from male–female relationships? Those who supervise initiation ceremonies and instruct the young initiates – the old women from the villages!' (ibid.) Indeed, the cultural committees never saw the light of day, and instead the kitchen party took over some of the functions of girls' initiations. Bridal showers had been introduced to Zambia during the 1970s by returning members of the diplomatic service and others who had lived abroad. They became popular with the rich before they were adopted among the less well-off during the 1980s. They were a means to 'show off', both by giving ostentatious parties and presents in the circuit of parties among friends. Mothers wished to give their daughters good kitchen parties as a good start to married life, suggesting on invitation cards the kind of presents expected.[27]

But a good start to married life was also supplied by giving the bride-to-be 'a few valuable tips on morals, good house-keeping and other varying do's and don'ts' (Kayamba 1987). Often the parties feature drumming and singing songs associated with girls' initiations. Depending on the mother, the bride has either been in seclusion for a week, when she is counselled, and the party takes place in lieu of the 'coming out' party. Alternatively, the party represents the initiation, and the young woman is taken aside during the course of the evening to be given counsel.[28] Hansen (1995: 140) has described Lusaka kitchen parties in 1992 as featuring 'as party manager a senior marriage counsellor who supposedly has instructed the bride-to-be in how to behave towards her husband, both sexually and interpersonally'. The climax of the party was the demonstration by the bride of her skills for 'dancing in bed'. Subsequently guests produced their gifts accompanied by a little dance and some advice related to their present.

The merging of 'tradition' and 'modernity' in kitchen parties, convenient as it might have seemed as a way to revive girls' initiations in urban areas, did not please all men and women, and as one man suggested in the local press they 'roused provoking debates' (Chibesa 1987). What disturbed men about kitchen parties was that they created spaces for their wives to socialise and enjoy themselves, and to get drunk and, by implication, to behave immorally. Married women for their part were concerned mainly about the role single women assumed at such gatherings, accusing them in turn of misbehaviour and immorality.

During Women's Week in Livingstone in 1985, UNIP provincial political secretary Hopkins Mwelwa urged the Women's League to monitor kitchen parties which had become breeding grounds for broken marriages, suggesting that social evils would result from uncontrolled women's parties. He voiced the concerns of married men who in letters to the local press called on the party and the government to ban kitchen parties altogether. They were concerned about the fact that their wives would hardly stay at home on the weekends to look after the children, leaving their husbands to tend to such matters (Mpengula 1987). In men's view, kitchen parties were certainly not advocating obedient wifehood if they encouraged their wives to stay out drinking and socialising with friends, thus far a prerogative of men only. An editorial of the *Times of Zambia* went so far as to directly link prostitution and kitchen parties, suggesting that women no longer went straight home after work, but that they are 'today permanent members of the destructive kitchen parties, and bars and streets have become their second home'.[29]

Married women defended the social space that kitchen parties had created for them. They confessed that the parties were their only opportunity for entertainment since their husbands would not take them out on social occasions. In the home care section of the *Zambia Daily Mail* Ina Kayamba (1987) defended the parties as enabling 'a lot of housewives to relax in an unrestrained atmosphere in the company of fellow women' and under the 'sensible organisation of the hostess'. Rather than attacking the institution of the kitchen party, married women blamed the presence of single women for introducing immorality to the occasions. There were complaints that single women were mainly interested in getting drunk and having 'show-downs with wives of their married boyfriends out of frustration resulting from desperation for marriage'.[30] 'In the olden days' single women were, according to this view, never allowed to attend kitchen parties (or rather initiation ceremonies) and it was certainly taboo for them to 'counsel the bride matrimonially'. If that was allowed kitchen parties had lost their meaning, having turned into 'social gatherings where [single] women . . . go to kill their boredom by getting stone drunk and taking out their frustration on others', and where they might even advise the bride to reconsider marriage (Mpengula 1987).

Although 'proper' women acknowledged that good kitchen parties needed alcoholic beverages to get going (Mpengula 1987), they blamed single women for abusing the licence to drink. Married women thus claimed the pleasures of the equivalent of a girls' initiation, where they could let go and show their authority over the bride-to-be. In identifying young 'modern' women as responsible for breaking 'tradition' and destroying family values, they tried to defend their authority and dignity as older women, and their marriages. Lacking authority and power over their husbands, who in their role as sugar daddies squandered their incomes on young girlfriends, they tried to assert themselves in an area they could legitimise through 'tradition', which also offered them a space apparently free of male interference.

Yet it was men who scapegoated urban women as immoral and called on the Women's League to revive and control initiation ceremonies and, later, kitchen parties. Women were blamed for their lack of 'traditional' values and at the same time they were seen as guardians of that 'tradition' that could 'stop the rot', as the local press invariably described it throughout the 1980s. In the urban context, recourse to girls' initiations proved a powerful tool in aligning older women to male interests, in that it offered a seemingly 'natural' way of blaming and dividing women, diverting attention away from the immorality and incompetence of men, because girls' initiations are about women enticing other women to accept the dominance of men. Thus the custodians of 'tradition' could be lauded for their 'traditional' demeanour and simultaneously ridiculed as 'conservative' and old fashioned.

Ultimately the discourse on the immorality of women and the need for girls' initiations offered men the possibility of placing the blame firmly on women's shoulders while claiming for themselves the right to be 'morally immoral'. When the participants of a Women's League conference in 1984 dared to evoke 'tradition' in their own right, suggesting 'that boys should undergo initiation ceremonies, like their female counterparts, for them to grow into disciplined men', and 'to curb the deterioration of moral standards'[31] they were simply ignored. Women were allowed to execute 'tradition', not to 'make' it.

Conclusion: traditional modernity or modern tradition?

Writing about the Baruya of the Papua New Guinea interior, Godelier has suggested that far from proposing a female counter-model of the social order, girls' initiations are 'merely another aspect of the men's strength, and an essential aspect of it, in that it is the work of women themselves. The women thereby add to the power that men derive from their permanent repression of women' (Godelier 1982: 50). His observations, although made in an entirely different geographical context, reflect the material presented from Southern Africa. Far from being the celebration of the 'strength of women, collectively, *vis-à-vis* men', as Arnfred suggests, the initiation ceremonies of girls were shown to perpetuate male dominance and boost the power men have over women. It is because men have power over women in the first place that the latter can be relied upon to encourage other women to consent to male domination, and to accept the order of things as legitimate.

In all the cases reviewed girls' initiations are informed by the needs and wishes of men. At no stage are women in control of the ceremony, and they cannot be, because girls' initiations are about becoming 'real women', who in Godelier's words are 'mothers of many children, hard working . . . proud of all that they do for their husbands, sons, brothers, and father' (Godelier 1982: 51) and, one might add, ready to subordinate younger women. Being able to define 'tradition' and its content, men have in all cases been able to further restrict women, either by wresting from them the opportunity to enjoy in whatever manner the company of other women, or by blaming them directly or indirectly for the deterioration of social values, a deterioration that many men so actively encourage.

The effects can be serious. The World Health Organisation has recently defined practices like the stretching of the clitoris and/or labia and the introduction of corrosive substances and herbs into the vagina as forms of genital mutilation (Kiragu 1995). These practices have been recognised as a serious health risk in South Africa. *Drum*, the popular magazine, outlined the dangers of 'dry sex' which involved the insertion of substances such as snuff, potassium permanganate, toothpaste, or salt into the vagina leaving the vaginal walls dry, swollen and tight. Men, the magazine states, prefer a tight vagina, and women comply even though they gain no pleasure beyond satisfying their partner. It is moreover a practice that increases the risk of contracting sexually transmitted diseases and it has been linked to the high prevalence of cancer of the uterus and cervical cancer in African women. Yet the advice to practise 'dry sex' has remained part of the woman-to-woman teaching such as that at puberty, when girls are told 'that vaginal juices contain dirt which has to be removed from the system'.[32] At the same time, 'tradition' also still prevents some mothers from discussing with their daughters such important matters as contraception and the dangers of contracting HIV.

Some such 'traditions' can have other effects on women, possibly subtler, but no less damaging. The already mentioned recent revival of virginity checks in South Africa was the initiative of a woman concerned with 'AIDS, pregnancies and other kinds of diseases'. She encourages girls to submit to a practice that was once enforced by the chiefs, and is now quasi-voluntary, involving gifts to those who remain virgins. She targets girls because 'there is no interest in boys: they don't need to change because they are not the ones to suffer'. Girls are thus made responsible for their chastity and ultimately for stopping the spread of AIDS, even though they are daily at risk of being raped. Being paraded around their neighbourhood dressed in little more then a bead apron covering their pubic hair and declared virgins increases the probability of being targeted as a rape victim.[33] When they avoid that fate they might be infected by their future husbands, who were under no moral constraint before marriage, and whom they cannot refuse, according to 'tradition'. The woman promoting the virginity drive admits the contradiction, but perseveres, deferring to the wisdom of 'tradition'.[34]

Meanwhile, in Zambia and elsewhere, women still wriggle their waists for visiting dignitaries and party officials at airports, in bars, and on national holidays,[35] and many women continue to suffer the pains and fatal effects of 'dry sex' and the beatings of their husbands and boyfriends, because a male-controlled and woman-transmitted 'tradition' wants it so. The fact that in a country like South Africa, with its commitment to gender equality and formal education, initiations continue to keep children away from school for months, and girls continue to be forced to accept a subordinate role, indicates the power of this 'tradition'. The age of girl initiates has fallen to minimise the effects of seclusion on formal education, but the content and style of the teaching has not been adjusted to suit the much younger charges. Moreover, the organisers of such camps who gain financially are often men even in the case of girls' initiations,[36] and, as was reported from a boy's initiation camp, they are not beyond abducting their charges and coercing them under threat of death to remain there.[37] This and the interests of older women do not leave much hope for an imminent change. In South Africa's Northern Province the initiative of an enlightened woman who tried to reform girls' initiations, suppressing the elements of subordination and terror, found no support except from the young women who ultimately have no say in the matter.[38]

Notes

1 *Drum* (Johannesburg), April 1995, *Pace* (Johannesburg), April 1995.
2 *Drum*, March 1996.
3 Responses of second year Anthropology students to an essay topic set by the author, 1995.
4 *Drum*, August 1995, p. 8.
5 Cross-cultural initiation surveys indicate that 50–60 per cent of societies initiate girls, compared to 30–40 per cent initiating boys; Terence Hays quoted in Lutkehaus and Roscoe 1995: XIV).
6 Personal information, University of Durban-Westville, February 1996.
7 Personal information, Durban 1996.
8 Personal information, Durban 1996.
9 Victor Turner, quoted in Jeannerat 1995: 22.
10 Personal information, Makunka, Zambia, 1981.
11 Women in Nampula and Niassa, quoted in Arnfred (n.d. 4: 4).
12 *Zambia Daily Mail* (Lusaka), 12 September 1972, quoted in Schuster (1979: 163).
13 *Times of Zambia* (Lusaka), 4 February 1988.
14 *Zambia Daily Mail*, 12 November 1985.
15 *Times of Zambia*, 9 October 1987.
16 *Times of Zambia*, 29 August 1972, quoted in Schuster (1979: 162).
17 *Sunday Times of Zambia*, 22 June 1986.
18 *Zambia Daily Mail*, 20 December 1986.
19 *Zambia Daily Mail*, 12 February 1982.
20 *Zambia Daily Mail*, 27 August 1984.
21 *Zambia Daily Mail*, 20 September 1983.
22 *Times of Zambia*, 16 January 1986.
23 *Zambia Daily Mail*, 18 June 1984 and 5 September 1984.
24 *Times of Zambia*, 28 May 1985.
25 *Zambia Daily Mail*, 18 July 1984.
26 *Zambia Daily Mail*, 5 March 1987.
27 Interview, Lusaka 1987.
28 Interview, Lusaka 1987.
29 *Times of Zambia*, 26 February 1986.
30 'Adolescents should not attend kitchen parties', *Times of Zambia*, 27 November 84.
31 *Zambia Daily Mail*, 18 June 1984.
32 *Drum*, May 1996, pp. 12–13.
33 Personal information, Durban 1996; see also Leclerc-Madlala (1995). Her data suggests that in Natal the rape of virgins has been on the increase, possibly because this is considered a cure or prevention for HIV.
34 Interview with Andile Gumede, 3 February 1996, Durban.
35 *Weekly Post* (Lusaka), 14–20 February 1992.
36 Personal information, Durban, 1996; Bushbucksridge 1997.
37 See for example the case of Amos Matsane in Bushbucksridge, who was beaten to death with an axe and garden spade when he made his

fourth attempt to escape from an initiation camp; *African Sun* (Bushbucksridge, South Africa), 30 May–12 June 1996.
38 Personal information, Bushbucksridge, June 1997.

Bibliography

Arnfred, S. (1989) 'Notes on gender and modernization', paper presented at ROAPE Conference, Warwick.

—— (n.d. 1), 'An analysis of the female initiation rites in Mozambique. Part 1: The content of the initiation rites', Roskilde.

—— (n.d. 2) 'Initiation rites in Mozambique. Part 2: Female gender identity and sexual socialisation', Roskilde.

—— (n.d. 3) 'Initiation rites in Mozambique. Part 3: Women and men debating female (and male) sexuality', Roskilde.

—— (n.d. 4) 'Initiation rites in Mozambique. Part 4: Morals of gender and age', Roskilde.

—— (n.d. 5) 'Socialism, development and gender – a philosophical and political discussion of modernization', Roskilde.

Casimiro, I. (1989) 'Contribution to the establishment of a data bank on Women and Development in Africa: some experiences from Mozambique', *Expert Group Meeting*, Addis Ababa: United Nations Economic Commission for Africa.

Chanock, M. (1985) *Law, Custom and Social Order: The Colonial Experience in Malawi and Zambia*, Cambridge: Cambridge University Press.

Cheushi, C. (1995) 'Zambia: culture versus women's emancipation', *Southern African Political and Economic Monthly* (Harare), 9 (1): 19.

Chibesa, D. (1987) 'Obstacles blocking women's advance aired', *Times of Zambia* (Lusaka), 22 June.

Colson, E. (1958) *Marriage and the Family among the Plateau Tonga of Northern Rhodesia*, Manchester: Manchester University Press.

Geisler, G. (1987) 'Sisters under the skin: women and the Women's League in Zambia', *Journal of Modern African Studies*, 25 (1): 43–66.

—— (1990) *Die Politik der Geschlechterbeziehungen in einer ländlichen Gemeinde in Zambia: 'Be quiet and suffer'*, Hamburg: Institut für Afrikakunde.

Godelier, M. (1982) *The Making of Great Men. Male Domination and Power among the New Guinea Baruya*, Cambridge: Cambridge University Press.

Isaacman, B. and Stephen, J. (1980), *Mozambique: Women, The Law and Agrarian Reform*, Addis Ababa: United Nations Economic Commission for Africa.

Jeannerat, C. (1995) 'The presentation of the Vhusha initiation ceremony in Tshiendeulu, Venda', paper presented at the Annual Conference of the Association for Anthropology in Southern Africa, Grahamstown.

Kachikoti, C. (1987) 'Dancing queens: stripteasers?' *Sunday Times of Zambia* (Lusaka), 27 March.

Kayamba, I. (1987) 'From kitchen parties to baby showers?' *Zambia Daily Mail* (Lusaka), 29 August.

Kiragu, K. (1995) 'Female genital mutilation: a reproductive health concern', *Population Report Supplement*, 41: 23.

Krige, E.J. (1966) 'Individual development', in I. Schapera (ed.), *The Bantu-Speaking Tribes of South Africa. An Ethnographical Survey*, Cape Town: Masew Miller.

La Fontaine, J. (1982) 'Introduction', in A. Richards, *Chisungu*, London: Tavistock.

—— (1985) *Initiation. Ritual Drama and Secret Knowledge Across the World*, Harmondsworth: Penguin.

Leclerc-Madlala, S. (1995) 'Infect one infect all: psychosocial response and impact of the AIDS epidemic on Zulu youth in South Africa', University of Durban-Westville.

Lutkehaus, N.C. (1995), 'Feminist anthropology and female initiation in Melanesia', in N.C. Lutkehaus and P.B. Roscoe (eds), *Gendered Rituals. Female Initiation in Melanesia*, New York/London: Routledge and Kegan Paul.

—— N.C. and P.B. Roscoe (eds) (1995) *Gendered Rituals. Female Initiation in Melanesia*, New York/ London: Routledge and Kegan Paul.

Mozambique Information Office (1984) *News Review*, London.

Mpengula, D. (1987) 'Planning good kitchen parties', *Zambia Daily Mail* (Lusaka), 15 August.

Pauw, B. A. (1962) *The Second Generation*, Cape Town, Oxford: Oxford University Press.

Richards, A. (1982) *Chisungu. A Girls' Initiation Ceremony among the Bemba of Zambia*, London: Tavistock.

Schuster, I.M.G. (1979) *New Women of Lusaka*, Palo Alto: Mayfield Publishing.

Urdang, S. (1989) *And They Still Dance. Women, War and the Struggle for Change in Mozambique*, London: Earthscan.

Van Gennep, A. (1977) *Rites of Passage*, London: Routledge and Kegan Paul.

Chapter 4

Kinship, gender and work in socialist and post-socialist rural Poland

Frances Pine

Changing weddings

I attended a wedding, in April 1996, in the Polish mountain village where I have been doing research since the late 1970s. I had been a guest at many weddings in the village before, and had written about them as the most important ritual event of Górale culture, reflecting and reinforcing the ideologies of gender, generation and kinship which underpin house and community identity and social personhood. This wedding was particularly important to me, as the bride was Beata, the daughter of the house in which I live when I am in the village, and I became more intimately involved in its progress than ever before. It was also the first wedding I had attended since the demise of the socialist state and the establishment of the market economy in Poland. During the week of preparation and the celebrations themselves, I was continually struck by both small and major changes, changes which I associate with the increasing affluence of the village, its greater engagement with national and global consumer culture, and above all with the shifting relationship between the house and the state.

Beata's *wesele* (wedding party) was not held in her family's house nor in the house of the groom's family, as it would have been in past years, but in a community centre. Although the food was prepared, as before, by the female kin, the work was organised by a local woman who had been hired at considerable cost by the bride's mother to oversee the process from beginning to end. Unlike brides at earlier weddings I had attended, Beata wore neither traditional Górale costume nor a dress copied by a village seamstress from a picture in a local magazine. Rather, her dress was a beautiful, elegant and extremely expensive garment imported from France. The *błogosławienie*, the domestic blessing performed by the parents over the young couple in the bride's house before the church mass, still took place, but no one seemed to know quite what to do or say. A major problem arose in the last minute planning – should the basket of blessed bread, salt and greenery with which the bride is greeted on her return from church be part of the initial ritual in her house, or should it only be produced as she crossed the threshold of the *wesele*? Part of the problem here was that the threshold she was crossing was not, as it had been in the past, that of a village house, but that of a public space, the cultural centre. The issue was more complicated than this, however: no one seemed to be certain what exactly this basket should contain, and even the old women shook their heads and appeared bemused. Eventually the bride's mother and I sat up late into the night before the wedding, pooling our memories, and managed to fashion a basket. In the end, even this was not necessary, for it transpired that the caterer had herself prepared a special, very elaborate loaf of ornamental bread (clearly for display rather than consumption) and had created a very professional 'rustic' looking basket to present to the bride.

Other small changes appeared similarly to be taking the wedding ritual out of the house, and placing it in a more public, anonymous domain. Where previously gifts of money were given to the bride on behalf of guest's houses, now individual friends and couples gave mass-produced, expensive presents, such as tea sets, crystal clocks and other household commodities. As in previous years, a band of local musicians played at the wedding party, but their tunes were at least in the first hours borrowed from television and radio, and reflected international popular taste rather than traditional Górale wedding melodies. The entire procedure, from the dressing of the bride and the greeting of the groom's party at her house, to the church wedding and the long *wesele* itself, was recorded on video by a professional hired for the occasion. Throughout the preparations and domestic rituals, and the *wesele* itself, there seemed to be an almost deliberate collective 'forgetting' of the way things had been done 'in the past', a somewhat surprising forgetting in view of the fact that the past in this case was less than a decade ago, and that all of the women involved had been participating in wedding preparations since they were small children. When villagers and I discussed other weddings which had taken place in the past few years, it became clear that this emphasis away from the rituals associated with the house was increasingly the norm. This raised the question of whether the changes brought about by the end of socialism had provided a new focus for social identity, and hence rendered the house less significant or relevant as the focus of the correct moral order of family, gender and generation. An alternative explanation, however, would be that the house remains at the core of Górale culture, but that this is now reflected more in terms of work and economy, and less in terms of ritual metaphor. In this reading, it can be argued that although the content of gender imagery and symbolism has shifted, keeping pace with increasing participation in the wider political economy, certain core metaphors are nevertheless maintained. This is what I want to explore in this paper.

Kinship and gender

I start from the premise that gender and kinship are two mutually constitutive symbolic systems (Collier and Yanagisako 1987) which change over time and in response to external events and processes, and that, at least in contemporary industrialised states, they are symbolic systems which may be constructed differently in ideology at local level and in state ideology. Following from this, I want to look at the idea of work, as it is linked to kinship and gender, and as it is both represented at the level of state discourse and practised at the local level. Finally, I wish to suggest that work, kinship and gender are inextricably linked in the ethnographic context with which I am concerned here, and can be seen as a set of practices which defines the person, confers personal, social and ethnic identity, and often stands in opposition to the wider cultural and economic discourse promoted by the state.

In very different ways the work of Connell (1987), Whitehead (1981), Butler (1990) and others has shown that gender can be seen as performance; for Whitehead particularly this performance is linked to labour and work. On another level altogether, Schneider and those influenced by him have shown kinship to be about practice and process; here too performance is important, for it is in the visible practice of kin-work, the public recognition of the kin link, that kinship is maintained over time. In yet a different kind of analysis, theorists of gender and the state, or gender and nation-alisms, have argued that the gendered (female) body can be seen to stand for the national or ethnic group; particularly in the context of the growth of ethnic identities and nationalism in the former socialist bloc, we can see a peculiar and not always consistent 'fit' between ideologies of nationalism, gender and kinship. In Polish history, the dominant discourses of gender are complex, and are inextricably linked to those of catholicism and nationalism, with the fatherland, the patriarchal father figure and the male nationalist hero standing side by side with Mother Poland, the nurturing mother/Madonna who saves and perpetuates the nation, and the mother who mourns, suffers, and endures (see Jaworski and Pietrow-Ennker 1992, Pine 1994a). I would argue, however, that the Górale do not completely subscribe to these images and that in terms of local ideology, gender identity is performed and made visible through work and ritual. For the Górale, being female, as much as being male, is about active agency demonstrated through labour.

The Górale

The Podhale, the Carpathian region stretching from the foothills to the high peaks of the Tatra Mountains which is the home of the Górale, has a long history of economic isolation and social marginality. As in many other remote, mountain borderlands, from the nineteenth century onwards the local economy has been fragmented, with villagers dividing their time between farming, petty commodity production and marketing, and travelling abroad as economic migrants. In the village in which I do research most households are extended, consisting of three generations at least; the work which the adults do, and the context in which they do it, is determined to a great extent by the needs of the farm, and those of the dependent children and old people, and is negotiated, among close kin, within the house or between houses.

In the mountains, the house and the local community have historically provided the basis for social identity (see Pine 1994b, 1996). Górale houses are named, and housenames are passed from generation to generation, from either parent to both daughters and sons, and are also extended to any one joining the house as an affine, a foster child, a lodger or a servant. Within the village community housenames confer social identity, placing the individual in a closely knit network of kinship reciprocity and obligation. Kinship and gender identity are integrally associated with work, both on the land and for the land. Farm labour revolves around the senior married couple of the house, the *gazda* and *gospodyni*, and it is the balance and complementarity between the labour of husband and wife, and the authority of the senior generation within the house and farm, which is reinforced in domestic rituals.

The socialist period

During the socialist period the Górale house could be seen as the site of resistance and opposition to the state in both economic and cultural terms (see Pine 1993).[1] It was only in the 1950s, with the socialist state's policy of full employment, that most Górale villagers, both men and women, first had the opportunity to enter into full-time, permanent waged work. Despite the economic stability and the access to pensions, benefits and a wide range of 'perks' associated with employment within the state sector, most villagers were at best ambivalent about this work. They tended to resent the authority exercised by Party managers in the workplace, and consistently represented their own jobs as a waste of time and of no value. This was in marked contrast to their attitudes towards agriculture: working on the land, for the upkeep and good of the house, was represented as correct and valuable labour, conducted within the proper context of the morality of the house and the reciprocity of kinship. Similarly, social relations within the village, the house and the farm were portrayed, not completely accurately, as being based on reciprocity and exchange, within an acceptable and correct hierarchical framework based on gender and generation. The Górale place very strong emphasis both on corporate identification with kin and family, expressed through house membership and reciprocal labour, and on distinctive individual enterprise, which although individualistic can also be seen as being *for* the benefit of the house. Their negative view of the (socialist) state as intrusive and authoritarian (particularly in terms of regulation of waged labour and agriculture), and as limiting to individual potential (particularly in terms of restrictions on private enterprise) should be understood in these terms. To a great extent, villagers expressed their attitudes to the local community and to the state through ritual.

The socialist state exercised enormous control over the public face of ritual, parading its symbols, and placing them in the context of nationalism, at every possible opportunity. The villagers responded by acting out their opposition through the conscious and deliberate rejection of socialist rites, and through concentration instead on alternative ritual elaboration centred around the house, family and catholic church. Hence, they would work in the fields on socialist holidays, ignore the parades on May Day and other commemorative festivals unless they were obliged to participate in them because of their jobs in the state sector, and would observe rather the holy days and festivals of the church and, above all, the domestic rituals of the house. In the case of weddings, for instance, the civil ceremony, which legitimated the marriage in the eyes of the state, was marked by minimal fuss and celebration, while the church mass was given the weight of more solemn and elaborate ritual; most elaborate, and most highly attended, however were the domestic blessings, which took place in the bride's house before the church mass, and the *wesele* which followed immediately after. Thus, in terms of both work and ritual the Górale continually opposed the inside – the family, house and farm – to the outside, above all the state.

The advent of waged work and a capitalist market has usually been associated in social theory with an increasing divide between the productive and reproductive spheres, or productive and reproductive labour. This distinction is in turn commonly presented as a gendered one; productive labour is linked to the public domain and historically to the idea of the working man's 'family wage', while reproductive labour is located in the domestic domain, within the household, and associated with women. I would suggest that in Górale communities, a rather different adaptation to waged labour, economic diversification and, since 1989, the capitalist market takes place. While the distinction between the realm of the house and that of the outside, which can be likened to the public/domestic dichotomy, is a central construct in Górale social order, it is not a gendered distinction *per se*. Rather, both women and men are associated with the public and domestic domains, and both have important and appropriate social activities to perform within each domain. In terms of the house and the farm, women are responsible for tasks such as cooking, cleaning, laundering, while men are expected to take on building, structural repairs, maintenance and so forth. In the fields, women and children do most of the arduous repetitive work, while men deal with heavier work involving horses and machines. Men slaughter animals, while women help to prepare meat and sausage under male direction. What this gendering amounts to, however, is a balancing of tasks and activities within each domain, rather than a rigid distinction between gendered domains. Equally important, these activities are *in practice* largely interchangeable; if there is no suitable woman about, a man may cook, clean and care for children without anyone casting aspersions on his masculinity; women can and do plough, drive horses, repair machines, and work on maintaining and repairing buildings.

Outside the domestic/farm economy, both men and women are expected to earn money to bring back into the house. This may be done through waged labour, through contract work in, say, construction, through craft production, through marketing and through economic migration. Work is an integral part of personal identity for both men and women, young and old. To comment positively on someone's industrious nature, their strength, and their skill at any kind of work is to give the highest possible praise; both females and males are on the other hand condemned for laziness, weakness and a lack of either skill or worldliness. For women, the ability and inclination to work hard is also part of being a mother, of providing for and nurturing the members of the house. Fatherhood is a more nebulous and detached quality, but to be good husbands and fathers, men must be seen to be able to work for, and physically protect, their own. Work is organised and negotiated first of all within the house on the basis of gender and generation, secondly between houses on the basis of kin and neighbour reciprocity and exchange, and thirdly in relation to the outside, in contractual relationships often organised through personal networks but nevertheless outside the morality of kinship and community. Even the gains from this 'outside' work, however, are often channelled back into the maintenance, improvement and perpetuation of the house (Pine 1999).

Following from this, I would suggest that in the Górale case the dichotomy between productive and reproductive labour is not a very useful one. During one day, a woman may clean the house, cook, work in the barn and in the fields, knit a sweater which may be for market or for home use, and go to clean in the local factory for wages. Villagers themselves clearly distinguish between work which generates income (*zarobki*) and labour which does not – for the former they usually use the word *praca* , for the latter *robota*. Some activities, however, such as working in the barn and the fields, and knitting, are impossible to classify in this way; even as they are being performed, it is often not clear whether they are directed towards subsistence/domestic consumption or sale on the market.

Both socialist ideology and the formal legislation of the Polish socialist state entitled women and men to economic equality in terms of access to work and pay. In practice, this often resulted in gender stratification (justified as 'protection' of women from hard or dangerous work, which was in fact often the most highly paid), and in a 'double' or 'triple' burden for women, who balanced full-time waged work with domestic labour and childcare and, in the countryside, agricultural labour as well (see Rai, Phizacklea and Pilkington 1992). For the Górale, while both dominant and local gender ideologies placed more value on what men do as work, and while women certainly carried a 'double' or 'triple' burden in terms of responsibility for domestic labour, farm labour, and waged or other outside work, women as well as men were active agents in all spheres of economic life and, perhaps equally important, were acknowledged to be so. Further, the fact that in the Podhale both men and women own land, and women's economic activities were visible and highly valued both in agriculture and, particularly, in the second economy, resulted in a greater degree of gender equality than in other regions. This was particularly the case in relation to the most lucrative form of work, economic migration. During the socialist period, because of the strict laws regulating passport control, and the equally stringent rules, particularly in the case of applications to North America, surrounding the issue of visas, it was often women who were the best candidates for economic migration: it was assumed, by both the Polish and the foreign authorities that women who left young children behind in the village would definitely return, while it was feared that men, particularly young, unmarried men, were likely to attempt to remain permanently abroad. The Górale played on these assumptions, and it was common even for women with very young children to go to work abroad, leaving their children in the care of other women of the house or of close female kin, and still to be seen as active and responsible mothers – because hard work and economic responsibility are themselves integral to the construction of motherhood.

Post-socialism

In both the socialist and the post-socialist periods, the state, and to some extent the nation, are part of the 'outside' against which local Górale identity is developed and transformed; relationships between the inside and the outside are negotiated largely through the medium of work. After the demise of the socialist state in 1989, the new government immediately embarked upon a path of rationalisation and restructuring of the national economy, in order to meet the requirements of the IMF and the World Bank. Throughout Poland unemployment steadily increased: in the mountains, official unemployment figures have been uniformly high, reaching 25 per cent in some sectors and affecting a disproportionate number of women (see Heinen 1992). However, the real economic decline which has affected other areas, especially one-industry towns, as the result of factory closures and unemployment (see Nagengast 1992), has not taken place to the same degree in the mountains. Neither has there been an enormous change in the types of work which people do. Rather, the emphasis placed on different kinds of work has shifted. In the post-socialist economy, many of the activities which under socialism people pursued informally or through the second economy have become legal and above-board; market women, for instance, can legally travel throughout the country on the purchase of a rather expensive licence, and small private businesses, often based in the house, are now far easier to establish and register than formerly. One middle-aged woman, for instance, used to provide meals 'informally' for tourists; she and her husband now run a full-time catering business from their kitchen and a small 'bed and breakfast' from their house; another middle-aged couple have converted their farm to a mineral water factory, employing local labour at rather low pay; other villagers have set up video rental businesses, small shops, and other such enterprises in their houses. Much of this work in the new entrepreneurial sector is done by the young and middle-aged, and much of it takes away from the farm labour force, and removes work from the domestic hierarchies which revolve around farming. Simultaneously, in an unsteady and unpredictable local market for agricultural produce, with rising feed costs and rapidly diminishing state subsidies, there is a general shift in the village economy, particularly among younger people, away from farming. Most village houses still work small farms, but the majority of these are increasingly for subsistence only; few villagers now deliver much milk to the local dairy, or raise meat for sale – the exception here is the small number of specialist farms which concentrate on meat or dairy produce.

During the socialist regime it was more likely to be men who worked away from home for short or middle-term periods (and the exception here was always economic migration abroad, which was equally likely to be female but was more long term) as construction workers, builders and drivers; now greater numbers of women are working regularly as long-distance traders and market women. This also has implications for the farming division of labour; in the socialist years, when men went away, women would run the farms, and there was some tendency towards a 'feminisation' of agriculture. Now the divisions of labour to be negotiated are more complex, as it is often women, and women with dependent children or parents to care for, who are in the position to bring most income back to the house by their travels and trading. All of these factors highlight the tensions and difficulties, which have been endemic for generations, in running a sustainable family farm; it is only as relations with the outside open up and broaden that these tensions are becoming explicit, and that simultaneously the established legitimate hierarchies of gender and generation within the house are being somewhat eroded.

Patterns of economic migration have also become more elaborate. While the labour is still largely carried out illegally in the host country, it is no longer difficult to arrange from the Polish side, as borders have opened and passports can be obtained without difficulty. While economic migration, through long-term kin links, to North America has been central to the Górale economy since the end of the nineteenth century and is still important, now migration to other parts of Europe, particularly Greece, Italy and Germany, is also commonplace. In the Polish popular press, and in popular representations generally, one of the most negative images of the new capitalism is the degradation and consumption of the nation by foreigners (westerners). A common and powerful metaphor for this is the seduction, rape or corruption of Polish women by predatory foreign men. The context for the corruption is usually work: a woman goes abroad expecting to work as a nanny, only to find herself snared into the sex trade, a woman working for a foreign businessman is seduced and abandoned after being offered marriage and a ticket to the West, and so on. The imagery here is of passive or helpless women, taken by wile or force from their proper roles as mothers, wives and homemakers. Underlying these stories, it seems to me, is a growing separation of work and family domains, and an increasingly powerful discourse of gender, in which women should be in the home, and men should be outside in the workforce; the horror stories consistently involve women leaving their families, leaving the nation, and attempting to act as independent productive agents. Less lurid but equally powerful discussions regularly take place in newspapers and women's magazines, blaming the breakdown of the family and moral values on socialism, and specifically on women's paid work, and advocating women's right to chose to remain at home and care for their children. These ideas coincide, of course, with rising unemployment and what is effectively the practical removal of large numbers of women from the workforce. What interests me about these gender narratives in the context of this paper is that, in terms of Górale categories of work, identity and personhood, they are simply not appropriate. Górale women are as likely as men, if not more likely, to be migrant workers, going to Greece, Italy or Germany as nannies, housekeepers or au pairs, and from there activating the chains which will pull other kin and friends after them, to do the same work or to work in factories or as labourers. Long-distance trade is the prerogative of women, and skilled market women travel throughout Poland and abroad, selling local products and bringing back goods with which to deal in the local market. Married women, single women, old and young, are equally likely to be involved in long-distance trade and migration, and they arrange this with the full support of their family and kin. In other words, the total pool of house and kin labour is continually balanced and rearranged, in order to allow the most pragmatic and lucrative divisions of labour between the sexes and the generations. Górale women are seen as interacting with the outside positively, through their work, rather than negatively or dangerously, through their sexuality. It is appropriate for them to leave their children and their home if they are going in order to bring back things which will add to the growth of the house; it is appropriate for them to work with foreigners and strangers, and this work is seen neither as threatening to their own bodies and persons, nor as dangerous for the boundaries and integrity of the community to which they belong.

It is in terms of this shifting relationship between work and state control that changes in the rituals of the house can perhaps best be understood. The centrality of the house economy remains consistent over time, as does the fact that both female and male personhood is largely expressed through labour, labour either directly within the house economy or *for* it. House rituals under socialism demonstrated house centrality accurately, and reflected the order of gender and generation and the hierarchies of labour which gave form to the social relations of the house and the farm. Work itself however was misrepresented during this period, or represented in terms that accentuated moral and cultural importance rather than economic or material importance. Thus, farm labour was emphasised above all other kinds of work, waged labour for the state was negatively represented, and dealings within the second economy, including economic migration, were veiled or hidden from public view. With post-socialism, these representations of work have changed, and have in many ways become accurate portrayals of economic reality. Farm labour, in terms of economic rewards at least, is now downplayed, and while waged labour in the public sector is still represented as negative and anti-social, with the continuing retraction of the state sector fewer and fewer villagers are involved in it. The emphasis of the rituals of the house has also shifted, from conspicuous house-based production to conspicuous consumption/purchase, which simultaneously negates to some extent the former farming/house order; much of the house-based ritual during the socialist period celebrated the divisions of the labour of the house, its productivity and its fertility, while the current emphasis appears to be more on purchase power, the hiring of outside labour, and the appropriation of styles and commodities from the outside. Whereas in the days of house-based production, the older generations were the keepers and transmitters of knowledge and expertise, and hence to a great degree the guardians of both economic and symbolic capital, it is the young, well versed in 'outside' cultures of consumption, who in the capitalist economy display the status of the house to the world.

Weddings, gender and generation

Here we can return to Beata's wedding. For this wedding, much of the labour which would formerly have been performed by the women of the house, and would have drawn attention to their industriousness, and to the fruits and products of the farm, was provided from the outside. The catering was paid for, many of the ingredients bought. The wedding dress was imported from France and as well as being extremely expensive, was consciously described as western and 'classic' rather than frilly in style. Many of the guests brought wedding presents of household appliances, glass and china, whereas formerly the appropriate, indeed mandatory, gift was a set sum of money to help to establish the new domestic budget. All of these points somehow have reverberations for the representation of labour, and suggest an increasing emphasis on commodification and on labour outside the house. Perhaps this was most clearly demonstrated by two very noticeable changes. The first was that, as I have mentioned, the *wesele* was in a community centre – and when I asked people about this, they all said, 'Well, it's so much less work; you don't have to do all the cleaning up – all that *mess* – someone else is paid to do it.' Similarly, professional waitresses served the food, formerly a task taken on with great pride by the bridesmaids, who were themselves demonstrating to potential suitors and mothers-in-law their strength, energy and skills in matters of the house. Thus, not only the symbols of the centrality of the house but also the public display of the correct gender order of labour within the house was being downplayed.

Finally, what was to me almost the most striking thing of all was the absence of the senior generation at this *wesele*. Although the grandparents from both sides did attend initially, they were clearly uncomfortable, and all left immediately after the first meal, stating that they had work in the barn or had to milk the cows. Again, the *wesele* was formerly an occasion where the integrity of the house work-force, under the direction of the senior generation, was on display. Here the split seemed almost palpable, as the younger generation created new ritual practices, based on more com-moditised consumption, in which the gender and generation hierarchies of the farming household have little or no place. At the beginning of the *wesele*, this was manifested in the music and dancing: the musicians played western pop tunes, and the guests, primarily the young, danced as they would in any disco anywhere in Europe. Old Górale tunes, and Górale style dancing, in the performance of which the old villagers would previously have played the leading role, were conspicuous by their absence.

And so it was the old people who sat, uncomfortable, and ill at ease, for the first, relatively sober hours of the party, and com-plained to each other that this was not a Górale *wesele* at all. Had they waited, however, they would have seen the bride's father's kin, from a 'more' Górale (more remote) village, begin to sing 'real' Górale songs more and more loudly as the evening progressed, led by the young male cousins who, as they consumed more and more vodka, became more and more vociferous in proclaiming that they were turning this into a 'real' Górale *wesele*. By the wee hours of the morning, the musicians were playing only traditional Górale music, and the bride and groom and all of the guests abandoned themselves to the old dances they had learned as children.

Beata danced with her husband, twirling, hands on hips, stamping her feet. The guests surrounded them in a tight circle, dancing, clapping and singing faster and faster, and Beata's most dangerous young patrilateral cousin danced the part of a bull, with his hands on his forehead like horns, charging at the bridegroom until the usurper was finally pushed out of the circle and the bride reclaimed by her male kin (the bulls). At this moment it was as if the archaeology of tradition and ritual was revealed. The bride danced in her expensive, imported modern white dress, embodying the new gendered consumerism, but through the dance itself she and her husband and her male kin played out in ritual form much older relationships of gender and kinship. It was as if after performing, and successfully appropriating, the new rituals of status and consumption, the young villagers thus reclaimed older, local cultural forms as their own.

Conclusions

Since 1989 the presence of the state has receded, and while the house continues to provide the economic framework for the organisation of labour, its ritual elaboration appears to be diminishing. Here I would argue that during the socialist period, when villagers straddled the boundary between the formal, state-controlled economy of waged labour, to which they were highly antagonistic, and the informal, house-based second economy of semi-legal and often hidden trading and dealing, the highly elaborate rituals of the house made its cultural centrality public and explicit. In the post-socialist period, a shift takes place. Work *for* the house, but in the 'outside' economy, is now clearly visible and economically central; work *within* the house takes on a more accurate and realistic position in the background of the represent-ation of labour. The rituals of the house which publicly display the relationship between gender and generation, labour and land, and which metaphorically emphasise its cultural and economic centrality as opposed to that of the state, are being relocated 'outside', and hence are shifting definitions of local identity towards consumption and commodification. However, this is not a simple replacement of the old by the new. The present generation are negotiating a complex era of change in their own way, taking on many of the ubiquitous symbols of the global market economy but at the same time retaining and even reinventing 'timeless' local practices which speak vividly of 'belonging' to the mountain landscape and culture. Gender acts as a cipher here: the bride's dress, the expensive, store-bought presents, the shifts from display of house labour to purchased help, are balanced against practices and processes which, although sometimes being reworked, are long established in village culture. The bull dance performed at Beata's wedding embodies the complexity of the cultural codes these villagers accommodate simultaneously.

Acknowledgements: The then SSRC supported my original fieldwork in 1977–9, and the ESRC funded further research in 1988–90 and 1992–6. I am grateful to Paola Filippucci and Deema Kaneff for reading and suggestions, and to the participants in the EASA panel for a useful and stimulating discussion. Particular thanks are due to Victoria Goddard for clear and perceptive editorial comments.

Notes

1 The arguments I am making about the house and the state, and the local antagonism to socialism, are specific to the Górale; in other parts of rural Poland, including the central region around Łódź where I have also worked, divisions of labour are quite different, as is the local gender order, and villagers on the whole were and are supporters of socialism.

Bibliography

Butler, J. (1990) *Gender Trouble*, London: Routledge.
Collier, J. and Yanagisako, S. (1987) 'Toward a unified analysis of gender and kinship', in J. Collier and S. Yanagisako (eds), *Gender and Kinship: essays toward a unified analysis*, Stanford: Stanford University Press.
Connell, R.W. (1987) *Gender and Power*, Oxford: Polity Press.
Heinen, J. (1992) 'Polish democracy is a masculine democracy', *Women's Studies International Forum*, 15, 1.
Jaworski, R. and Pietrow-Ennker, B. (eds) (1992) *Women in Polish Society*, New York: East European Monographs , Columbia University Press.
Nagengast, C. (1992) *Reluctant Socialists, Rural Entrepreneurs: class, culture and the Polish State*, Boulder, Colorado: Westview Press.

Pine, F. (1993) ' "The cows and the pigs are his, the eggs are mine": women's domestic economy and entrepreneurial activity in rural Poland', in C. Hann (ed.) *Socialism: Ideals, Ideologies, and Local Practice*, London: Routledge.

—— (1994a) 'The process of privatisation in post socialist Poland: peasant women, work and the restructuring of the public sphere', *Cambridge Anthropology* 17, 3.

Pine, F. (1994b) 'Maintenir l'économie domestique: travail, argent et éthique dans les montagnes polonaises', *Terrain* 23, October: 81–98.

—— (1996) 'Naming the house and naming the land: kinship and social groups in the Polish highlands', *JRAI* 2, 2: 133–56.

—— (1999) 'Incorporation and exclusion in the Podhale', in S. Day, E. Papataxiarchis and M. Stewart (eds) *Lilies of the Field: Marginal People who Live for the Moment*, Boulder, Colorado: Westview Press.

Rai, S., Pilkington, H. and Phizacklea, A. (1992) *Women in the Face of Change: The Soviet Union, Eastern Europe and China*, London: Routledge.

Whitehead, H. (1981) 'The bow and the burden strap: a new look at institutionalised homosexuality in native North America', in S. Ortner and H. Whitehead (eds) *Sexual Meanings: The Cultural Construction of Gender and Sexuality*, Cambridge: Cambridge University Press.

Chapter 5

Properties of identity

Gender, agency and livelihood in Central Nepal

Ben Campbell

When I first walked up the Trisuli Valley of Nepal in 1980 I was struck by the quality of gender relations in Tamang communities,[1] which appeared relatively non-oppressive and permitted a surprising openness of erotic expression. The women there seemed to be in many ways remarkably free agents. Their interactions with men were seemingly uninhibited by the predominant South Asian attitude of feminine modesty (*laaj* in Nepali). Years later, during fieldwork, these initial impressions were developed as I came to understand the considerable strategic possibilities women exercised in the achievement of their productive livelihoods and in their personal relationships.

The general 'status' of Himalayan women and their relative freedom in sexual morality and remarriage have been commented upon in attempts to compare systematically elements of ethnic societies with those of Hindu high-castes.[2] There tends to be an assumption of functionalist coherence to the associated features in these analyses, which does not recognise the dimensions of personal agency behind representations of cultural practice, and the kinds of differentiated qualitative social meanings and articulations attached to features of property and personhood.

In this chapter I discuss women's access to property in one of the 'ethnic' communities of Nepal as a way into understanding strategic practices of gendered personhood. Dowry is often cited as an instrument of women's oppression,[3] but the ethnographic case discussed here is in many ways exceptional to the politics of gender normally associated with dowry in South Asia. The practice of dowry is often listed as a typical feature of the Hindu high-castes (Gellner 1991: 108). That a dowry system can co-exist with bride-service might seem anomalous (Collier and Rosaldo 1981: 321), but that is perhaps an effect of thinking in terms of tables and ideal types rather than the variety of ways people can and have to make their social worlds. Both dowry and brideservice relationships are significant aspects of Tamang women's realisation of personal agency, and it is through an appreciation of differently positioned social actors that the processual vitality of relationships and their exchange dynamics can be understood.

The area under discussion has a history of central neglect. Rasuwa District is a relatively sparsely populated, borderland mountainous region of Central Nepal through which an important trans-Himalayan trade route once ran. It was kept off limits to British military recruitment into the Gurkha regiments. Historically, this region acted as a labour reserve for the Kathmandu elites, and surplus value was extracted more through labour corvee and portering services than taxation of produce. Culturally, the Tamang-speaking people are significantly different from the Hindu main-stream: being Buddhist in religion, practising cross-cousin marriage, and with most of the clans eating beef. In terms of cultural gender politics, the honouring of wife-givers is also contrary to Hindu logic (March 1979, Holmberg 1989).

Despite the construction of a road through the district to a mine (that has remained largely unproductive), the area remains little 'developed', as the creation of a national park in the 1970s set in place severe restrictions on productive intensification. The value of land is not high, and attempts to promote temperate fruit produc-tion have not significantly caught on. Trekking tourism provides income to a limited number of villages in the district, though men and women frequently earn small amounts from portering. The predominant economic activity remains transhumant agro-pastoral production with a limited section of the households managing some surplus sale of dairy, livestock, and potatoes. Given the relatively unproductive character of economic resources, it is rather in the mobilisation of extensive social networks for co-operation in labour, and in managing livestock, that much effort is invested (Campbell 1994). It is in this context that dowry transfers of productive property can be especially significant to the Tamangs' marginal livelihoods. Seasonal or permanent outmigration for work is increasingly the response to domestic production insufficiency. Disparities of wealth are not enormous, except for the few poli-ticians with connections at national level, and there is no cultural support for the reproduction of status elites.

Rather than track back systematically across previous debates on dowry and brideservice, the point of this contribution is to present gendered gifts of property as an active process of identity negotiation. The argument is developed in an ethnographic context where the 'domestic domain' is one that is constantly being reconfigured to include actors that are not usually in the picture in standard anthropological treatments of dowry as to do with the devolution of household 'estates' (e.g. Goody and Tambiah 1973). For the Tamang, dowry is a factor in enduring relationships between a woman and the men she calls brother/father (with whom she may or may not share the identity of actual clan membership). The identity of clan, and more broadly classificatory parallel kin, provides Tamang women with a solidity of relational personhood retained in frequent life histories of serial marriages.[4] The identity of a classificatory sister/daughter can be exercised in a whole range of contexts that generate significant transfers and ritual recognitions, usually initiated by the woman bringing gifts of alcohol and special foods, resulting in various reciprocations. From the simple acquisition of a bundle of wool from brother/father shepherds at shearing time, to the handing over of a mature animal, or an area of terraced fields, Tamang women invoke a moral economy particular to the relationship of *phamyung-busing* (male–female parallel kin). These transfers are, however, not seen as automatically generated from kinship prescriptions, and need to be actively worked at in the quality of relationships over time.

Tamang women's claims to property entitlement as a sister/daughter are dialectically related to the issue of erotic freedom in a double-sided ontology of personhood, given shape through the rigorous logic of Dravidian kinship reckoning. The kinds of exchange appropriate to parallel kin exclude erotic possibility. A woman's *phamyung* are the men she can turn to in situations of marital separation or violence, to exert collective moral pressure over her brideservice-obligated husband. With reliable, close *phamyung* she can expect to be supported and welcomed in their house as 'her' house. By contrast, classificatory male cross-cousins, husbands' younger brothers, and older sisters' husbands, constitute a set of relationships in which she can expect to engage in two-way erotic joking and ritualised, combative seduction, even well into old age.

It might be reasonably questioned to what extent and in what cases keeping distinct these two aspects of personhood can be challenged. First of all, how standard for women is the receipt of material support from male kin in practice? And secondly, what factors of change influence the sustainability of property redistribution to women, and tolerance of their moral independence? To answer the first question I analyse statistics for types of dowry received and the significant variable of women's residential proximity to male kin affected by post-marital domicile. The second question leads to discussion of a test situation: the effects that the commoditisation of sexuality has on the extent to which Tamang women prostitutes' moral identity as sisters and daughters can remain independent from their livelihood careers. Bringing together the contrasting experiences of women finding livelihood security in the density of local networks with those of their sisters tossed about in the South Asian experience of economic migration forces the argument away from a simple, localised materialist reductionism. The agency involved in making livelihood in one context is not wholly different in the other. Both dowry and prostitution are rarely discussed in terms of agency. They tend to be seen as passive effects of gendered inequalities. Here I attempt to treat them as part of the active making of livelihoods for the women involved, who seek to maintain a sense of self that is not overshadowed by their marital or sexual relationality.

If kin give dowry, dowry gives kin

Investigating the terminologies and practices of property transfer, it became clear that the Tamangs' borrowing of the Nepali word for 'dowry' *daijo* (pronounced *deidso* in Tamang), to describe gifts of property to women, did not correspond to what I knew of discussions on the practice and meaning of dowry in South Asia.[5] The ethnography opened up problems with definitions of dowry, revealing it as an arena of strategic agency in which women's commentaries and motives can be contrasted to men's, and in which the giving of productive resources to women does not necessarily flow from ascribed entitlements of kinship proximity, but can actually reconfigure alliances and relationships in a transformative process of creative kinship.

If one takes dowry to be defined as a transfer from a woman's natal family to herself, her husband or his kin, at the time of marriage (paraphrasing Agarwal 1994: 505), then much of what happens with Tamang women does not fit this kind of definition. Such definitions over-privilege specific notions of women's identification with both natal and marital domestic boundedness, and I would prefer a broader definition of dowry or another category to cover gifts made to women by kinsmen. Surely an important aspect, often ignored in the literature, is how people talk about dowry. What does it mean to them, and how does it affect their lives? What emerged in this respect was that property gifts to women were used to make or assert kinship, almost as much as following from it. Starting from a perspective of dowry as the channel for the diverging devolution of household property to female heirs (Goody 1976: 6) will not work here. With the Tamang, its giving can be far more strategic, where dowry is seen as a substantial statement of support to female kin, a statement of relationship. The key social reality underlying this strategic practice is the openness of Tamang notions of the 'house' (the same Tamang word, *tim*, also applies to 'lineage'), and its effective encompassment in the local kinship discourse on the classificatory solidarity between male and female parallel kin (*phamyung-busing*).

By far the most common gifts of *deidso* to Tamang women are of livestock. This is interesting because Bina Agarwal (1994) argues against Goody's homogenising of dowry as pre-mortem inheritance, and insists there is a world of difference in the experience of women, between societies in which movables such as livestock are given to women, and those in which women can claim by right significant portions of land. This may indeed be true for most of agrarian South Asia, but as is so often the case when comparing the Himalayan fringe to the rest of South Asia, qualifications need to be made.

Most Tamangs of Rasuwa District, Central Nepal live on relatively poor, unirrigated land, and keep herds of cattle, cattle–yak hybrids, water buffaloes, sheep and goats, that are taken in seasonal movements through forests, pastures and harvested fields. For them the major indicator of relative wealth is livestock rather than land,[6] (and this has become even more the case as milking animals provide dependable income to families selling to the increasing demand for fresh milk in the district capital). Up until a generation ago, land could still be cleared from the forest,[7] or long-fallowed fields could be bought up relatively cheaply. The limiting productive factor was rather adequate numbers of livestock to ensure the continuing fertility of the soil. The main limiting factor on keeping herds was insufficient labour. Giving away livestock as dowry relieves the pressure of labour intensification on families with successful herds over-burdened with fodder collection.

This background demography of labour had various historical consequences for gender and property relations. In the past (particularly before the restrictions on movements across the Tibetan border after 1959), wealthier households diversified economically into trade and long-distance pastoralism. They attracted male herders (*gothalo*) from poorer villages to the south, several of whom ended up marrying into the village. This created a specific identity complex of the immigrant *mha* (son-in-law) which I will elaborate on here. There are no longer any wealthy long-distance trading and herding families, but the phenomenon of uxorilocal in-marriage persists at a lesser frequency. The in-marrying *mha* symbolises male dependence and subservience, a condition of untrammelled brideservice. He would be agnatically landless, indebted to a family for initial years of employment, often marrying a daughter (or at least a classificatory daughter) of his employers, and indebted for their provision to her of *deidso* land and livestock. It is not, though, simply the poor immigrant men to whom obligations of brideservice apply. Tamang society and culture exhibit many of the features of brideservice elaborated in Collier and Rosaldo's (1981) remarkable study of this way of making marriage and the networks of co-operation that follow from it. Apart from expectations of help in subsistence activities, and house building, all domestic and community rituals require a *mha* in attendance: to carry the dead, to feed the guests, to replenish the lamas' drinking cups, and when the night is over, to carry home the drunken father-in-law.[8]

Now, how does the immigrant *mha* raise his head above the fate of perpetual brideservice? What agency can he exert to alter his status? What all Tamangs try for is to counterbalance the number of men you call *kyen-shyangbo* (WF-WB) with those you call *mha* (ZH-DH). The way to do this for men is by accumulating relationships of 'sisterhood' (*busing*). It is often the case that there would be no one the herder, as an incomer, could trace an exact genealogy with. But there probably would be a woman of a clan with a similar enough name to one in his natal village with whom he was parallel kin (*phamyung-busing*).[9] Once established with a productive herd of his own household, he has the opportunity to disperse young buffaloes, cattle, sheep or goats as *deidso* among the village women with whom parallel kinship can be in some way claimed, or quite simply, and legitimately, invented through formally entering into a relationship of ritual/fictive kin (Tamang – *leng, robo*; Nepali – *mit*) for instance with the women's brothers in their natal villages. Women who have married into the village are often similarly eager to have men they can call 'brothers', to avoid their predominant categorisation as lowly daughters-in-law (*tsang*). Eventually, with the preference for cross-cousin marriage, these newfound brothers' children can provide spouses for the sisters' children, and so the layers of village reciprocity networks deepen as marriage consolidates the original creation of kinship. Future generations of the herder's clan acquire broader alliances of parallel kin, leading to classificatory claims of wife-giver status to other clans. Dowry is therefore a slow but convenient way out of symbolic poverty in relationships characterised by the condition of exclusive brideservice.

Accounting for kin

What I want to emphasise is the need to look at dowry from actors' perspectives of claim, contestation, alliance, and situated strategy located in dynamic processes of property accumulation and transfer in the local economy. At the time of my fieldwork it was clear that land was in increasingly limited supply. The numbers of men marrying in to the village had dropped significantly since the national park ban on new clearances of forest in the 1970s, and land was circulated through women in a minority of cases. In a survey of land tenure I discovered that 12 per cent of the land in cultivation was acquired as *deidso* (virtually the same percentage as land acquired by purchase). In most cases the women who received *deidso* had natal families with well above average holdings. All of these women had moreover married in their natal village, apart from two women who were provided for with *deidso* in the absence of a husband, thus dismissing the necessary linkage of *deidso* to marriage and, *pace* Agarwal, suggesting that inheritance is the issue.

Obviously the term *deidso* covered a variety of personal circumstances. These could be clarified by other expressions, such as a woman inheriting in the absence of brothers saying she had 'eaten father's property'. In some cases women spoke of doubt as to the nature of their rights to the land they were working: was it merely usufruct, or a genuine transfer? It may have been said 'by mouth', but was not in their 'name', i.e. legally recorded. The costs of legal registration can be virtually as much as the value of the land.[10] Villagers tended not to register changes in land title until after the death of the named holder, or in the event of sale. Pragmatically,

this enabled certain adjustments to occur as to which heirs cultivated which particular plots in the inheritance. Given that holdings
are widely dispersed in parcels of terraces across the mountainside,
domestic labour circumstances for the heirs and changes in their
preferred herd compositions and crop specialisations often mean
that brother heirs would swap around particular fields to their
mutual convenience. Brothers received equal shares, and they
would not want to deny a share to a brother who perhaps went to
India for several years but had not been heard from. Registration
imposes an inflexible absoluteness of tenure contrary to the needs
of periodic readjustments.

Curious about the decision-making circumstances in which land
might be given as *deidso* I asked a woman who had already given
land to one daughter whether she would do the same for her
youngest. Her reply was 'If she marries a man with no land, it will
be given'. From this and other responses it follows that the logic
was clearly redistributive across economic inequalities and not the
pattern reported elsewhere in South Asia of dowry being used to
maintain socio-economic differentiation (Goody 1976). However,
the social relations around *deidso in land* do conform more
recognisably to the formulation of a conjugal estate provided by a
wife's natal family. By contrast, it is the gift of *deidso in livestock*
where the transfer of resources requires greater cultural explanation
of productive alliances extending beyond the logic of simple
domestic devolution.

I surveyed all adult women of the village of Tengu about their
receipt, or not, of *deidso*, and about their husbands' or brothers'
dispersals. The results were most revealing about the relationship
between what people say should be the case, and what actually
happens. The most commonly stated principle governing the
timing of gifts of *deidso* was that they should be given once a
couple go through with the marriage rite known as *rit cheeba*.[11]
This is a nocturnal meeting of bride and groom's relatives, usually
sometime after a previous rite of formal hospitality (*dolchang* or
nyetchang) that first recognises the union. The ingredients for *rit
cheeba* include gifts from the groom's party of: a large wooden
cylinder of fermented mash, a container of millet beer, fifteen
bottles of distilled alcohol (*raksi*), a shoulder of goat, and fried
doughnuts. 'The father and male kin of the wife have to eat the *rit
chee*.' The bride's agnates take pride of place during *rit cheeba*, and
enjoy addressing the groom's agnates collectively as *mha* (oblig-

ated wife-takers). Ostentatiously wiping the drink from their moustaches in their seats of honour, they dispense advice to the groom, and warn him not to beat their daughter too much. If they have not already done so, this is when promises of *deidso* should be made.

Deidso is the most significant exchange between *phamyung* and *busing*, apart from the possible marriage of their children. After promises have been made for the gift, the actual transaction is said to be initiated by an agnate asking a woman to come bringing a standard quantity of thirty bottles of *raksi* and a basket of doughnuts. (These items are also brought by *busing* for their *phamyung* every year at the autumn festival of *tiwar* in return for money, particularly if the man has been lucky in the brief, preceding gambling season.) The *deidso* animal may not even be handed over at this stage, especially if it is still suckling, if the woman is not set up to look after it, or in the case of sheep and long-haired goats it will stay anyway with the village flock and be tended by agnates or hired shepherds.

I have collated the responses to questions about *deidso* into two graphs (Figures 5.1 and 5.2). Figure 5.1 shows that there is a 100 per cent correlation between the giving of *deidso* and the performance of *rit cheeba among women who have remained in the village on marriage*, though several of them had also received *deidso* before *rit cheeba*. For women who married in from outside the village on the other hand the relative poverty of agnates and their living far off were the most commonly given reasons for them not receiving anything. Poverty was also cited by men as their reason for not having given *deidso*. 'If you're poor, whose going to give it?' or 'I'll give it when I'm rich' (meaning rather, 'in my dreams'). Other women said their *phamyung* give it 'with their mouths', i.e. in words, not in deed.

The observation made above about women receiving dowry if they marry within their natal village indicates the importance *deidso* can have in intra-community life. But surprising twists to the relational logic of exchange can emerge where the density of crosscutting paths of kinship and affinity offers village-endogamous women tactical possibilities for 'spinning' the interpretation of dowry transfer. When it comes to looking closer at the narratives people have of actual attempts to elicit promises of *deidso*, and the rationale of motives and levels of social commentary provided for

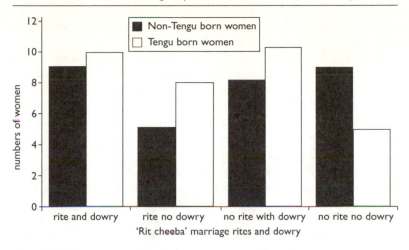

Figure 5.1 Tamang '*rit cheeba*' marriage rites and dowry.

particular exchanges, the formal rhetoric that privileges the transfer of property from real or classificatory father-brother to sister-daughter on marriage has to be seen as just one among several perspectives. For example, when I spoke with one woman about a report I had heard that her husband was going to give a buffalo to one of his *busing*, she responded with a quite different version of the linkages in the exchange. She did not privilege her husband's same-clan relationship to the woman recipient, who was of a different lineage altogether. Instead she spoke of the *deidso* as a case of herself arranging the transfer of an animal to *her* 'sister's daughter' (in this case her FBDD).

Thus, while public representations favour views of dowry as generous male gifts from *phamyung* to their *busing*, bestowed at a ritual which sets up marriage as a deal between groups of men in which the groom's side is obliged to defer to the providers of a wife *and* livestock, the private conversations over dowry which can be heard outside formalised ritual contexts provide occasionally more convincing accounts of women keeping livestock passing among their own *nanchen* (the collective term used by women to refer to their parallel women kin). It is precisely because of the repeated cross-cousin marriages between the *children* of *phamyung-busing*, or, as men more commonly say, repeated marriages between the same patrilineal clans, that alternative discourses are possible: that women of the same clan, *nanchen*, find themselves in a position to give animals to each other's daughters.

Figure 5.2 indicates the extent to which women resident in the village had received *deidso* from men beyond their natal household. While two-thirds of all women received at least some *deidso*, just over one-third also received an animal from beyond the natal household. But it is this one-third which demonstrates the definitional problem of understanding dowry. Are we discussing a practice adequately described as 'dowry', or are we dealing with something quite different? Not to treat these gifts as dowry would be to ignore the importance of ties that bind people as kin in Tamang society across divisions into multiple households. It would also downplay several things: the structural centrality of parallel kin in a society organised around a moiety distinction between kin and affines; the importance of kinship reckoned through the matriline; as well as the seriousness with which ritual kinship is viewed. Several of the gifts of *deidso* were made to women counted as *busing* through descent 'from one mother' (not through patrilineal clanship), and what might seem the most tenuous case of all, the village's head lama gave a sheep to a woman of another village whose grandfather had been ritual kin (*leng*) with his father. I was told 'She came calling him "father", and he gave her *deidso*'.

The important anthropological point, surely, is to ask what can it mean to call someone 'father', 'daughter', 'sister', and 'brother' in different societies, and to see the sorts of practical and symbolic relations these entail. The fact that significant productive resources (from one small buffalo calf, great milking herds can grow)[12] are given across core domestic boundaries indicates relational identities of considerable value. I have tried to show how these identities figure from a variety of positions. Dowry features as a strategic practice of marking and sustaining these identities, which is as important to the poorer families (both as receivers and givers) as it is to the rich. It would be wrong to attribute purely instrumental economic motives to the giving of dowry (another hugely significant function of 'sisters' is to provide food in rituals for the dead, and to nourish brothers undergoing initiation as religious specialists), but clearly, the ongoing effective co-operative disposition of people who can be called on in times of need is a factor in the survey's conclusion that all women who remain in the village after marriage have received some form of dowry. The people in Tengu need all the help they can get.

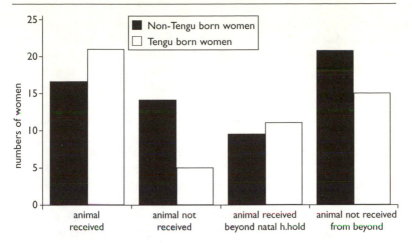

Figure 5.2 The variable of village origin and women's receipt of livestock dowry.

Property and associations of freedom

The flip side of the coin whose face of kinship and property value we have been looking at so far also needs to be kept in view, as it reveals the dialectically reverse identity of the sister and daughter: namely the erotically significant cross-cousin (*samdi-shya*), wife (*be*) and elder brother's wife (*tsang*). Just as a woman's extensive classificatory *phamyung* relationships are capable of substantial realisation in the domain of property, so it is with non-*phamyung* in the domain of sexuality. In the same way as *deidso* operates well beyond strictly defined domestic boundaries, expectations of erotic relations are similarly extensive beyond conjugal and household confinement. It is not so much that pre- and extra-marital sex are 'tolerated' to use Agarwal's terminology, they are positively encouraged, in the right circumstances, and with the right category of people.[13] When a woman's husband's younger brother comes to plough her field the atmosphere is thick with erotic potential, and not-so-subtle innuendo. At mourning feasts in which a period of taboo-marked grief is finally overcome through a collective celebration of sexual frenzy, even septuagenarian men and women can be seen chasing their cross-cousins, meddling with others' clothing, and cracking unrepeatable jokes.[14]

To understand how Tamang dowry is worked and has effect requires focusing on the agentially relevant social categories, those primarily of *phamyung-busing*, and not a confined vertical transfer of discrete domestic patrimony. But the relative gender parity characteristic of Tamang communities is also bound up with women's erotic freedom. Tamang sexual morality is not dominated by a regime of male surveillance and control. Women's sexuality is not subjected to exclusive domestic appropriation. It was commonly mentioned that the wives of men who spent long periods outside the village would seek pleasure elsewhere. Self-restraint in this matter is not considered particularly virtuous or healthy.

I would not suggest that gendered identity can simply be reduced to a function of property rights, but there does seem to be a morphic correspondence in the fact of both the circulation of productive resources and the realms of erotic freedom being characterised by similarly extensive ranges of agency beyond domestic confinement. It is rather these social parameters of legitimate action in themselves, a particularly scaled ontology of community and personhood, that facilitates the creativity of kin-based property transfer on one hand, and the relatively extensive freedom of erotic life on the other. Both facets depend on their mutual dialectical inversion to make a division of moral clarity that bifurcates all gender relations. I concur with Hildegard Diemberger's statement from research on another Himalayan community in east Nepal that:

> There are no distinct female and male worlds for the Khumbo ... when discussing the position of women and men in general, one must always specify exactly which women and which men, in which social position and in which context of life.
>
> (1993: 100)

and that 'It is not just the kinship system but the place kinship has in society that affects its impact on women's lives' (ibid: 96).[15]

The argument I have developed about dowry and creative identity therefore depends on an analysis of kinship agency within a particular form of redistributive community.[16] By contrast, Bina Agarwal's remarkably comprehensive study of women and land rights in South Asia is designed to inform political arguments about changing structural gender inequalities in the sub-continent. While she takes pains to distinguish dowry from inheritance proper as against Goody's conflation of the two, she also recognises that practices of dowry vary considerably as to their effect on women's control over their lives depending on the additional presence or absence of other features. Basically, she sees dowry as most coercive where women are in the position of marrying strangers in far-off places, and most positive where women marry by choice in their natal villages and exercise some effective control over their property. If dowry can be a positive factor for women here, it 'cannot be separated from other elements of strength in women's situation' (Agarwal 1994: 482). It is these other elements – of residence and erotic freedom in particular – that I have tried to include as complementing the transfers of property in giving women some scope for achieving a degree of control over their lives.

In order to explore further the relation between identity and agency among the Tamang, a few comments about the contemporary moral dilemmas confronting them in the form of sex work and trafficking in girls and women are instructive. Since the late 1980s organisations working with community, health and women have brought attention to the number of Nepali women working in India's sex industry (Seddon 1995). A large number of them were recruited from the Tamang heartlands of Central Nepal. The predominant representation of their condition is as passive victims of trafficking, abuse and coercive prostitution. In no way do I wish to belittle the terrible human sorrow which has befallen many of these women, but it is hard to reconcile the narratives of passive victims with the culture of Tamang women's agency outlined above.

A strict materialist interpretation might argue that the rising population and shortage of land in the hills has produced a crisis in the rural economy, such that a proportion of village women can no longer be adequately cared for by the system of gendered redistribution within their communities, and the pressure towards transnational economic migration cannot be resisted. This is indeed the case, but it does not adequately explain the dimension of women's agency within the process, or help in understanding the continuing value of kin networks to the women who return from Bombay (Mumbai). Rather than representing a wholly new situation of commoditised bodies and alienated kin, the prostitution networks taking Tamang women to India amount to a further historical stage in a process that for over a hundred years has involved a seepage of concubines to the palaces of the Nepali elite. (It is said that the concubines' fathers used to receive employment in return for a daughter.) When moral outrage is now voiced at men trading their daughters for the price of a new tin roof on the house, the total context of economic impotence in this area can be too easily forgotten. Thousands of boys and girls are placed by their families in situations of debt bondage, to live with animals on the mountainsides, clean and cook in Kathmandu restaurants, or work in carpet factories.

The point that needs to be made is that sex work can *appear* to be not so bad an option to girls, who see some of the Bombay migrants returning with savings to set up shops, and again *some* of whom manage to successfully reintegrate with community life, get married, and achieve status as independent entrepreneurs. Of course this is by no means the fortune of most of them and the AIDS epidemic is growing, but 'to sell vagina' (*pissya tsungba*) abroad and then to redistribute some of the proceeds among hard-up parents and *phamyung-busing* back home can be seen as morally commendable. Given the cultural conditions of pre- and extramarital sex not being intrinsically reprehensible, women who are skilful negotiators of strategic kinship can act in such a way as to deflect moral condemnation, and prove themselves as independent providers worthy of estimation as valued *busing*. This has been a livelihood scenario of some time depth as the history of ethnic sexual predation on the Tamang communities emphasises.[17]

A couple of examples might help to elucidate the general point of this chapter. Anga Chyangba married in her mid-teens to a village man twenty years older who took her to India where he worked as a coal miner. She had a son by him, but returned to the village complaining of mistreatment. She then kept a shop in a variety of places: in the village in a room of a brother's house; in the local town; and later in Kathmandu. She went through a number of relationships, some of which lasted a couple of years or so. In these cases the man would be called a brother/son-in-law by her own *phamyung*. At one stage, with the backing of her mother, her brothers arranged for dowry of half an acre of land to be registered in her name, so she could get a bank loan to invest in pots and pans and stores for the tea shop. Through all her ups and downs, failed commercial enterprises, and despite her widespread reputation as a loose woman, her *phamyung*, though occasionally severe with her, never abandoned her as a sister. She would come for annual brother–sister ritual at *tiwar*, and make them generous gifts of alcohol and food always presented in ways that incorporated a more sophisticated style and elaboration than that of the regular village *busing*. Being a skilful raconteur and flamboyant dresser, she would be a favourite of her younger *nanchen* who would borrow her fancy shoes and scarves, and she would be on mostly good terms with her brothers' wives, who enjoyed the hint of glamour she brought to life in their houses.

Anga Chyangba was not a prostitute as such, but her networks in the towns and city included some of the Tamang women who had returned from the Bombay brothels. One of these, Maili, she became ritual friends with. Maili was a super-confident shopkeeper/entertainer who moved into the village and attracted a flow of soldiers, teachers and bureaucrats from the local town. She won people over to rent rooms to her for a shop with great panache, charm and a touch of Bollywood glitz. She liberally distributed desired items of clothing to create a following of adoring younger girls, and used her ritual kinship with Anga Chyangba to assert a *busing* identity with Anga Chyangba's *phamyung*. As long as she paid her rent and kept the *phamyung* happy with occasional hospitality of fried smoked meat and alcohol, and gifts at *tiwar*, for a while she effectively maintained a credible local persona with an identity that enabled people to use kinship terminology with her. Eventually trouble with police and ructions with another shopkeeper led to her leaving the village. As I write she is in jail on charges of trafficking in girls.

Maili pushed to the limits the tolerance that the Tamang culture of personhood can offer a woman making her livelihood from the dissociation of sexual morality from kinship responsibility. Her skilful agency in attending to the performance of parallel kinship kept the 'fiction' of kinship alive for a period, while her financial solvency assisted in her identity as a successful independent woman. (On reflection it was through very similar processes of fictive kinship attendance and exchange that I too was able to achieve an identity as an incorporated incomer.) Where sexual morality is not linked to the performance of kinship, the problem of commoditising sex is not so culturally disastrous as it can be to women for whom such a livelihood career implies outcaste status. Where the domestic appropriation of women's sexuality by male surveillance is dominant, clearly women are denied the personal agency represented by the two individuals' cases described here.

My final argument then is that the linkage of productive property distribution to kinswomen and the possibilities for women to be relatively independent social actors, including the field of sexuality, hinges on a separation, on a particular moral division of relational personhood (though it turns out there is little guarantee of either property or freedom). In the ethnographic case discussed both facets of property and sexuality depend on a cultural context of agency in which kinship on one hand and sex on the other provide an arena for creative sociality and the processual transformative potential of what Carsten has called 'the relatedness which people act and feel' (1997: 290). Focusing on the practices of possible engagement of positioned actors in their strategies of livelihood and relationality offers a different kind of understanding of identity to the view of passively prefigured gender roles and mechanistic property transfer. The inter-agency of distinctive persons gives redistributive practice its dynamic relevance to people in making their lives. It has to be questioned whether the freedoms associated with the division of relational personhood can be maintained in the absence of property, and women have to rely materially on their erotic and marital personas alone.

Glossary

be   wife
busing   (a man's) female parallel kin
deidso   dowry
gothalo   herder
kyen-shyangbo   wife's father/brother
leng   male ritual kin
mha   daughter's/sister's husband
nanchen   (a woman's) female parallel kin
phamyung   (a woman's) male parallel kin
raksi   home-distilled alcohol
rit cheeba   central marriage rite
romo   female ritual kin
samdi-shya   female cross-cousin
tim   house/lineage
tiwar   Hindu brother–sister ritual usually in November
tsang   son's/brother's wife

Notes

1 'Tamang' as used here refers to a linguistic group. The information this chapter is based on was collected in fieldwork, supported by the ESRC, during 1989–91 in Tengu village, Rasuwa District.
2 See Gellner (1991) for a discussion of the problems of such stereotyping.

3 See Agarwal (1988, 1994) for her extensive review.
4 This solidity of personhood is itself expressable 'dividually' through the 'path of the father' and the 'path of the mother'. The solidity rests in the contrast to affinal identity.
5 Of the relatively more recent contributions to the discussions of dowry in South Asia, I found Gloria Raheja's (1988) important study of the issue of inauspiciousness in *dahej* gifts in Northern India to bear no relation to the ideas of dowry in the situation described here.
6 There is nothing comparable to Agarwal's study in regard to women's property rights in pastoral economies of the region, though Graham Clarke (1992) provides an analysis of Tibetan herders that stresses the dependence of inheritance practice on economic change, as 'matrilineal' practice seems to increase with relative poverty.
7 It was banned with the establishment of the Langtang National Park in 1976.
8 The role of brideservice in relation to other forms of co-operation in production is discussed in Campbell 1994.
9 One such cluster of in-marrying cognate clans in the village of Tengu were the Lo, the Loptsen and the Lapten.
10 Some astute women with no interest in cultivation had managed to get agreement for their share of *deidso* land to be legally registered so as to procure a bank loan on it.
11 *rit* means ceremony, custom. Turner 1980: 537. It is considered that if this rite is not performed, after death people cannot find the path to the place of the dead, and so it must be performed for the deceased during the mourning feast.
12 In the current articulation of village production with the cash economy, the greatest income is possible through selling fresh milk in the bazaar of the district capital. The household which benefits most from this has a buffalo herd of five adult females entirely produced from an original *deidso* animal. A typical blessing given at a wedding asks for the winds of the Tibetan plateau to blow away all disease, and for herds and flocks of animals to multiply from single beasts.
13 In the case of an unmarried girl falling pregnant, the issue is not her lost virginity but the clan identity of the child. If a marriage cannot be put together, then a man has to be found to admit paternity, however fictive or coercively achieved. The idea of someone being without clan is simply not an option. It would be a condition of non-social being. This paternity arrangement does not though avoid later reference to the child as 'a clan X bastard'.
14 Christina Toren's (1994) fascinating account of love and sex in Fiji also relies on the erotic tension between cross-cousins, which she stresses as egalitarian. But unlike her description of hip-thrusting, older women publicly mimicking the sexuality of youth in ridicule, I would suggest that many Tamang senior citizens of both sexes are not interested in mere showy simulation.
15 Diemberger's discussion of the Khumbo people has many cultural continuities with the Tamang, but in certain key respects the Khumbo are more 'Tibetan': in their prohibition of matrilateral cross-cousin

marriage and the priority given to households over wider kin groups in conceptions of alliance (1993: 95). It is the very looseness of the household in Tamang cultural practice which makes the issue of dowry so interesting in terms of agency. Diemberger appears to say that Khumbo women cannot receive dowry as land. For yet another excellent treatment of the varieties of property-gender complexes in the Himalayas see Levine (1988).

16 Henrietta Moore writes: 'It is through the negotiations that shape the outcome of the system of redistribution that social identities are themselves reproduced and opened up to potential change.' And further: 'Engagement in the system of redistribution provides individual persons with an experience of the meaning of gender, and with the meaning of other forms of differentiated identity – meaning is only given to difference through practical engagement. However, the very fact of practical engagement in the system of redistribution ties the experience of social identities, and of their construction, both to processes and relations within the domain of the household and to wider economic and political networks.' (1994: 105).

17 These issues are discussed further in Campbell (n.d.)

Bibliography

Agarwal, B. (1988) 'Who sows? Who reaps? Women and land rights in India', *Journal of Peasant Studies*, 15, 4: 532–81.

—— (1994) *A Field of One's Own: Gender and Land Rights in South Asia*, Cambridge: Cambridge University Press.

Campbell, B. (1994) 'Forms of cooperation in a Tamang community of Nepal', in M. Allen (ed.) *The Anthropology of Nepal: Peoples, Problems, and Processes*, Kathmandu: Mandala.

—— n.d. 'Sexual Values: erotic culture, personal strategies and market forces in the lives of Tamang women', paper presented at the meeting of the South Asia Anthropologists Group on Sexuality, SOAS, 1997.

Carsten, J. (1997) *The Heat of the Hearth: The Process of Kinship in a Malay Fishing Community*, Oxford: Clarendon Press.

Clarke, G. (1992) 'Aspects of the social organisation of Tibetan pastoral communities', *Tibetan Studies. Proceedings of the 5th Seminar of the International Association of Tibetan Studies*, pp. 393–411, Oslo: NARITA.

Collier, J. and Rosaldo, M. (1981) 'Politics and gender in simple societies', in S. Ortner and H. Whitehead (eds) *Sexual Meanings: The Cultural Construction of Gender and Sexuality*, Cambridge: Cambridge University Press.

Diemberger, H. (1993) 'Blood, sperm, soul and the mountain: gender relations, kinship and cosmovision among the Khumbo (N.E. Nepal)', in T. del Valle (ed.) *Gendered Anthropology*, London: Routledge.

Gellner, D. (1991) 'Hinduism, tribalism and the position of women: the problem of Newar identity', *MAN* 26, 1: 105–25.

Goody, J. (1976) *Production and Reproduction: A Comparative Study of the Domestic Domain,* Cambridge: Cambridge University Press.

Goody, J. and Tambiah, S. (1973) *Bridewealth and Dowry,* Cambridge: Cambridge University Press.

Holmberg, D. (1989) *Order in Paradox: Myth, Ritual, and Exchange among Nepal's Tamang,* Ithaca: Cornell University Press.

Levine, N. (1988) *The Dynamics of Polyandry: Kinship, Domesticity, and Population on the Tibetan Border,* Chicago: University of Chicago Press.

March, K. (1979) 'The intermediacy of women: female gender symbolism and the social position of women among Tamangs and Sherpas of Highland Nepal', unpublished thesis: Cornell University.

Moore, H. (1994) *A Passion for Difference,* Cambridge: Polity Press.

Raheja, G. (1988). *The Poison in the Gift: Ritual, Prestation, and the Dominant Caste in a North Indian Village,* Chicago: University of Chicago Press.

Seddon, D. (1995) 'AIDS in Nepal: issues for consideration', *Himalayan Research Bulletin,* 15, 2: 2–11.

Toren, C. (1994) 'Transforming love: representing Fijian hierarchy', in P. Harvey and P. Gow (eds) *Sex and Violence: Issues in Representation and Experience,* London: Routledge.

Turner, R. (1980) [1931] *A Comparative and Etymological Dictionary of the Nepali Language,* Delhi: Allied Publishers.

Chapter 6

Gendered houses

Kinship, class and identity in a German village

Gertrud Hüwelmeier

The subject of this essay concerns the linkages between buildings, social groups and cultural categories in a German village.[1] Up until the present day houses are named after ancestresses born around 1850.[2] When considering the emergence, continuity and meaning of the village naming system I will first outline the economic and social transformations of the last century. I will then concentrate on changing male and female identities within the processes of industrialisation and labour migration. The discussion will contribute to an understanding of the construction of local identity which focuses on the house as a central category in peoples' thinking about belonging.

As an anthropological category, the concept of the 'house' was discussed by Lévi-Strauss (1983; 1987), who defined it as a moral person, as

> a corporate body holding an estate made up of both material and immaterial wealth, which perpetuates itself through the transmission of its name, its goods, and its titles down a real or imaginary line, considered legitimate as long as this continuity can express itself in the language of kinship and affinity, most often, of both.
>
> (1983: 174)

Yet although the debates on 'houses' had been rekindled recently (Carsten and Hugh-Jones 1995), its usefulness as an analytical tool for the anthropology of European societies has been widely neglected (Waterson 1995: 63).[3] This may be due to the fact that the anthropology of Europe has concentrated on the Mediterranean area (Goddard *et al.* 1994). Here kinship has been treated as a marginal subject and received some attention mainly in relation to marriage and inheritance, or, on the political level, to patron–client relationships (Bestard 1991: 8). Moreover, the neglect of kinship may be connected with the 'familiarity' of bilateral kinship systems, that appears not to require further research (Davis 1977: 198, quoted in Bestard 1991: 8). Compared with kinship studies in 'primitive' societies, which played a crucial role in anthropological theory, kinship seemed to be of little interest when studying European societies.[4]

In European societies, characterised by a cognatic system, anthropologists felt 'obliged to abandon the study of larger groups and to focus instead on the family and on marriage' (Goddard 1994: 68). Citing Fox (1967: 51) on English society, 'which lacks descent groups of any kind', Strathern notes that 'an unfortunate consequence of the terminology of cognatic kinship, so-called, lies precisely in the implication that the most interesting difference in the English case must be the absence of groups' (Strathern 1992: 69). Instead, analysis focused on the nuclear family as a unit of consumption and on the household as an element of locality. Yet the category of the household remains unsatisfactory, because its analytical power appears too weak in examining processes of historical transformations. As Sabean pointed out (1990: 98), 'the notion of the household is a substantialist concept, that sees the farm family as a total unit and less as a category of complex alliances and reciprocities'. The category of the household, while focusing on residence, does not explain, for example, if and in which way absent members, particularly in the case of labour migration, are included or not.

In this chapter I would like to emphasise the necessity of making use of the concept of the house, first of all, because my informants talk endlessly about it. As a 'native' category it seems to be highly relevant in discourses on belonging and in creating individual and collective identities. My attention will focus on villagers' ideas of the house, and the analysis of their images and representations will be centred less on the structure and function of the house, and more on the symbolic aspects and the relevance of the house within the context of social change. In answering the question: 'What do people mean by using the concept of the house, how are they talking about it and in which way does the category of the house represent the wider social and political system?', we must focus on kinship as a cultural system (Schneider 1980) and its constitution for various identities.

Special interest will be given to class and gender in discussing the concept of the house as a social unit. In the processes of significant economic and social change, for example industrialisation and labour migration within rural communities in Germany, male and female identities have been shaped continuously. Debates within the anthropological literature on changing identities therefore must include a historical perspective, as has been pointed out by many colleagues (for example Segalen 1990; Segalen and Zonabend 1987; Bestard 1991), combining work in archives and church registers with participation and observation in the classical sense. Without the recognition of peoples' thinking about the past and without reference to the wider society anthropological analysis will be of little heuristic value.

The nineteenth century and the impact of labour migration

In Central Europe, the agrarian revolution led to a broad change, which above all resulted in the mobilisation of women in agriculture. This process could be dated between 1700 and 1870, when most of the population in Germany was engaged in agricultural production. Following Sabean, who discussed processes of change during this period in a south-western region of Germany (Württemberg) comparable with my research area (Hessia), the increasing mobilisation of women depended on reforms in agricultural practices and the introduction of new crops, which led to intensive stock raising. In regions characterised by smallholdings, during the eighteenth century, new agricultural technologies, for example the three-field rotation, innovations in cropping, substituting oxen for horses, and the introduction of stall feeding (Sabean 1990: 21), required new forms in the gender division of labor. Women were primarily occupied with the intensive hoeing of the new fodder crops in the fields.

Throughout the nineteenth century, the living and labour conditions in rural areas changed significantly, especially in regions in which, because of population growth, the soil quality and the consequences of partible inheritance led to pauperisation and did not allow all household members to rely solely on subsistence production. The rise of industrial capitalism in Germany since the middle of the nineteenth century brought new income-earning opportunities, allowing many men from rural areas to work as wage-labourers in remote industrial zones. Most of them left their villages during the summer for seasonal migration while simultaneously maintaining their smallholdings. They were commuters between city and village and this led to a double position represented in the term 'worker-peasant' in the literature on rural lower-class people (*Arbeiter-Bauer*; Kaschuba 1990: 75). This strategy involved working outside the village for money while simultaneously conceptualising oneself as a peasant with a smallholding. Within the social sciences this term, which represents the transition from agrarian to industrial society, betrays an implicit male bias. For example, no suitable term has been coined for the women remaining in the villages, even though they were the ones who would work in the fields and be responsible for subsistence production. In most areas this was the main resource of the household compared with the relatively unstable income of men, who worked as building and construction workers.

The temporary absence of men from rural areas is known to anthropology from various societies (Moore 1990: 124) and has been well documented. But still too little attention has been given to the European context, especially in regard to the emergence and development of women-centred households. Household networks go beyond the nuclear family and serve as material and moral support for their members. The question is, however, what consequences resulted from increasing socio-economic differentiation, especially in relation to changes in individual, collective and local identities? To answer this question we have to look at the micro-level and concentrate on social and economic conditions of living and working as well as on cultural concepts of village identity in rural areas.

Goat, cow and horse farmers[5]

The processes of transformation outlined above occurred also in Eschau, which at the turn of the twentieth century was a little village of 700 people.[6] With the construction of the railway from Frankfurt am Main to Cologne in the 1880s, the number of migrants from Eschau and surrounding villages increased significantly. Since the walk to the next train station took two hours and the distance to the remote work places in the Rhineland was significant, men did not return to their villages for months, earning some money as construction workers, masons and painters during the summer.

At this time, nearly every family owned a tiny house or a half of a house, some goats, and a very small piece of garden land as well as a bit of field land. The quality of the soil was extremely poor and because of partible inheritance land parcels were so small that the majority of households could not survive from agriculture alone. Corresponding to the number of fields and according to the size of the house, the social hierarchies within the village were based on classifying households according to whether they had a horse (in addition to some cows and pigs), at least one cow or only some goats. The goats were considered as 'the cows of the poor people' and were used mainly for the daily consumption of milk and butter, which were considered inferior to products derived from cows' milk. The owners of the goats were called 'goat farmers/peasants', and this term was also used as self-reference. In other words, landholding size and the type of stock symbolised the status of households. In addition social hierarchies were reflected in the architecture of houses.[7] Horse farmers' houses included a kitchen, a living room and several other rooms. The stalls and barns surrounded the farmyard and were separate from the house. Cow farmers' houses were also separate from the barn, though the houses, barn and stall were significantly smaller than those of the horse farmers. In contrast, goat farmers had very small houses, often only half a house, consisting of a kitchen and one, sometimes two, small bedrooms. Often there was no barn, and the goats were housed in the basement. Land ownership was as follows: goat farmers had between 1 and 5 acres of land, cow farmers between 5 and 20 acres (depending on the number of stock) and horse farmers had an average of 30 acres of land.[8] Compared with the northern regions of Germany with no partible inheritance, where farms had 200 to 500 acres, even the 'rich' horse farmers in Eschau could be designated as 'petty peasants' (*Kleinbauern*). Cash income in horse farmers' houses was small and they produced mainly for the local market. In order to earn some more money, members of the wealthier farmers' families practised a craft, and two of the families ran an inn.

Goat farmers represented both the largest group in Eschau and the lowest economic status. They were considered to be poor and dependent on others for the horse-cart services required during harvest. In contrast to the goat farmer households, who paid the horse farmers cash for the services of their horses or – because in many households cash was very short – provided their labour in compensation, the cow farmer households worked in a relatively favorable position: they could either till their fields alone with their oxcarts or they formed yoke teams (*Spanngemeinschaften*) with their relatives or neighbours while yoking together two cows (cf. Wagner 1986: 142). In the houses of the horse farmers and also in some of the larger cow farmer houses, one male member remained at home, while others looked for work as craftsmen. On the other hand, most husbands and sons of the goat farmer families left the village to work as masons and painters at distant construction sites. Women remained home with the children, managed their work on the smallholdings and additionally worked collectively as day labourers in the horse farmers' fields.[9]

The division of labour

In the context of labour migration, which expanded significantly in the last third of the nineteenth century, it is no exaggeration to speak of a feminisation of the village (Sabean 1990: 153).[10] In Eschau this was a consequence of the departure of male labour. Because of the absence of men, women of the goat peasant households took over all work arising in the house, the garden, the stalls, the field and the woods. They carried out tasks that had been characterised as the 'typical sphere of women' in agricultural regions: care of small animals, gardening, baking, milk processing, cooking, washing and caring for the children (Mitterauer 1992: 30). In addition to these tasks, they took on hard physical labour in the fields which formerly belonged to what was considered as the male domain, such as ploughing. They were likewise responsible for feeding the goats and often had to transport the grass a great distance to the village. Many women helped with the harvest and with threshing. Moreover, they worked collectively in groups of five to ten women as day labourers in the horse farmers' fields. Some women organised financial affairs with the horse farmers, and this is another indication of women's responsibility, not only for guaranteeing the survival of the household through subsistence production, but also for administering cash and managing financial transactions.

These activities went well beyond the so-called domestic domain, a term vividly debated in anthropology (Moore 1990: 51), concentrating broadly on the 'natural' bond between mother and child, which led to the problematic dichotomisation of public and private or domestic domains (for a detailed discussion see Collier and Yanagisako 1987; Comaroff 1987). Women in Eschau were not just concerned with the care of their children, but thought of themselves as working women.[11] The absence of men (fathers, temporary husbands and sons) increased their realm of free activity and strengthened their influence, their self-confidence, and their decision-making authority.

Symbolic representation: the name of the house

The economic and social significance of women in rural lower classes has been expressed through their names, which attached to the house and to all those born or married into it. Thus, houses are conceived of not only as physical but also as social units that correspond to property and intra-village hierarchies as well as to gender. While tracing genealogies with people during fieldwork, I was confronted with a double naming system that can be summarised as follows. Villagers refer to the official family names, as recorded in communal and church registers as 'written' names, which are of little importance in intra-village discourses. In contrast, the non-official system of 'spoken' names is of central significance. When talking about others, kin groups and individuals, women as well as men, houses are designated still today by names which can be found neither in communal registers nor in church ledgers.[12] Only those born in the village and those married into it (the latter, however, only after many years) are familiar with the categories of classification. Thus, 'strangers' (or '*Fremde*', a term used for those who have no ties of kinship within the village) are excluded from the flow of information, chatter and gossip. Heide, a 50-year-old woman who moved to the village in the 1970s, reported:

> I have now been living here twenty years and have worked in the post office for many years. So I know all the people in the village by name, but only by their 'correct' names. But when I'm with the other women for coffee or so, I can't join in the talk because they use names I've never heard. I don't have any idea who they're talking about.

It is interesting that the 'spoken names' frequently use female first names preceding the first names of the person in question, whether man or woman.[13] Female house names do not, however, refer to mothers, but rather to female ancestors born in the middle of the nineteenth century. Elisabeth, a 40-year-old woman explained:

I belong to the Margret'sches. The house has long since disappeared. But I must say I'm rather proud of this name. What this woman must have accomplished is fantastic I think. My mother always told me about it, about this Margret'schen, who must have been born around 1840. She was the mother of my father's mother and had heaps of kids. And her husband worked somewhere as a switchman for the railroad. Then he ended up between two trains and died in the accident. This Margret'schen had to do everything alone, supporting the children, and doing what farmwork there was. My Grandma, Margret'sches Käth, she married my Grandpa then, he came from a neighbouring village. He was a house painter. And Margret'sches Liss, that was my Grandma's sister.

My interview partner was conscious of belonging to a house and a group of relatives, whereby the house as a building as well as a social unit has been called by her great-grandmother's name until today. Even though Margret'schen became a widow through a tragic accident, widowhood cannot be used to explain the naming of houses with female Christian names, for the number of such houses is comparatively large. Furthermore, in many other areas of 'traditional' Europe, widowed women became heads of households and represented the house to the outside (Mitterauer 1990: 38). The interpretation for the passing down of female names in Eschau is rather to be found within the framework of village economy and kinship relations.

Nearly all the women after whom houses, kin groups and individuals are named were wives of painters and masons, of men, then, who as goat farmers and therefore worker-peasants only lived in the village periodically, spending several months each year as migrants in distant cities. Houses were mostly called by the Christian names of women. Some were given the name of the place of origin of women who married in from neighbouring villages, so that the practice does not relate to inheritance patterns. Only a few goat farmer houses were named according to other criteria, for example for some special feature of the house (such as 'high porch'), or for some character trait of its members, or for musical abilities (for example 'bass fiddle'). In contrast, cow farmer houses were often identified by the occupation of male villagers (tailor, wagoner, blacksmith, etc.), while horse farmer houses were called by the first names of deceased male ancestors or in some cases by influential positions (mayor, church treasurer).

Names change with marriage. Both men and women who marry into other houses receive, in the course of their marriage, the 'spoken name' of the house they move into without however losing the 'spoken name' of their house of origin. This double identity is important for the membership of a house as social unit as well as for intra-village discourses about origin, reputation, ownership, piety, and the work ethic of its members. The differing usage of 'house names' in designating a person leads to no confusion whatsoever; the names vary according to who is speaking about whom, for example a member of the same age group as ego will use a different name than a member of ego's kingroup (cf. Zonabend 1980: 232) and naming depends on the social context in which villagers talk about someone.

Even though women take on the 'official' family name ('written' name) of their husband at marriage, this name is almost exclusively for bureaucratic purposes, for example the issue of a birth certificate from the communal administration whose offices today lie outside the village. Calling married women by their maiden name (their father's surname) even after marriage is known in other European societies. Marilyn Strathern observed this kind of naming in the English village of Elmdon (Strathern 1981: 164) and Mary Bouquet confirmed this observation in another region of England (Bouquet 1986: 27) where children were also called by their mothers' maiden names. The interpretation of this as a 'kind of dual affiliation' (Bouquet 1986: 27) appears at first glance convincing, but the question remains as to whether the house is being identified as of special significance. Bouquet points out that 'it is customary to distinguish families with the same surname by reference to the farm's name: for example "Herds to Leigh" or "Herds to Galsham"'. Here locality is superimposed upon family as means of classification *internal* to the population' (Bouquet 1986: 23; emphasis from Bouquet). As Bestard lucidly pointed out for the island of Formentera, house names are 'social names *par excellence*' which are given by others, designate 'the island as a community and name households as units of residence which reproduce in the same space' (Bestard 1991: 33). In contrast, the surname is

> an official name *par excellence*, registered in written form, yet virtually unrecognised in the oral system, and transmitted to a child automatically at birth to relate it to matrilineal and patrilineal lines of descent, whereas the christian name is an element of individual life used orally as a term of address and transmitted through a ritual which marks the differences of natural birth. . .
>
> (ibid. 33)

The naming system in Formentera represents a system of classification connected with kinship ties that, as in the German village discussed here, corresponds with male labour migration.

Regarding the house names in relation to gender, differences seem to be obvious. According to Strathern in the English case, the men's 'written' names do not change with marriage. 'Attention is specifically drawn to the contrast between women's natal and conjugal status in a way that does not, of course, apply to men; they do not change their names on marriage' (Strathern 1981: 164). However – and this is a point of significant difference in Eschau – men's 'spoken' names do change with marriage if the husband moves into the woman's house of origin. Both women and men, as made clear by the naming practice in intra-village discourse, receive new or additional names several times in their lives. The assignment of names corresponds with membership in a peer group (here nicknames are assigned), with residence, marriage and kinship. Marriage however does not lead to the couple being considered a unit after the wedding. Women and men are conceptualised as autonomous individuals each with their own name. This autonomy is expressed in the individual naming system.

Gender constructs and gender identities

Male identities

One of the crucial gender constructs characterising the nineteenth century is based on the concept of the male head of the household, the house father (*Hausvater*). The house father has been defined by some historians, above all in the German-speaking area, as the politically and legally sole decision maker who represents the members of the house to the outside, is responsible for their actions and dealings, and can also be made accountable for members' infractions of rules (Rosenbaum 1993: 85). In the village investigated here, the male head – if he indeed ever exercised such power in and over the house – lived far away. David Sabean criticised the figure of the house father as an invention of officials. House father and house mother

> were the lenses through which the village, state, and church officials viewed the family. They had a hierarchical connotation and authorised the male head of the house as the address of various communications. The state's guarantee of general order, proper behavior and diligence was the Hausvater.
>
> (Sabean 1990: 113)

Yet none of the villagers used the term in the court records he investigated. Rather, the concept corresponds to the ideology of the state and maintained its relevance in the context of fiscal interests, the drafting of tax lists, and state interest in the exercise of power, influence, and control. Furthermore, the construction of the figure and concept of the house father blurs the lines of conflict, difference and power between the sexes.[14]

At the turn of the twentieth century village life reveals separate, rather than common, realms of life and work for women and men. In most houses, male identity was particularly marked by labour migration. Often, several men from the village worked together in small groups on distant construction sites. Since they had to pay for food and lodging, even though they were housed in very poor conditions in so-called 'sleeping spaces', little remained from the money they earned. Women reported the frequent conflicts about money arising between spouses. The men were all too eager to spend their money in taverns and 'wasted' (Bataille 1985) the wages they had earned with so much effort in an extensive male drinking culture.[15] During the winter months, nearly all men regularly gathered in the two village pubs where they sang and drank. The community of men associated through singing clubs, could be interpreted as staging and performing masculinity and male competition.[16]

Moreover these voluntary associations must be analysed within the framework of political transformations in Germany, particularly in the founding of the nation-state in 1871 and the Bismarckian laws against the labour movement in Germany (*Sozialistengesetze*). Singing clubs and other voluntary associations provided opportunities for clandestine political activities.

Additionally the spread of singing clubs must be discussed within the context of economic change, industrialisation and the emergence of capitalism in the last decades of the nineteenth century (cf. Hüwelmeier 1997a). On the local level, this kind of popular culture contributed to the reconstruction of collective male identities. Social relations as well as marriage patterns based on property and intra-village hierarchies were levelled out through the common club membership of horse, cow, and goat farmers and to an extent counterbalanced the collapsing social and economic relations caused by seasonal emigration. The unity of men was symbolised in two singing clubs. Because of intra-village power conflicts between large kin-groups, the men's singing club split up shortly after its foundation in 1882. It is interesting that houses and respective kingroups have formed the basis for recruitment into the clubs until the present. The continuity of this kind of dual organisation was maintained by marriages within each club and, consequently, the succession of sons within their fathers' clubs (Hüwelmeier 1997b). Moreover, political party affiliation is connected with club membership and even the village economy is divided along club lines. Women, either despite or because of their formal exclusion from the singing clubs, strongly identified with their fathers' and husbands' clubs, which were generally the same.

Female identities

Female identity was mainly conceptualised within the framework of the village economy. The self-image of older women to whom I spoke was defined first and foremost by their work in the fields.

Subsistence production guaranteed daily survival, particularly in periods of unemployment and decline in the earnings of the men in the winter months when they found no work as masons and earned only a little in forestry work. Women were producers[17] and worked collectively in groups of female relatives as day labourers in the horse farmers' fields, and individually when tilling their own plots. Hard physical labour was expected of women who were regarded with respect and high esteem by men.

Middle-class ideals of the loving wife and mother who remained in the home and devoted herself to the care and rearing of children played no crucial part in conceptions of female identity among the lower classes of rural regions. In peasant societies, it was 'less the mother than much more the active woman who was highly regarded' (Segalen 1990: 264). Because of child 'neglect', the village priest of Eschau requested the presence of catholic nuns to settle in the village in 1901. They treated and visited the sick and the poor and took care of the children in the newly built *Kindergarten*, while mothers worked on their distant plots free of care. On Sundays, young unmarried women gathered in the Congregation of the Virgin Mary where they spent some hours without being controlled by brothers and parents. In the house of the nuns or sisters (*Schwesternhaus*) young women had the only opportunity for gathering weekly in a female dominated space (Hüwelmeier 1999). With the support of the nuns, young girls put on performances that were presented to the village community once a year. They also went on outings in the surrounding area, were trained in needle-work, knitting and sewing. Later, in the 1920s, women were engaged in outwork. Some of them worked individually, others met collectively within their houses. Outwork, based on needlework, was organised by an entrepreneur, who came regularly from outside the village to deliver new work and to collect the finished products, which were mainly tablecloths. Because of the great economic crisis and unemployment during that time (end of 1920s), many women were the only providers in the goat farmers' households. This was important during the Second World War, when most of the male villagers served as soldiers. Some lost their lives and others returned to the village after captivity in the late 1940s. Thus women had been responsible for their families, earning money while doing outwork and additionally managing the work in the fields.

These facets of female identities, as heads of households, day labourers, outworkers and activists in the Congregation of the

Virgin Mary were subsequently affected by the decline of agriculture and the departure of the nuns.

New communities of women

Beginning in the 1960s, a far-reaching process of change occurred in German rural society, particularly in regions with small-scale agricultural production. In Eschau as well, occupational and social differentiation, the relinquishing of petty peasant activities through the sale or leasing of small plots due to land reallocation,[18] agricultural production for the market, the daily presence of the men who now left the village in the morning and returned in the evening on special 'workers' buses', the closing of the convent and departure of the nuns, the construction of new houses, and women's individual outwork all contributed to changing gender relations, particularly in regard to new communities of women. At the beginning of the 1970s, two large women's clubs were founded. Members were recruited along the lines of the two men's singing clubs. Wives of singing men gathered collectively to balance out the isolation caused by outwork, which now was organised by a local entrepreneur and was no longer based on needlework but producing equipment for the car industry. The new communities of women generated conflicts between the sexes, particularly because women now occupied the space of the male-dominated inns, talking loudly, drinking alcohol, smoking cigarettes and spending money. Some years later a women's bowling club was founded, its members meeting weekly and using their 'bowling money' for an annual trip to Majorca or some other spot. In 1990, shortly before I carried out my field research, a women's singing club had been founded which included more than 60 women members.

The founding process of the women's singing club was affected by vehement disagreements between women and men (Hüwelmeier 1996a; 1996b). The conflicts were mainly about control over money (membership fees), but were also to do with political power. Women insisted on electing their own committee and refused to be reduced to a sub-group of the men's singing club. Because of the dual organisation of the village choir, the women's choir is almost exclusively composed of women whose husbands and fathers belong to the same singing club, while women connected with the competing men's singing club could not be recruited as members. The rivalry between the men's singing clubs was reproduced among the women and demonstrates their strong identification with their fathers' and husbands' clubs as well as the difficulties of building a community of women beyond male club networks. Both male singing clubs are composed of large kingroups and thus houses as social units are the basis for recruitment. Nearly all the male inhabitants (except for those considered to be 'strangers' or *'Fremde'*) who had been born or had married into the village, belong to one of the two groups. The same could be affirmed to be true of the women's choir: members belong to women-centred kinship networks. Mothers sing together with their daughters and sisters; aunts, nieces, cousins and sisters-in-law attend choir rehearsals collectively.

Conclusion

Social scientists have stressed the importance of nuclear groups within the processes of transformation of peasant societies in Europe, 'as if this type of conjugal family were a logical consequence of modern society' (Bestard 1991: 69). Moreover the purported decline of extended families and kinship ties has been linked directly to processes of urbanisation and labour migration. Theoretical perspectives have broadly developed in line with the dichotomies of 'traditional' and 'modern' social forms borrowed from Weber, Durkheim and Tönnies. Categories such as *'Gemeinschaft'* and *'Gesellschaft'*, 'mechanical solidarity' and 'organic solidarity', derived from evolutionist conceptions, have played a crucial role in theoretical elaborations regarding social change in Europe and beyond. Urban society has been conceptualised as being opposed to rural communities and the latter have been discussed in terms of simple social structures, egalitarianism and social and cultural conformity. Anthony P. Cohen lucidly analysed these theoretical implications as 'myths' (Cohen 1985: 28f) and pointed out the symbolic construction of community.

Undoubtedly changes in household and family relations occur within processes of change but these changes do not support a hypothesis of inevitable decline. Agreeing with Yanagisako (1979: 182), I would argue that kinship relations do not necessarily weaken or disappear with migration. On the contrary, I would suggest that kinship relations and idioms gain a new importance within the context of change. Here kinship is not just a means of organising new kinds of relations in the urban context, as Baumann

(1995) has pointed out for ethnic communities in London. It is also significant for those who remain in their villages of origin, since here too new forms of social relations and discourses are established, based on kinship and 'houses' as social units.

Notes

1 Financial support for writing this essay was provided by the Förderprogramm Frauenforschung des Senats von Berlin. I would like to thank Michael Mitterauer, Edith Saurer and Claudia Ulbrich for comments and discussions as well as Gerd Baumann and Victoria Goddard, who read an earlier version of this chapter.
2 Thus we find a village naming system that could be designated as opposed and contrasted to the official naming system of the state bureaucracy based on patrilineality.
3 Pina-Cabral (1986) mentioned the house as a peasant institution in Portugal; Bestard (1991) discussed houses as units of kinship in Formentera.
4 Even lineage models have 'no value for anthropological analysis' (Kuper 1982: 92). Kuper argues for the 'house' as an alternative model for the understanding of the structure and historical development of the Zulu State (Kuper 1993). Fortes (1949: 10) remarked very early, that the Tallensi's own term for the lineage and that of other West African groups significantly means 'house'.
5 The term *bauer* can be translated as either farmer or peasant. Both terms are applicable to the small-scale land-owning groups discussed here.
6 I carried out fieldwork from 1991 to 1993. At that time the village, whose name is a pseudonym, had about 1,000 inhabitants. My main interest was directed to two male singing clubs, through which the village has been divided in half. Kinship and marriage, village economy and politics are associated with the two choirs and are up until the present day crucial aspects in the social organisation of the village (for a detailed analysis cf. Hüwelmeier 1997a). Parts of this essay have been published in Hüwelmeier 1997c.
7 For the significance of house architecture as symbol of power and as a metaphor of bodies cf. Carsten and Hugh-Jones 1995: Introduction. A critical review was offered by Holy 1997.
8 Four acres are the equivalent to one hectare.
9 Since around the turn of the century many young women of goat farmer families also left the village after school and worked as domestic servants in urban households. Upon marriage they returned and worked in the fields with their mothers. Some of them married a spouse they met in the city, but most of them married into another goat farmer household. Marriage patterns and village endogamy changed after the First World War, when 50 per cent of the marriages were endogamous. After the Second World War, in the 1950s, when many refugees came to the village, 14 out of 37 marriages were endogamous. In the early 1970s, again 50 per cent were endogamous.

In contrast, in the early 1980s, only 5 couples out of 22 married within the village (Hüwelmeier 1997a: 101).

10 In regard to African societies undergoing change, Moore (1990: 145) speaks of a 'feminization' of the subsistence economy. Here a crucial element in the process of capitalism lies in the commercialisation of small-scale peasant production as a consequence of male labour migration. In Eschau production was under-commercialised. Crops were needed for feeding stock and the more animals one possessed, the more crops were needed. Horses did not serve as status markers, but did bring in some cash and labour to the horse farmer families. Finally, 'driving for others' (*für andere fahren*) always implicated reciprocal services and strengthened the ties between houses.

11 The women's right to vote was established in Germany in 1918.

12 Seiser (1999) stressed the importance of house names as opposed to 'written' names in her study on inheritance and marriage in an Austrian peasant community. Mitterauer (1997) analysed the practice of name giving based on autobiographical sketches.

13 Segalen (1990: 40) reported that in some regions of France each member of a stem family receives an epithet, the name of the house, which had been added to his official name. In contrast, in Eschau the name of the house precedes the individual's first name without mentioning the surname. Thus, one speaks of Änn'sches Reinhold, Lisse Hermann and Katte Schorsch. In these cases Änne, Liss and Katt are village dialect names for the first names Anna, Elisabeth and Katharina, which precede male first names.

14 In her micro-historical study of an Alsatian village in the early modern times, Ulbrich (1999) stressed the lines of conflict and power that had been acted out not only between women and men, but also within groups of women and groups of men. Property, economy, kinship and religion (Jewish and Christian) had been important elements in these conflicts.

15 Hans Medick analysed the changing patterns in drinking practices within the 'plebeian' culture of the eighteenth and nineteenth centuries, which corresponded with increased spending and a lack of saving (Medick 1982: 157–96). He interpreted tavern culture as a completely 'rational' economy which allowed the lower classes to transform their money into communicative and symbolic acts.

16 Cornwall and Lindisfarne (1994: 10) focused 'on the negotiation and plurality of masculinities' and supposed that 'indigenous notions of gendered difference are constantly created and transformed in everyday interactions. Relations of power are constituent parts of these interactions.'

17 See Lenz and Luig (1995: 15) for African societies.

18 Land reallocation was supposed to make agriculture more effective. In regions with partible inheritance the plots had become so small that the use of tractors was difficult. Land reallocation implied a new distribution of the smallholdings and the merging of others for better farming and market production. The 'winners' of reallocation were the few horse peasants.

Bibliography

Bataille, G. (1985) *Die Aufhebung der Ökonomie*, München: Matthes & Sietz.

Baumann, G. (1995) 'Managing a polyethnic milieu: kinship and inter-action in a London suburb'. *The Journal of the Royal Anthropological Institute*, 1(4): 725–41.

Bestard-Camps, J. (1991) *What's In a Relative? Household and Family in Formentera*, Oxford: Berg.

Bouquet, M. (1986) ' "You cannot be a Brahmin in the English country-side". The partitioning of status, and its representation within the farm family in Devon', in A.P. Cohen (ed.) *Symbolising Boundaries. Identity and Diversity in British Cultures*, Manchester: Manchester University Press.

Carsten, J. and Hugh-Jones, S. (eds) (1995) *About the House. Lévi-Strauss and Beyond*, Cambridge: Cambridge University Press.

Cohen, A.P. (ed.) (1982) *Belonging: Identity and Social Organisation in British Rural Cultures*, Manchester: Manchester Universitty Press.

—— (1985) *The Symbolic Construction of Community*, London: Routledge.

Collier, J.F. and Yanagisako, S.J. (eds) (1987) *Gender and Kinship. Essays toward a Unified Analysis*, Stanford: Stanford University Press.

Comaroff, J.L. (1987) 'Sui generis: feminism, kinship theory, and structural "domains" ', in J.F. Collier and S.J. Yanagisako (eds) (op. cit.).

Cornwall, A. and Lindisfarne, N. (eds) (1994) *Dislocating Masculinity*, London: Routledge.

Davis, J. (1977) *People of the Mediterranean. An Essay in Comparative Anthropology*, London: Routledge & Kegan Paul.

Fortes, M. (1949) *The Web of Kinship among the Tallensi*, London: Oxford University Press.

Fox, R. (1967) *Kinship and Marriage. An Anthropological Perspective*, Harmondsworth: Penguin Books.

Giddens, A. (1995) *Konsequenzen der Moderne*, Frankfurt a. Main: Suhrkamp.

Goddard, V.A. (1994) 'From the Mediterranean to Europe: honour, kinship and gender', in V.A. Goddard, J.R. Llobera and C. Shore (eds) *The Anthropology of Europe. Identities and Boundaries in Conflict*, Oxford: Berg.

Goddard, V.A. Llobera, J.R. and Shore, C. (eds) (1994), 'Introduction', in V.A. Goddard, J.R. Llobera and C. Shore (eds) *The Anthropology of Europe. Identities and Boundaries in Conflict*, Oxford: Berg.

Holy, Ladislav (1997) 'About the house', Book review. *Social Anthropology*, 5(1): 109–10.

Hüwelmeier, G. (1996a) 'Frauentöne-Männerstimmen. Konkurrenz, Kon-flikt und Kooperation zwischen den Geschlechtern', *Feministische Studien* 2: 91–100.

——— (1996b) ' "Kreischende" Frauen-singende Männer. Geschlechter-beziehungen in einem deutschen Dorf', in W. Kokot and D. Dracklé (eds) *Ethnologie Europas. Grenzen, Konflikte, Identitäten*, Berlin: Reimer.

——— (1997a) *Hundert Jahre Sängerkrieg. Ethnographie eines Dorfes in Hessen*, Berlin: Reimer.

——— (1997b) 'Kirmesgesellschaften und Männergesangvereine. "Rites de passage" in der dörflichen Kultur Deutschland', *Zeitschrift för Sozialisationsforschung und Erziehungssoziologie* 1: 30–41.

——— (1997c) 'Frauen und Männer als Hauschaltsvorstände. Geschlech-terverhältnisse in ländlichen Unterschichten Deutschland', in G. Völger (ed.) *Sie und Er. Frauenmacht und Männerherrschaft im Kultur-vergleich*, Köln: Rautenstrauch-Joest-Museum für Völkerkunde.

——— (1999) 'Ordensschwestern und Jungfrauen', in: U. Krasberg (ed.) *Religion und weibliche Identität*, Marburg: Curupira.

Kaschuba, W. (1990) *Lebenswelt und Kultur der unterbürgerlichen Schichten im 19. und 20. Jahrhundert*, München: Oldenbourg.

Kuper, A. (1982) 'Lineage theory: a critical retrospect', *Annual Review of Anthropology*, 11: 71–95.

——— (1993) 'The "house" and Zulu political structure in the nineteenth century', *Journal of African History*, 34: 469–87.

Lenz, I. and Luig, U. (eds) (1995) *Frauenmacht ohne Herrschaft. Gesch-lechterverhältnisse in nichtpatriarchalischen Gesellschaften*, Frankfurt a. Main: Fischer.

Lévi-Strauss, C. (1983) *The Way of the Masks*, London: Jonathan Cape.

——— (1987) *Anthropology and Mythology Lectures 1951–1982*, Oxford: Blackwell.

Medick, H. (1982) 'Plebejische Kultur, plebejische Öffentlichkeit, plebejische Ökonomie. Über Erfahrungen und Verhaltensweisen Besitzarmer und Besitzloser in der Übergangsphase zum Kapitalismus', in R.M. Berdahl (ed.), *Klassen und Kultur. Sozialanthropologische Perspektiven in der Geschichtsschreibung*, Frankfurt a. Main: Syndikat.

Mitterauer, M. (1990) *Historisch-anthropologische Familienforschung*, Wien: Böhlau.

——— (1992) *Familie und Arbeitsteilung*, Wien: Böhlau.

——— (1997) 'Vom "Judenkind" zum "Schloßmoidl". Lebensgeschich-ten also Quelle der Namenforschung', in R. van Dülmen, E. Chvojka and V. Jung (eds), *Neue Blicke. Historische Anthropologie in der Praxis*, Wien: Böhlau.

Moore, H.L. (1990) *Mensch und Frau sein: Perspektiven einer feminis-tischen Anthropologie*, Gütersloh: Gütersloher Verlagshaus Hans Mohn.

Ortner, S.B. (1974) 'Is female to male as nature is to culture?' in M.Z. Rosaldo and L. Lamphere (eds) *Women, Culture and Society*, Stanford: Stanford University Press.

Pina-Cabral, J. de (1986) *Sons of Adam, Daughters of Eve*, Oxford: Oxford University Press.

Rosaldo, M.Z. (1974) 'A theoretical overview', in M.Z. Rosaldo and L. Lamphere (eds) *Women, Culture and Society*, Stanford: Stanford University Press.

Rosenbaum, H. (1993) *Formen der Familie*, Frankfurt a. Main: Suhrkamp.

Sabean, D.W. (1990) *Property, Production, and Family in Neckarhausen 1700–1870*, Cambridge: Cambridge University Press.

Schneider, D.M. (1980) *American Kinship. A Cultural Account*, Chicago: The University of Chicago Press.

Segalen, M. (1990) *Die Familie. Geschichte, Soziologie, Anthropologie*, Frankfurt a. Main: Campus.

Segalen, M. and Zonabend, F. (1987) 'Social anthropology and the ethnology of France: the field of kinship and family', in A. Jackson (ed.) *Anthropology at Home*, London: Tavistock.

Seiser, G. (1999) 'On the importance of being the last one. Marriage and inheritance patterns in Upper Austria', in P. Schweitzer (ed.), *The Dividends of Kinship*, London: Routledge.

Strathern, M. (1981) *Kinship at the Core*, Cambridge: Cambridge University Press.

—— (1992) *After Nature. English Kinship in the Late Twentieth Century*, Cambridge: Cambridge University Press.

Ulbrich, C. (1999) *Schulamith und Margarete. Macht, Geschlecht und Religion in einer ländlichen Gesellschaft des 18. Jahrhunderts*, Wiren: Böhlau.

Wagner, K. (1986) *Leben auf dem Lande im Wandel der Industrialisierung*, Frankfurt a. Main: Insel.

Waterson, R. (1995) 'Houses and hierarchies in island Southeast Asia', in J. Carsten and S. Hugh-Jones (eds) *About the House. Lévi-Strauss and Beyond*, Cambridge: Cambridge University Press.

Yanagisako, S.J. (1979) 'Family and household. The analysis of domestic groups', *Annual Review of Anthropology* 8: 161–205.

Zonabend, F. (1980) 'Namen–wozu? (Die Personennamen in einem französischen Dorf)', in J.-M. Benoist (ed.) *Identität. Ein interdisziplinäres Seminar unter Leitung von Claude Lévi-Strauss*, Stuttgart: Klett-Kotta.

Chapter 7

Gender and politics through language practices among urban Cape Verde men

Guy Massart

The data analysed in this paper relate to my fieldwork in Praia, the capital of the Cape Verde islands, during 1990 and 1991. This was a time of very significant change on the islands: the PAICV (*Partido Africano da Independência de Cabo Verde*), at the time the ruling (and the only) party, publicly announced that elections would be held for the first time in fourteen years. My research covers this important period, following events as they unfolded during the elections and the first six months of the new republic, now led by the victorious MPD party (*Movimento Para a Democracia*).

It is tempting to approach political processes and behaviour armed with quantitative methodologies and searching for causal explanations based on essentialising categories and definitions (Stolcke 1995; Crapanzano 1992). Such an approach would find wide acceptance, not least in the media. But despite the convenience of surveys and statistics, this genre has, in my view, an important drawback. By focusing on structural determinations it ignores the ways that agents deal with structural conditions, or how different agents experience life and produce and manage various identities. In my research I am concerned to break away from this framework and explore ways of highlighting issues of agency and identities.

The shift in my theoretical and methodological orientation towards agency was all the more pressing since, as a participant among young urban Cape Verde men, I was faced with numerous questions arising from the ways in which these young men expressed their relationship to the political arena. I was particularly interested in why they talked in the same way about politics as they did about women. Or in other words, why did these young men mix elements of political genres with fragments of masculinity genres when talking about politics? My approach, based on a theory of discursive practice (Hanks 1996; Hall 1996), will highlight the concept of agency, addressing the question of what constitutes agency.

The research context

I started working in Cape Verde as a sociologist, rapidly turning to anthropology. Together with two Cape Verdean sociologists and another Belgian I was engaged in a new sociological research centre. In our sociological practice we constantly confronted the limitations of categories, especially in the analysis of political polls. Clearly, some respondents were not expressing 'opinions' but instead were giving 'the right answers' to questions, according to their assessment of the political system. They were giving the answers they thought the authorities expected. The interviewees were conscious of the 'effects' of their answers, and deployed them pragmatically. We were aware of discrepancies in the survey results but those reading our analyses were reluctant to see the ambiguities inherent in the responses, since they rejected the pragmatic functions of language and were persuaded by the evidence that 'people have said it!'. But a more significant dimension emerges from this relating to the issue of power.

People who gave the 'right answers', the 'less critical ones', belonged to the 'lowest socio-economic group'. These were the terms most commonly used to categorise and so interpret the situation. The group identified in this way was characterised as having a 'very low level of formal education '. This reproduced the common idea that formal education, sanctioned by some kind of diploma, was essential to gaining power and high social status and to be competent (or critical and politically active). In short, the level of formal education (kem ki tem scola, the formally educated) was an essential criterion for discrimination in the political arena.

In fact, this interpretation legitimated a central criterion of inequality in Cape Verde society. Furthermore, the emphasis on education precluded an alternative understanding that recognised this behaviour as an expression of resistance of the 'low socio-economic' groups, and their recognition of the differential distribution of power in their society. The essentialisation of categories was therefore related to power. This entails the denial of agency, as if the political were a realm of life just beyond the reach of the majority of Cape Verdeans – according to our polls, these outsiders constituted close to 70 per cent of the population.

The question is not whether categories or identities are true or false – we know that they are relevant within specific situations of utterance. The question is what are identities 'doing' so that they fit – or not – within a specific interaction? If to categorise is to organise hierarchically, whose power is being applied against whom? I will show in this paper how categories and identities are being reproduced and therefore how power relations are produced and reproduced. I will concentrate on identities relating to sexual distinction and to political authority, identities that are highlighted and linked in the discourse of the agents themselves, and show how the reproduction of those different identities is interrelated.

My research interests and approach were informed by political opinion or ethics and by the experience that interpretations in terms of structure not only reproduced inequalities but were also descriptively inadequate (Sharrock and Anderson 1982). In my opinion, the categories used here by sociologists and the highly educated (*os doutores*) were suspect. Categories are embedded in power, and the use of categories is the exercise of power. I concentrated on the categories used by the actors in their daily lives and focused on the 'lowest socio-economic' or 'popular' groups. I was interested in a different sociology of Cape Verde society, one that would not reproduce the old clichés that were intimately bound to an ideology of inequality and precluded the possibility of thinking about the changing experiences of subjects. The inadequacy of negative definitions of these groups as ignorant and therefore passive, as non-agents, an image associated *inter alia* with the notion of '*o Povo*' ('the people') was clearly evident. Instead, the interesting question was where did the agency of the marginalised apply and how was it expressed? Focusing on the categories used by the '*povo*' in everyday life I undertook to take seriously the 'folk sociology' of members of this group and in doing so discovered elaborate categories that were particular to this group, as well as some that were common to groups across 'classes'. What follows provides an example of these issues.

A friend/informant and I went to the island of Fogo to visit his mother, who still lives in the family home. One of the neighbours, D., a 25-year-old man, 'had gone crazy', as they said. D. locked himself in, refusing to talk to anybody, and living in his parents' house 'as a child'. My friend talked to him and told him in front of his parents: '*D., bu tem ki ser ômi na tudu kuza: bu tem ki trabadja, pega menina*' – 'D., you have to be a man in all things: you have to work, to "catch" girls'. As my research proceeded, I noticed repeatedly that as in this case, the relations between male and female were a frequent theme in male discourse. Here lay a trap: the young man is not a 'man' (*ômi*) and what is it to be a man? To work and to catch girls! Wasn't D. a man? According to my friend he was not – he was merely a male – not a woman (*mudjer*) either. D. is a male who had to become a man. So a male *should* be a man! D. was therefore in an undefined gender category, 'without gender'. In any case it was clear that a male (*matchu*) was not the same thing as a man (*ômi*).

The parents of the young man were witnessing the whole scene. I wondered whether my friend was not simply talking to D. (there seemed to be a consensus in the fact that D. was not communicating) and was talking (also) about himself contrasting himself to D., addressing D.'s parents as his neighbours in the past, from whom he could gain confirmation of his competence as a man, as an ideal typical hegemonic[1] man (Cornwall and Lindisfarne 1994 ; Vale de Almeida 1996). That is to say that this is a relatively prosperous person, wise and informed, authoritative and a 'fucker'. Once again, my sociological expectations were caught out.

Here too the categories were expressing inequalities, used to make several points in a single utterance. This definition of a man, besides commenting on D.'s behaviour, was meant to apply to other contexts, or bring to mind other contexts, such as my friend's supposed success in the capital as an '*ômi*' – a man. I was struck by the 'doctoral' tone of my friend's speech. I could only understand it as the exercise of an authority derived from his return from the capital to his native zone, to the prestige that accrued to him by coming from the 'centre'. The '*coitado*' (poor), the '*trabadjador*' (worker) from Praia had turned into the one giving advice with authority in the community where he had grown up and which he had deserted years ago.

This encouraged me to take seriously the reflexive efforts of the layman and to approach these from an anthropological, comparative perspective. I had to reconsider the question of analytical units and the issues of power, inequalities and agency that are embedded in the discursive practices of everyday life. More broadly I came to see language in everyday life (in the field) and in our anthropological activity as practices that imply relations of power and inequality and produce an economy of identities. Different identities expressed in different contexts were paradoxical (i.e. the one to preach advice was also a poor worker) although they made sense in the situated experience of the individuals (and probably of the group). Therefore, I could only understand an utterance and an identity, a position, in terms of power expressed in relations as they reflected other positions, behaviours and identities experienced in other contexts.

If identities are of central concern to sociologists and anthropologists, it is because they are essential[3] tools for western social scientists and for westerners in general. But identities[4] have received so much conceptual attention that they have become isolated from the specific cultural language practices in which they are expressed – what Crapanzano (1992) and Silverstein (1976) would define as the negation of their pragmatic and indexical function. Identities cannot be defined in a positivist way as notions referring to some 'thing'. They exclude and include, are used to distinguish, to refer to relations and are naturally associated with others through the practices of agents. In this sense it becomes clear that identities are not only descriptive but also pragmatic devices, implying hierarchical relations and therefore power (Strathern 1988; Cornwall and Lindisfarne 1994). From now on, to enhance their performative and pragmatic dimensions, following Giraud (1992), I will refer to identities as *identifications*.

Identifications, contexts and genres

One cannot assume that identification will always refer to the same thing or have the same meaning regardless of the context, time or place. The referential function of identifications stems from their metonymic character: they concentrate meaning, they are the actors' 'short-cuts'. Identifications must therefore be seen as linguistic signs associated with – because embedded in – the experience of those using them. That is to say, identifications are always experienced from a particular position.

Yet a focus on the linguistic dimension alone is incomplete. The oral interactions between actors must be approached as the study of the experience of these actors. For the actor, then, linguistic communicative practices are experiences and as such must be looked at in their different dimensions. In communicative practices there are associations with places, settings, addressees, super-addressees, tones, linguistic features, contents, emotions. It is within this complex network that the meanings of identifications must be studied.[4] Thus the anthropologist must be culturally competent to understand and relate the identifications to their broader frame of use, given that the meanings of identifications lie within experience. We are no longer dealing with words alone but with elements constitutive of experiences.

This in fact relates to the search for a relevant 'unit of analysis' that would both authorise a focus on the text and on the context (Bauman and Briggs 1990; Fabian 1995). This unit constitutes the basis from which categories used by the actors are considered. The question is not so much one of situating a word, a text reduced to its simplest expression, a category in a context, but to place a symbol in a broader 'enduring mode of practices' present in inter-actions. To do this, I will use the notion of 'genre' as developed by Hanks (1996):

> Analyzed as modes of practices, [genres] . . . are among the best examples of habitus as a set of enduring dispositions to perceive the world and act upon it in certain ways . . . They articulate with social fields through indexical centering, orientation to reception and dominant structures, and different kinds of finalization.
>
> (Hanks 1996: 246)

In its classical acceptation, genre refers to a conventionalised discourse type. Here it is a framework informing ways of producing and interpreting discourse (Pratt 1982). Beyond its classical use in literature genre is open-ended, flexible. Genre supersedes the notion of context and emphasises both the referential and pragmatical functions of language, as it entails a way of seeing the world and acting upon it. Rather than words referring to something, I propose to see identities in a broader framework of conventions and expectations of communicative practices.

In this sense, identifications have become secondary in my analysis. For instance, gender must not be restricted to dicho-tomous categories essentialising males and females and affirming the domination of the former over the latter, although this is an experienced reality. Instead, gender is to be found within a genre that I will call the masculinity genre, which tends to assert the predominance of male entities and objects over female ones. Gender in language practices as analysed in this paper marks a way of talking about different relations: relations between men and women and political relations. My argument is that there is an affinity between power relations characterising both aspects of male–female relations and relations between *doutores* and *povo*[5] (doctors/people), 'those-who-command' and 'us' (what I will call the political relations). Therefore the same 'genre', the masculinity genre, is equally applicable in all instances. I argue that in the ethnographic case analysed here, the different layers of meaning are related in an economy of identifications experienced and produced by the agents.

The masculinity genre is not the only way to talk about male and female relations in Cape Verde, nor for that matter to talk of political relations, nor is it restricted to men. The masculinity genre is a gendered discourse that reflects upon power relations as experienced by different agents, which asserts one's position in relation to dominant and dominated and tends ultimately to provide identification. This genre offers a way to reflect on inequalities, as they are experienced. It is also used to respond in those contexts where the speaker endorses a downgrading identification. In this process, identifications are of central concern to the actors: they touch on the capacity to be somebody in this unequal society. Here genre tells us about a specific, collectively shared way to be in the world, about valued ways to behave for and among urban popular groups. It is significant that this gendered genre is used and re-enacted in situations in which the agent strives to assert her/himself.

The masculinity genre described below implies reflexivity on the part of the actors. The genre itself is characterised by the semi-public setting of equals in which it is used[6] and by the assertiveness of its tone. Its very form, functions, tone and settings imply a seduction of the listeners by the speakers. A speaker gains the floor, establishes an authority, which entails an assessment and hence reflexivity by the participants in that the words are judged relevant or otherwise. As Bauman and Briggs (1990) claim, there is a negotiation between the participants of the discourse. The discourse is not therefore a construction of reality but a collectively approved performance; its relevance constitutes the discourse as a somehow valid account of reality. This validation must in turn be understood as an effect of power, as the authority to speak and the power to define reality are intertwined in practice.

The question of authority and the focus on actual language practices reintroduce the anthropologist into the picture as her/his work is carried out through interaction practices with the 'subjects'. In this process, the anthropologist loses her/his external standpoint. Ethnography is therefore seen as writing about actual interactions, comparing different interpretations and reflexive endeavours and through them questioning the power relations that they legitimate. The accounts of the masculinity genre given below began as predominantly based on a specific theme within discourse, that is to say male discourses about females to other males. I soon realised that those conventions and expectations applied to other themes and relations. So my objective is neither the themes nor the relations, nor identifications *per se* but an economy of those identifications as seen through the language practices of the actors.

The masculinity genre versus other genres

I want to look at political process through the actual discursive practices of Cape Verdean men. My fieldwork in Cape Verde was concerned with the young urban men living in Praia, capital of Cape Verde during a period of dramatic political change. These young men were in their early thirties. They were first generation migrants to the city and were either married, living with a partner or were bachelors living with kin of their generation.

The PAICV (*Partido Africano da Independência de Cabo Verde*), the ruling party since independence from Portugal in 1975, publicly declared its intention to open up the political system to other parties in February 1990. In fact, only one other party took part in the elections and it won more than 60 per cent of the national votes: the MPD (*Movimento para a Democracia*). The opening up of the political system created a great deal of political effervescence in Cape Verde. The exclusion of young so-called Trotskyists from the PAICV ten years earlier was brought up again and it was recalled and commented on as a crackdown of internal opposition within the PAICV. It was remembered especially vividly, given that several key founders of the MPD were among those who had been expelled. This effervescence was especially strong among the young men referred to in this chapter. Two of the so-called

Troskyists were successful men from their area of town. One was an advocate praised for his defence of poor people and another was a leader of a local development organisation working for the socio-economic emancipation of the poor in their area and in rural zones of Santiago Island where Praia is located.

During the campaign the young men supported the MPD, as did the majority of Cape Verdeans. Among the groups of young men I frequented it would be difficult to make a statement in favour of the PAICV, although I know that some of them actually voted for the PAICV. It was generally accepted that those who were part of the gigantic network of the PAICV (through kinship, but also through the *Movimentos de massa* – Youth, Women's and Worker's Organisations) voted for the PAICV. The *Povo* – the 'people', the common people, or in sociological terms, the 'marginals', 'not participating' in actual political terms and not linked to this network , or those who simply objected to single-party rule – claimed to support the '*Partido da Mudança*' (Party of Change), the MPD. The campaign was a time of revelation of the hidden manoeuvres of the PAICV, and the leaders of the MPD stated repeatedly during the campaign that the PAICV would be '*desmamado*', 'weaned'. During this period, the PAICV was openly losing face in public, as alleged manipulations of people and money were unmasked. What were also unmasked were the hidden efforts of its leader to remain in charge of the party and the state (party and state were merged during the fourteen years of single-party rule). Leaders were accused of having dominated Cape Verdean society. The 'people', including my informants, felt empowered by those revelations.

The campaign, the elections and the large victory of the MPD inevitably created great hope and a great messianic climate. 'People', including my interlocutors, felt empowered by the revelations and became vehicles of this information in their usual private and semi-public spaces of performance. The autonomy of the individual based on her/his knowledge, her/his capacity to *know* was boosted throughout the electoral process. The PAICV, which quietly accepted its defeat, was a scapegoat in this process as criticisms of this party fomented an atmosphere of messianic expectation.

However, the mood changed rapidly as the immediate and tremendous changes that had been expected did not materialise. Tensions within a political movement as heterogeneous as the MPD were not slow to appear. People came to blame the bicephalous political situation, the MPD versus the PAICV, as the first was accused of being a new PAICV that controlled all the political institutions through its large electoral victory. Those at the top seemed not to have changed and the gap between the '*povo*' or the people and '*kem ta manda*' or those who rule was reproduced. If anything, people were perhaps more bitter and conscious of their marginality after the elections and their experience of the contradiction between the messianic expectations and the reality of the rule of the movement that triggered them.

The everyday discourse of young Cape Verde men

By 1990 I had been living in Cape Verde for two years, working in the research centre and as a development agent in a Cape Verdean NGO. As a man, I was going out after work or at night with friends and colleagues, drinking in small popular bars, playing cards and visiting friends. My leisure time with Cape Verdeans was gendered. Men went out with men, meeting other men. I soon learned to recognise the right tone to use in these settings, and I could feel the pleasure the men felt when talking with their peers. The men one met in bars were friends, or friends of friends who would soon become close. You would address them by *bo* in Creole, which is the equivalent of the Portuguese *tu* as opposed to *nho* (*o senhor*). The tone was always assertive, and it seemed that the drinking pushed the assertiveness and the loudness of the voices. The utterances were centred around the person of the speaker, always putting a strong emphasis on his own opinions and adventures. The speaker would refer to himself through the term *mi*, a more affirmative singular personal pronoun than the *N'* that precedes a verb. A usual form of address from one man to another would be *A mi, mi, N' ta flaw* – 'I, I am telling you . . .'. The other common personal indexical found in that particular genre was *es* 'they', marking a certain distance between the interlocutors and 'others'.

Conversation centred on the speaker. This effect was achieved through rhetorical devices as well as through the content of speech. The emphatic style was central to gaining the floor. As in story telling, seduction of the other participants was crucial in order to be heard, and being heard was the means to being an actor. As the men put it: *Kem sabi mas ta kanta medjor* – 'Who knows more, sings better'. The importance of being heard drew my attention to the performative character of the talking, of the telling. It showed that talking was not a mere description but constituted a form of action upon the world and that this very action was gendered.

Women were presented as dependent on the man's good will (Massart 1992). Beyond illustrating men's dominance over women the stories also expressed men's *independence* of women, not of any women, but of potential sexual partners of the speaker. In fact a man wants to make clear his autonomy from any one that can fool him. In those stories the point being made (Godzich 1984) was that women should not and could not fool men. Men get their way: '*Es ka ta enganam*' – 'They [women] won't fool me', implying a competition which requires one to hide his/her 'real' desires from the one that can satisfy them – just as we encounter in the political arena.

Talk about politics in this period of political campaigning, of the emergence of the opposition and of the approaching elections, was carried out in similar terms. Knowledge demonstrated by the speaker was crucial in establishing his authority, revealing a new truth to his interlocutors, untying political strategies, bringing in remote or new information about what, from my perspective, seemed to be private issues, and therefore of no relevance to the political debate. But the very dynamics of the interactions informed what was being achieved through it, asserting a valuable identification.

The more assertive the man, the more attentively he was listened to. In other words, gaining the right to speak in the men's group was just like gaining the right to participate in the society, as if it proved the social competence of the man in the larger society. To emphasise the point, I would like to return to the saying that *Kem sabi mas ta kanta medjor*, who knows more, sings better. I will show that the authority gained in the interactional group is extensive to society in general and that it was about being a man, displaying an identity, in this case masculinity. The form of masculinity displayed by these men shows how being a man in this Cape Verde environment applies equally to political, economic and gender relations.

Masculinity genre and other genres: *Kem sabi mas ta kanta medjor*

Superior knowledge guarantees a good talk. Knowing, and knowing the right way to speak (*kanta*, to sing), gave the participant the authority to speak. Knowing was opposed to *engana* (to fool).

Being fooled was therefore a key issue when it came to being a man. In political as well as in gender and in economic relations, a recurrent utterance was *A mi, es ka ta enganam* – 'Me, they won't fool me'. 'They' referred either to women, politicians or employers, in short, those agents who were not peer men. The fear of a man was of being *enganadu* – fooled. For a man *'Ka ta toma abusu de ninguem'*, he does not tolerate being taken advantage of, exploited by anybody. To be fooled and taken advantage of is a source of shame – *vergonha*. Shame as one man explained to me (addressing the anthropologist in this instance), gave a man *raiba* – rage. It was unbearable. If it were not possible to overcome shame by revenge or compensation it could be a reason for suicide. This complex of *engana/abusu/vergonha* (to fool/to take advantage of/shame) applied to gender, political and economic relations. It was re-enacted among men and for men, because it constituted the core of being a man, the core of his masculinity. Once this masculinity was put in doubt or threatened, a man had to save face. This was achieved by being able to impose one's will, reaffirming one's masculinity through the dominance of the offender or through marking one's independence from that person, that is, cutting one's relation with the offender.

The *engana/abusu/vergonha* complex underscores a conception of the person as a strategising actor willing to shed her/his dependence, hence vulnerability. It relates to a game where the winner receives from the loser, and wins at the cost of another. The very social existence of the individual is jeopardised by extreme social as well as physical vulnerability, the nature of which changes over time. Indeed vulnerability is central to this representation. The desire for autonomy is constantly challenged by concrete conditions (as is hegemonic masculinity), frustrating the agent. This sense of vulnerability is particularly strong among the young men considered here, as it is embedded in a long historical experience of extreme vulnerability towards nature, feudal and colonial masters, and earlier slave traders.

What was at stake in the relations discussed among men, was *poder* – power. In this setting, power was presented as a language practice: *manda* – to command, to give orders. *Manda* is a central verb in this genre and is also a positive action that affirms masculinity just as *sabi* – to know. As with the other terms, it applied to all three types of social relations. A man is said to command in his house: he would say to a 'rebellious' woman wishing to have her way '*Kem ta manda li, é mi*' – 'Who commands here, is me'. Similarly, the politicians were those '*ki ta manda*' – 'those who command'. After the parliamentary elections came the municipal elections. Insulting pamphlets were common, mainly on the island of São Vicente. As we were discussing one of these pamphlets with a friend at home, my wife asked him why he thought that politicians acted this way, insulting other candidates. His answer was immediate: *Pamodi es ki ta manda* – 'Because, it is they who are in command, giving orders' (using the word 'command' as a verb in Creole).

Other genres and other identifications directly addressed political relations. In other words, the very same boastful males participated in other kinds of genres and in other settings. These different genres impinged upon the political processes just as the masculinity genre did. I can think of two other instances, one of which was the public-political genre. Here, identifications were collective rather than individual, based on the nation and its ideology. Politicians were the main speakers in this genre; at least they were perceived to be the ones who were strategically modelling their utterances and therefore powerful, as they were thought to determine the 'project' for Cape Verde. In terms of content it centred on the future of Cape Verde. The main feature of this genre is its utopian character, driven by two main symbols, 'development' and 'democracy', and its main achievement is that of creating hope. An example of this genre is provided by the two parties' campaign slogans. For the PAICV, the party in power since independence, the slogan was: *Nada de aventuras, somos o futuro* – 'No adventures, we are the future'. And for the MPD, the winners by a large majority: *Vota mudança. A competência no governo* – 'Vote for change. Competence in the government'. The MPD was commonly referred to as *O partido da mudança*, the party of change.

The election campaign took place as the country emerged from a long period of single-party rule during which the formal media was, if not censored, certainly controlled by the PAICV. For fourteen years the public space had been monopolised. The opening of spaces for communication to the *publico* through the newspapers and the radio represented a significant change. National radio and television, newspapers, posters, graffiti, pamphlets and rumours all provided means of communication. There were also the public meetings organised by the parties, *os comicios*, and local meetings. In this small country where kinship relations create dense webs between the 350,000 inhabitants, local and face-to-face campaigning, such as the *comícios* and personal relations with politicians, were especially successful. Finally, public space in the most literal sense also played a part, as for several days after the election results were announced, the streets of Praia were taken over by people celebrating the MPD victory. Slogans and banners displayed symbols of the victors and ridiculed the defeated PAICV.

Interviews – combination of genres and new revelations

Another genre in which men were 'doing' politics was the narratives of interview situations. Once again one would have to take into account the different features of the genre. The identifications and the addressees were different. Here interviewees were talking to an anthropologist and defined themselves through socio-economic categories (poor – *coitados, pobres*; worker – *trabalhadores*), dictating access to power (*poder*) conceived as the 'capacity to impose one's will'. Through the following excerpt taken from an interview I want to show how in practice different identifications are used and related, making sense of the very paradox of various identifications.

Interview excerpt:[7]

G:	*Bu nunka ka gosta di PAICV?*	You never liked the PAICV?
Paulo:	*A mi, não, nunka.* *Podi ser ki sa ta fazeba tcheiu kuza ki passa despercebida*	I, PAICV, never . . . Might well be that they were doing a lot of things that went unnoticed.
	Pa mas ki bu sabi, ma bu ka sabi.	You might know a lot, but you do not know.
	Dipos, doutores é so kes di caneta assim,	And then, doctors are only those with a pen [the ones of pen].

	ago, doutores go ta monda padja	Now, doctors weed the fields
	Chuba ka bem go, é modi?	Rain didn't come. How do we stand?
	E por isso.	That is why.
	N tem ki odja pa nha camada.	I've got to look for my stratum [class, 'layer'].
	Mi é camada di trabalhador.	I am from the workers' group.
G:	*Bo é di camada trabadjador?*	You are from the workers' stratum?
Paulo:	*Nós é pa nu desenvolvi, mas não massacras trabalhadores, nunka também el tem direitu, pamodi ele é ser como tu, como qualquer também, ele tem, meu*	Us, we have to develop, but do not slaughter the workers, never, he has rights too, because he is a being like you, as anybody, he has the same rights, man.
G:	*Enquantu trabadjador, bu ta chinti diferensa entre MPD e PAICV? I bu ta chinti diferente di kes gaju ki sta la?*	As a worker, do you feel any difference between the MPD and the PAICV? And do you feel different from the guys who are there?
Paulo	*Isso N'ta atcha normal, problema é ki es sta lá naquele carro lá. Es sta lá. MPD é igual, só boca ssim.*	I find this normal, problem is that they are in this car there. They are there. MPD is the same, just words

The first part of the excerpt that I analyse is a short narrative; it tells a story. The expression 'might well be' develops a series of logical affirmations and ends with a conclusion, making the point that 'I am from the workers' group'. Paulo explains how in the field of politics he is ignorant (i.e. not male) and instead of using the corresponding term of the dichotomy between doctors/*povo*, he uses another term taken from the political genre, and an old one, not quite contemporary to the ethnographical moment, 'the workers'.

The utterance is initiated by a classical move within the interview situation. The anthropologist, in order to reorient the course of the interaction, provocatively elicits a political opinion. Paulo talks about possible successes of the PAICV that might have gone unnoticed. He follows by offering a paradoxical utterance that comes to explain why he is saying that they might have done much without his knowing: 'you might know a lot, but you do not know' (the *bu,* usual second person of a personal pronouns as a rhetorical device associates the addressee to him, the hidden I). By this paradoxical statement, he affirms he is someone who 'knows' (a man – somebody of value in daily life), and at the same time shows, in a reflexive statement, that he does not know (*sabi*). Both identifications coexist here and are clashing in the linguistic form *as they do in his life*. He affirms to me that he *is* a man and he is someone of value (he knows a lot) but in spite of this, he does not have power.

Paulo reorients my question on political opinion. The point is not whether he ever 'liked' the PAICV but rather that he ignores things about them, about politics! Ignorance associated here with political relations brings up in this utterance, as in so many others, gender relations and the identification of '*ômi*' – man; the political relations are in themselves gendered. The identity of the party does not seem to be that important. Instead, he stresses that he is ignorant, that he does not have his say in the business of politics, he cannot even see clearly into it. Those who can and do are distant from him, socially and economically. In fact, the problem is declared in the last sentence in a clear parallel between the 'haves' and 'have-nots' in terms of power and wealth. Much could be said about the image of the car in Paulo's last sentence as a symbol of masculinity, of wealth and prestige. The question is, therefore, what is the power that is left to him as a man and also – therefore? – as a person in the relations he lives through.

The masculinity genre is used here as a tool to mark inequality, and at the same time it shows the irrelevance for the arena of politics of being powerful in another setting: the encounters of Paulo's daily life. In this sense, the gendered power position is used to evoke an arena (daily life) not restricted to men but common to all the Cape Verde *povo*, evoking the most valued position in this arena (to be someone who knows, or to be a man), and to emphasise the gap existing between the two spheres, and ultimately, his recognised powerlessness. It is because he recognises his powerlessness that he evokes relations of daily life, where as a man he has power over women.

In the same utterance two identifications are expressed: as a man and as a worker, a man who is not a 'doctor'. A doctor is an educated person, someone with knowledge, recognised by his '*caneta*', his pen (the new symbol of power as seen from the perspective of a man/worker). It is clear here that the power of knowing is in the hands of the educated. He uses '*doutor*' in two ways, 'the doctors are those with a pen' so that the powerful are now those who have a certain level of education. He let me understand that this is a new situation, or at least associated with the PAICV and therefore with the post-colonial period.

He also explains why his powerlessness is important and that leads him to define himself as a 'worker' who has to defend his own social stratum (*camada*), the workers, associating another order of reality to his own position: the country. This 'additional dimension' is drawn from the political genre, where 'worker' is a new category compatible with the Marxist discourse of the one-time single party as well as its nationalist ideology. The '*doutores*' are the ones 'weed[ing] the fields', doing the work in the fields, this being an image of taking care of the country and its subsistence.[8] But the rain had not come, which means there is no food. The lack of rain refers to the precariousness of life on the islands and to a past of hunger. The discourse on rain and agriculture is a reminder that the whole country, regardless of socio-economic position, is weak in resources. From this point of view, the fact of having '*doutores*' running the country does not make any difference (a fact that derives from the climate that one does not control: the rain does not come), although it implies as well that the '*doutores*' are the ones disposing of the wealth (they are responsible for the fields). The rain which guarantees the future is of such concern in the political discourse and therefore central to the responsibility of the doctors – those who command. The absence of rain refers to the absence of a secure future that is, after all, the promise of all the political parties. Hence, the obligation to be a worker. Various interpretations are possible.

Those 'who rule', are those with formal education, yet they cannot guarantee the well being of the whole people. They are widely seen as ruling for the sake of power itself. The category '*doutores*' is embedded in a logic that links it inevitably to the category of 'worker' – the link is forced on Paulo by the *doutores*' power over the entire society. Once again we return to his initial point: the issue is not which party rules the country at any given moment, but rather the category of people ruling it and imposing their logic on him. The problem is one of the monopolisation of power and wealth. This gives rise to the anxiety of survival, referring back to historical traumas such as famines and slavery. There is also a hint of regret here, rendered by ending the story with the Creole expression of '*É modi?*' that I have translated as 'how do we stand'. The issue of rain refers to a 'we', it concerns the reproduction of 'us', the humans on the islands. '*É modi?*' marks an anxiety (where do we go from here?) and an accusation, demanding a justification ('you tell me now!'), so that these words express anger and powerlessness. Being a man in private cannot ultimately compensate for powerlessness in the 'public' sphere.

Politicians are accountable for the secure reproduction of the people. This accountability is of particular relevance here, given the vicissitudes of agriculture and the climate, which have stricken Cape Verde with a history of famines that have left thousands dead. The last great famine of 1949 is still vividly recollected in popular songs and impinges on the representations of the Cape Verdeans. The issue of their reproduction causes anxiety about the future, and influences the way they look to the future. When facing the fatality of poor yields and consequent scarcity of food God was blamed and prayed to as the One to ensure the rains necessary to secure food. In the nineties, aid and private investments are the new messiahs, but equally beyond reach. This is where the politicians are responsible. The reminiscences of these deep anxieties contributed to creating both the messianic climate and the consequent disappointment and feeling of having been cheated, experienced after the elections. In the saying of the powerless, those contradictions led them to define themselves as workers, and as '*ómi*'. This identification as men is acted out in private and semi-public spheres, and can be seen as compensation, corresponding to the failure to integrate oneself in an open political field, and probably in the economy as well.

The opening up of the political system, the experience of free, fair and peaceful elections were not sufficient conditions to bring about the opening up of new public spaces. Power remained distant and there was no real progress in gaining access to the public sphere. From the perspective of the *povo*, the political practices of the leaders did not seem to change, nor did the living conditions of the *povo* improve. In their view, the politicians were still primarily concerned with their own well-being and power. The closure of the usual spheres where a man can perform his identification as a man has disastrous effects on women. It entails a focus on women in terms of exchanges of sexual access for material security or compensation, reinforces the non-accountabililty of men (*Ki ta manda*) and the assignment of women to the sphere of domestic life and the control of all other spaces by men. Women from the same '*bairro*' also expressed disappointment a few months after the elections. Their comments regarding 'those who rule' were similar to those of the men. But in spite of the shared views of men and women, men continued to assert their identifications through an opposition versus women in the private and semi-public spaces as an integral part of their political commentaries.

Conclusion

Masculinity is used here to mark a valorised identity in a specific context. In the example above Paulo reaffirms himself as a man – or we could say as a highly valued individual outside of the public sphere of life. But he explains that his political opinion must be understood in other terms. He is a worker. He is identified in another way, as an unequal in terms of power, understood in this context as power in relation to party politics. The paradox is being yet not being a man. The struggle is to assert autonomy, knowledge and therefore manhood.

My argument is that the 'cultivation' of individual autonomy, with all the gendered boastfulness that this entails, must be seen in relation to other genres (and their respective experienced identifications), in this case, linked to the political arenas we have seen in Paulo's comments. The peer group ('*a malta*') remains the locus of the specific expression of valued identifications and of the presentation of the self. The peer group recreates itself through the years and exists in private and semi-public spaces such as homes and bars and in other activities friends carry out together, but always in face-to-face situations. There were no other associations offering a space for agency to these young men. It seems clear from the agents' point of view that a gap has to be bridged between '*povo*' and '*kem ta manda*', a strategy for 'ruling' and at the same time 'changing the living conditions of the majority', which entails a different conception of power.

New gender relations have to be fought for, new spaces created, new solidarities forged. Because gender is a classificatory principle that applies to relations of power between autonomous individuals it is 'good to talk about' political relations in the sense of the *res publica*. This is because gender relations are political relations *tout court*. The young men in my ethnographic material default on the values of hegemonic masculinity, that is why they are both re-enacting their claims to hegemonic masculinity in private and semi-public settings with peers *and* conceiving alternative classificatory principles suited to their age and conditions. Paulo's statement offers an alternative: the workers' stratum.

Contrary to common generalisations regarding the relationship between the private and the public, in the case of Cape Verde the private sphere remained the basis for discussions about politicians during the period of research. This is because politicians were not distant in the private sphere. The private sphere is the sphere where there was equality between men (in their relationships to women), where the young men could in fact know something about politicians, where they were powerful enough. '*Kem ta manda*', the '*doutores*', are individuals and during the election campaign their sexual life was scrutinised as much as their professional life. The private or the semi-private space is well suited to the political. This is because the political is saturated with the relations of reproduction of a gendered genre as seen in the use of 'bits of political genre with fragments of masculinity genre'.

The reproduction of the same power relations that exclude *de facto* a major part of the population shows that '*democracia*', democracy, has not been achieved in Cape Verde with the first 'democratic elections'. But if democracy is to be understood from the perspective of the aspirations and desires of the *povo*, it would entail better living conditions for the majority. It would make possible the creation of new, more egalitarian social relations and a society where people are more accountable in the public sphere and where all can aggregate along new lines of interests. In the meantime, however, the significant contradiction for these Cape Verdean men stems precisely from the fact that their ultimate political action in the political arena, voting, is constrained by the power of distant others – the 'doctors'. The *doutores* offer discursively the option between utopia and security and leave the men feeling powerless. The power of the 'doctors' thus contributes to the reproduction of discourses and practices that aim to make men feel empowered, like 'real' men – as real as the 'doctors'.

To conclude, I would like to return to the question of agency. In this chapter agency is linked to a theory of discursive practice. My argument is that agency is achieved through communication and through the performance of genres indexed by identifications. These performances in turn lead the actors to identify 'new positions from which to act' (Strathern 1988: 320). In the cases analysed in this chapter performance was intended to demonstrate knowledge and, through knowledge, autonomy. This could only be achieved through the incorporation of the personal, the private and the gendered dimensions of the actors' experience into the discourses of the political. In the context of a democracy where participation in the public sphere was unequally distributed, where economic inequality prevailed and where vulnerability was built into the collective imaginary, the masculinity genre provided a way to perform and assert self-worth and validate individual experience. However, the consequence of this strategy of validation was the continued dichotomising of male and female spaces, responsibilities and opportunities and the perpetuation of gender inequalities.

Notes

1 Relatively – and this is the point – hegemonic in relation to the advantage my friend has over D. in political relations as we will see further.
2 I use the term 'essential' on purpose to refer to an essentialism that has been much criticised from a political point of view (Stolcke 1995 among others).
3 It is very tempting indeed to spell this 'Identities' in order to enhance the connection between the concept, the broader episteme in which this concept was forged, and the concrete politics in which those concepts evolve and which they transform.
4 My use of the notion of network is deliberate. I want to emphasise the relations that exist between different identifications and therefore their meanings as established through the communicative practices of the actors. This includes a consideration of how different emotions or experienced paradoxes summon certain ways of speaking and interpreting.
5 *Doutores* in Cape Verdean Creole is one of those identifications that concentrates meaning. *Doutores* [Doctors] refers to an academic level, everybody holding a B.A. is formally called *doutor*. But in the setting where it is used it talks also of power relations. To get a formal education abroad remains in Cape Verde the best preparation for acquiring power, responsibilities and money.

6 This is not so much a previous condition as a result.
7 I will analyse the first part of the excerpt as it forms a narrative (it is in bold). I decided to annex the four interactions which followed in order to give the reader more elements to understand the text.
8 This allegorical passage draws on the lyrics of a popular song called 'Doutorado' by a local 'funaná' band, Finaçón, itself a sarcastic critique of the doutores.

Bibliography

Abu-Lughod, L. (1986) *Veiled Sentiments. Honor and Poetry in a Bedouin Society*, Berkeley and Los Angeles: University of California Press.

Bakhtin, M. (1986) 'The problem of speech genres', in Holquist, M. (ed.) *Speech Genres and Other Late Essays*, Austin: University of Texas Press.

Bauman, R. and Briggs, C. (1990) 'Poetics and performance as critical perspectives on language and social life', in *Annual Review of Anthropology*, 19: 59–88.

Bonniol, J.-L. (1992) *La couleur comme maléfice. Une illustration créole de la généalogie des Blancs et des Noirs*, Paris: Albin Michel.

Bruner, E. (1986) 'Experience and its expressions', in E. Bruner and V. Turner (eds), *Anthropology of Experience*, Chicago: Chicago University Press.

Cabral, N. (1980) *Le Moulin et le Pilon. Les îles du Cap-Vert*, Paris: L'Harmattan. ACCT.

Carreira, A. (1983) *Cabo-Verde. Formação e Extensão de uma Sociedade Escravocrata (1460–1878)* (2a edição), Com o pratocínio da Comunidade Económica Europeia. Instituto cabo-verdeano do livro.

Connell, R.W. (1995) *Masculinities*, Cambridge: Polity Press.

Cornwall, A. and Lindisfarne, N. (eds) (1994) *Dislocating Masculinity – Comparative Ethnographies*, London: Routledge.

Crapanzano, V. (1992) *Hermes' Dilemma and Hamlet's Desire. On the Epistemology of Interpretation*, Cambridge and London: Harvard University Press.

Fabian, J. (1995) 'Ethnographic misunderstanding and the perils of context'. *American Anthropologist* 97, 1: 41–50.

Ferreira, M. (n.d.) *A Aventura Crioula*, Lisboa: Platáno Editora.

Giraud, M. (1992) 'Assimilation, pluralisme,"double culture": l'ethnicité en question', *Information sur les sciences sociales* 31: 395–405.

Godzich, W. (1984) 'After the story teller . . . comes the storyteller', in R. Chambers (ed.) *Story and Situation Narrative Seduction and the Power of Fiction*, Minneapolis: University of Minnesota Press.

Gumperz, J.J. and Cook-Gumperz J. (1982) 'Introduction: language and the communication of social identity', in J.J. Gumperz (ed.) *Language and Social Identity*, Cambridge: Cambridge University Press.

Hall, S. (1996) ' Introduction: Who needs identity?' in S. Hall and P. du Gay (eds) *Questions of Cultural Identity*, London: Sage.

Hanks, W.F. (1996) *Language and Communicative Practices*, Boulder, Colorado: Westview Press.

Lavie, S. (1990) *The Poetics of Military Occupation. Mzeina Allegories of Bedouin Identity under Israeli and Egyptian Rule*, Berkeley: University of California Press.

Massart, G. (1992) *Life Histories and Stories about Women from the Life of Cape Verdean Urbans: An Anthropological Story Telling*, unpublished M.Phil. thesis, School of Oriental and African Studies, University of London.

Nagel, J. (1994) 'Constructing ethnicity: creating and recreating ethnic identity and culture', *Social Problems* 41: 152–76.

Pratt, M.L. (1982) 'Conventions of representation: where discourse and ideology meet', in H. Byrnes (ed.) *Contemporary Perceptions of Language: Interdisciplinary Dimensions*, Washington: Georgetown University Press.

Schutz, A. (1979) 'Bases da Fenomenologia', in R.H. Wagner (ed.) *Textos escolhidos de Alfred Schutz. Fenomenologia e Relações Sociais*, Rio de Janeiro: Zahar Editores.

Sharrock, W. and Anderson, R. (1982) 'On the demise of the Native: Some observations on and a proposal for ethnography', *Human Studies* 5: 119–35.

Silverstein, M. (1976) 'Shifters, linguistic categories, and cultural description', in K. Basso and H. Selby (eds) *Meaning in Anthropology*, Albuquerque: University of New Mexico Press.

Stolcke, V. (1995) 'Talking culture. New boundaries, new rhetorics of exclusion in Europe', *Current Anthropology*, 36, 1: 1–13.

Strathern, M. (1988) *The Gender of the Gift*, Berkeley, Los Angeles, London: University of California Press.

Vale de Almeida, M. (1996) *The Hegemonic Male. Masculinity in a Portuguese Town*, Providence, Oxford: Berghahn Books.

Chapter 8

Out of the house – to do what?

Women in the Spanish neighbourhood movement

Britt-Marie Thurén

Introduction

Spanish women do not participate in formal politics to any great extent. For example, the number of female parliamentarians hovered around 6 per cent during most of the 1980s. This fact reflects a long history of conditions that have tended to alienate women from the political sphere. However, there is one political context in Spain in which women and men participate in practically equal numbers. This is the so-called neighbourhood movement or citizens' movement (*movimiento vecinal* or *movimiento ciudadano*) which was born as a semi-legal resistance movement during the Franco regime. Its express purpose was to improve conditions in the areas of towns and cities (*barrios*) where poor people lived, but since this entailed a struggle against the dictatorship, 'participatory democracy' became an integral objective. It was around the time of the transition to democracy, in the late 1970s, that women started joining the movement in greater numbers, and they are still increasing. The study of this movement is important because it can elucidate the relationship between the gender order, the political order and cultural change.

This chapter discusses the possible reasons why Spanish women who decide to participate in political activities usually prefer a neighbourhood association to a political party or a labour union and how they can act once there and what it means to them and to society. The aim is to describe relevant factors of various kinds in such a way as to make the specific Spanish experiences interesting and relevant to broader feminist debates. The examples discussed shed light on processes of redefinition of private and public domains and the location of the separation between them. They also show that the role of gender as a major principle of social organisation is being renegotiated. Such negotiation is not un-problematic. Men's resistance to certain gender changes result in conflict but also cultural innovation. So do women's fears, ambivalence, enthusiasm and learning as new stages of activity come within reach. The analysis will show interconnections between the organisation of time and space and gender in the *barrios*, and what they mean for political activities and how women and men negotiate among themselves for space in their partially common, partially different political struggles. There are gender-related differences, within the working class, in people's view of themselves as agents of change.[1] Following an outline of the historical background to the movement, the chapter will examine examples from four towns.[2]

Background

Spain has undergone dramatic economic and social transformation during the last decades. In the 1950s it was predominantly agricultural, with difficulties feeding its population. During the 1960s it was urbanised and industrialised at a rapid pace. Of all OECD countries, only Japan had a faster rate of growth during that decade. This meant that a large proportion of the population moved from villages to cities. Around the largest cities, self-built shacks mushroomed in the 1960s and slowly disappeared during the 1970s.

There was an improvement in average living standards, but it came at a high social cost. Not only was village social life destroyed, workers' health strained by pluri-employment, and so on, but all of these processes of change took place under conditions of dictatorship. But then a political change came too. Franco died in 1975. More or less democratic general elections were held in 1977 – for the first time since 1936. A new constitution was approved in 1978, and after new general elections a socialist government took over in late 1982. The degrees of democracy and socialism are certainly issues for debate, but it is a very different country from the one Franco governed. Cultural change was as dramatic as economic and political change, and individual experiences and expectations had to be reinterpreted.

In the Mediterranean area, gender is frequently used as a root metaphor to express other social phenomena. The relationship between women and men is used in proverbs, poetry, song, jokes, drama, gestures, insults and so on, to illustrate political power, religious feelings, philosophical abstractions. Important events inevitably affect the gender order just as the gender order shapes processes of change. And change is culturally perceived in gender terms. During the 1970s and 1980s, discussions regarding 'change' often sparked debates about sexual morals or mothers working outside the home. The tendency is weakening now, because gender is retreating from its privileged cultural place. The gender order *is* really changing.[3]

History of the neighbourhood movement

After the civil war (1936–9) Spain was exhausted in every way, and the resistance against the dictatorship was largely wiped out during the 1940s. However, after 1956 resistance grew again. A new generation had grown up, and the political parties in exile changed their strategies from confrontation to infiltration. In this way, for example, the Workers' Commissions were organised. They were illegal but powerful enough to organise important strikes already in the early 1960s and they were recognised de facto in many settlements towards the end of the decade. Because they worked through the legal vertical trade unions of the regime, they could reach and recruit more people than the underground parties could.

According to the political philosophy of the Franco regime, society rests on three fundamentals: union, family and locality. The vertical union structure, controlled from the top, constituted the regime's first pillar. As to the second pillar, the regime coincided with the majority view, that the nuclear family is the basic building block of society. More than 90 per cent of all Spaniards live in nuclear families, which are strongly solidary.[4] The third pillar was the locality and here too there was correspondence between fascist theory and Spanish tradition. Beyond the family, the village or the urban *barrio* usually provided the individual's frame of reference.

Small villages were effectively defined through a local adminis-tration and an appointed mayor, but the cities presented a problem. To be sure, the city equivalent of the village was and is the *barrio*. Spaniards identify with their *barrio*, just as they identify with their village. It is a place of safety, where one is known, and where one's social networks are based.[5] But the *barrios* are not administrative units. With the sudden influx of migrants to the cities during the late 1950s, new *barrios* spread and old ones changed. The local identity of urbanites grew diffuse. Culturally, this was experienced as a loss. Politically, it made the regime nervous.

The response of the regime was the 1964 law of neighbourhood associations. This aimed at constructing organisations similar to the unions, but on a territorial basis. The only legal party, the Falange, would act as an umbrella organisation and design the statutes. Each association was to have a clearly defined territory. Permitted activities were carefully specified and distinguished from forbidden ones. In other words, the regime's intention was that the structure of the neighbourhood associations would emulate the union structure to control and influence everyday life. Unlike the unions, it would reach all, even women, the young and the elderly. But the neighbourhood associations, like the unions, also offered opportunities for infiltration and resistance. The legal purposes of the associations were soon inextricably mixed with illegal ones. To improve conditions in poor neighbourhoods meant, in practice, to protest against land speculation, lack of infrastructure and services, bureaucratic inefficiency and corruption, and so on. The former purpose was legal, the latter illegal, but they were intimately linked.

The first associations emerged on the outskirts of Madrid, Bilbao and Barcelona, in *barrios* that lacked such basic services as water and transportation. The inhabitants also demanded schooling for their children, electricity, health care. For many, the hope of such facilities had motivated their move to the city (Molina 1984). There was a need to devise ways of organising collective action, whether for protest or self-help. A semi-legal resistance movement emerged. The neighbourhood associations were soon infiltrated by the underground political parties, and became increasingly daring. They began to express their demands, especially for housing. There were a few successes. The regime realised that the cities needed workers, and commercial builders could not build affordable workers' homes so housing schemes were set up and the associations acted as channels for communication between the schemes and the workers, so that their needs and wishes could be taken into account.

Having lost the stable social organisation of the villages, people found themselves living among strangers in an urban context they were ill equipped to handle. '*Hacer barrio* ' – to make the *barrio* into a living social reality – soon became a central slogan. A yearly *fiesta*, usually on a saint's day, sports and games for the young, a place for the elderly to play cards, co-operative food outlets to

provide cheap staples, perhaps a literacy course. So the neighbourhood association became a political, cultural and social centre, in
one *barrio* after another. The associations spread to older *barrios*,
even to middle-class *barrios*. It has been suggested that the dictatorship created common interests across class barriers (Castells 1986).
The middle class, too, suffered from the lack of schools and the
deficient health care system, from noise and air pollution. They too
lost out to land speculation and building fraud and needed fora for
debate, places to learn about politics. Periodically, the regime
became nervous and closed them down, but the movement as a
whole grew steadily.

In the mid 1970s it seemed that the regime would be transformed once Franco died, and as if that day was not too far off.
The neighbourhood associations had by this time federated themselves in the largest cities (which was illegal), and the movement
was spreading to smaller cities. For the plethora of small leftist
parties that was coming into existence, the movement provided the
opportunity to measure their strength and to act semi-openly. The
movement became something of a political prize. But most movement activists were not party members. Their aim was to improve
their *barrio* or the living conditions of their families . For many, the
neighbourhood associations became a political school, the only
legitimate one. The insights gained led many to join a party; others,
however, were put off by the party tactics of infiltration and in-
fighting that they observed first hand as, towards 1980, many
associations became battle grounds between different parties.

From many perspectives 1977 was a critical year. Political parties
were legalised, so party activists who had used the movement as a
front could resurface and militate openly. Many of the most active
and experienced leaders abandoned the movement. Some thought
the end of the regime signalled the end of the struggle and there
was work to be done elsewhere. The socialist and communist
victories at the first democratic local elections in 1979 confirmed
this view, and some ex-leaders of the movement even became town
councillors or mayors. But not all the movement's objectives had
been achieved. It was still necessary – and fun – to try to 'make
barrio'. Someone had to co-ordinate the yearly *fiesta*, the senior
citizens' clubs, photo contests, *barrio* marathons, film clubs,
women's committees, language courses. For some activists, the
movement had become a home, a place that had cost years of work,
money and sometimes, jail.

Such a hard-won space could not be given up easily. It also became clear that the political fight was not over. There was a need to maintain a check on the fledgling democratic institutions, including the parties themselves. There was still corruption and speculation, *barrio* facilities were still deficient and the neighbourhood associations could make valuable contributions.

Once basic needs like housing and water were largely resolved, there was transportation and health care to consider. Then came schooling, traffic safety, better street lighting, playgrounds and parks. These blended into more general issues, such as local industrial politics, bureaucratic corruption, unemployment, air pollution and noise. Then in the 1980s there were drugs (working class *barrio*s were hard hit), the 'Gypsy problem' (old ethnic animosities found a new vocabulary, as the Gypsies were thought to be the principal drug dealers) and crime.

In the 1990s the movement was still growing but also changing. 'Confrontational' tactics were increasingly considered 'old-fashioned' and a shift towards voluntary work was encouraged. Social work, sports and local festivities absorbed ever more of the activists' energies and time. But there were still many burning issues that could bring thousands of *barrio* inhabitants into the streets at a moment's notice. The movement continued to have *poder de convocatoria* – the capacity to generate support far beyond its regular membership.

In the early years the focus was on resistance to the destruction of self-built housing. Then came an era of oscillations between cautious negotiations with the authorities and massive illegal protest meetings. Collecting money for fines and bails was important too. During the transition towards democracy, negotiations became friendlier and symbolic actions less violent. Demonstrations, street vigils, occupations of municipal offices, and traffic stoppages were common, as were petitions to local politicians, letters to editors and securing sympathetic press coverage. As democratic institutions stabilised, association work increasingly consisted of visiting municipal offices, meeting with politicians and the press, keeping an eye on official bulletins.

There was also always the creativity of each association. Humour is a congenial weapon. I lived in a *barrio* in Madrid where a beautiful park that used to belong to a duke was now city property. The *barrio* had no green area, so the association claimed the park for public use. Since the city did not respond, we 'opened' it with a mock ceremony and a *barrio* picnic outside its walls every spring (after five years of this the park *was* opened!). Another *barrio* in Madrid organised a 'rat hunt' modelled on English foxhunts. Satire, poetry and costumes, songs and sketches were features of the *fiestas.*

During the 1980s the neighbourhood associations were recognised by many towns and cities as 'interlocutors' or 'public interest organisations'. In the media and in private conversations, the movement was often mentioned together with other 'new' social movements, especially feminism, pacifism and environmentalism. It was usually considered more mainstream than these, but less so than political parties or trade unions.

Organisationally, the movement had established stable structures. Most associations now have their own premises and many produce regular bulletins. The city-wide federations work on city-wide issues, such as the organisation of traffic and public transport, and for the co-ordination of *barrio* issues. The various federations have formed a countrywide confederation and some experienced activists claim a national role for the movement alongside political parties and trade unions. In 1996 the movement had nearly two million members, of which perhaps one tenth were activists. There were around 2,000 associations, organised in over one hundred federations.[6]

Time, space and gender in the *barrio*

During the early years the movement was almost exclusively male, with a few exceptional women, but the proportion of women has steadily increased. In fact, most of the newly recruited activists in the 1980s and 1990s seem to be women, and mostly average *barrio* women. The confederation has set up a 'women's structure' and a few country-wide women's congresses have been held. The relationship between these structures, the confederation and women themselves is unclear, but what is important is that there is now one political forum in the country where women are present at a level close to the 51 per cent they represent in the population as a whole.

The gender order in Spain has traditionally separated women and men into different life styles, domains and spaces, all marked with contrasting gender symbols. The key metaphor here is that 'women are of the house, men are of the street'. The house stands for family life, maternal duties, privacy and intimacy. The street stands for everything else: economic activities, friendship and sociability, formal education, and all decision-making that affects units larger than the nuclear family.[7] The separation is decreasing, and is under constant debate, but it is still a structural and cultural fact with clear consequences (cf. Thurén 1988 and forthcoming). Most women's lives are very different from those of most men. Different life experiences produce different subjectivities, so women's political priorities often differ from those of men, as do their styles of interaction and communication. This makes it difficult for women and men to work together, even when goals are shared.

Many women undoubtedly see the neighbourhood associations as suitable places for an extension of their duties as mothers and homemakers. In this sense, the movement has played a role for women similar to movements elsewhere that they have been compared to (Castells 1986; *Salida* 1989), such as the *ollas comunes* in Latin America.[8] Women tend to see political parties as male spaces, whereas the neighbourhood movement is seen as closer to home, easier to understand and an instrument for improving the home surroundings and the life of one's children. It is not seen as 'politics' and women militating in more traditional political organisations may add that therefore it is of little consequence. Political or not, the associations constitute a public space. And unlike other activities where many women participate, such as parent teacher associations or church groups, the neighbourhood movement is not a predominantly female space, since half of the participants are men; it is not quite gender-neutral, but it is more so than almost any other public context in Spain.

There is tension within the movement between those who want to use it as a platform for radical social change and those who see it as an instrument to solve everyday problems, and this tension is reflected in debates on women's issues. There are several reasons for women's increasing presence in the movement.[9] When the leaders left during the early days of the transition, it was men who left, since very few women were party activists.[10] As the proportion of women rose , it became easier for other women to join. There is also the fact that the movement is territorially defined. It is in, of and about the *barrio*. And this is where women live and work. Women do not stay indoors, even in places like Linares (cf. below, page 180), where they are supposed to remain within the confines of the 'house'. They are on the streets as much as men, or more, because while men are at work, women's family duties take them on errands all around the *barrio*. It is not quite legitimate to walk around for pleasure, but during the daytime, typical *barrio* streets are full of women and only a few men, and full of activities that form part of family life, such as children walking to school and housewives shopping for food. In other words, the *barrio* is a mediator between 'home' and 'street'. It is outside the home, but it is close to home; and it is a women's space during much of the day.

An association based on the *barrio* is thus suitable for women interested in public life. The decision to go into the 'street' is not so momentous, since they are still in or near the 'house'. There may be opposition to their presence, but less than in other political contexts. From a practical angle, too, it is easier for a woman to be active in a neighbourhood association than in a party or a union. The premises are close to home, so going to a meeting takes less time, which is important for most women, especially mothers of small children. Proximity is also an advantage for older women and/or people who do not read very well, who are not comfortable moving far away from their neighbourhood.[11] The timing of meetings suits women and men. They are held early in the evening, when most people are back from work, but before dinner and children's bedtime.

However, women cannot easily socialise after meetings, which places them at a disadvantage. It is not common for husbands to take over home duties, so most women have to hurry home after meetings. Furthermore, women are not comfortable in the bars where the socialising takes place. Downtown cafeterias are gender-neutral, but *barrio* bars continue to be clearly male spaces. But pleasure is a motive, too, especially for women, since they have fewer alternative meeting places. In spite of the serious objectives, frustrations and conflicts, most activists have *fun* in the movement and many said all their friends were in the movement. (See below, page 176, on stories of participation.) The pleasurable atmosphere of the meetings, at demonstrations, at the bar also influence women's participation.

Perhaps the main reason for women's presence in the movement is their superior knowledge about the *barrio*, and this legitimates their participation to some extent even among traditionalists. Only about one-fourth of working-class married women work outside their homes.[12] For the others the *barrio* is their daily territory. The content of women's family work has much to do with the *barrio* as a space: they know where the children play and what dangers there are and what they would need to grow up happier and healthier; they know the food stores, prices and quality; they know if drug dealers gather on some corner.

One aspect of the traditional gender order that remains relevant, though not explicit, is the feeling that women are unable to *represent* anyone but themselves and possibly their children. This probably lies behind some of the difficulties women encounter in other political contexts or in the movement beyond the *barrio*. The proportion of women decreases drastically as one moves up the organisational pyramid. Already at the level of city federations, there are few women. Activists tend to elect men to represent the *barrio* and women tend to avoid being elected. I am inclined, however, to see practical reasons as foremost for the absence of women in the federations. Federation premises are farther away and attending meetings is too time-consuming.

In the *barrio* association activists represent only themselves. They are there as individuals. It has been argued that women are less individuated than men in western countries, and this is certainly true for Spain. One major obstacle for women's participation in any aspect of public life is their close connection with the family, and the relatively lower degree of legitimacy accorded to their actions as individuals, outside the family context. But if and when they overcome this obstacle, it is still easier to act as individuals than to represent larger collectivities.

As more women enter the movement, it becomes easier for others to join. The style of interaction and the issues become more 'woman friendly' and their participation becomes less controversial, provoking less gossip, suspicion and resistance. The importance of gender as such also decreases as women move in. When I asked about the division of labour according to gender, it was always vehemently denied; whether or not it existed in practice, it was clearly not acceptable in theory.

Interaction in the association

The interactional style of the movement is generally relaxed and down-to-earth, humorous and ironic. Styles of working and talking are becoming more formal as the movement becomes institutionalised but are still looser than in the political parties and labour unions. Many women (and some men) felt out of place in such organisations, because they had to learn pre-established ways of speaking and acting.[13] In the movement greater spontaneity is possible.

The movement also lends itself well to innovation, because it is relatively new itself and has always experimented with styles and methods. The friendly style is related to the fact that many of the activists know each other in many roles and most of them have overlapping networks. The style is also compatible with the issues as they are culturally perceived: 'small' 'everyday' things like street lights and bread prices; 'family' issues like health care and schooling; even 'dirty' issues like drugs, rats and garbage collection. There is nothing elegant, nothing momentous about them. For all these reasons, meeting procedures have to be informal and the atmosphere is usually friendly. Tasks are assigned pragmatically to whoever has the time or inclination. Most associations have annual meetings that elect a board, but election is not a requirement for being active; usually whoever comes to the meetings with some regularity is considered active and is listened to. Voting is extremely rare. Minutes are hardly ever kept. Experience counts, veterans are listened to, but claims to prestige on the grounds of experience, education or income are avoided. Formal signs of hierarchy are scrupulously avoided. Presidents try not to invoke their authority to keep order. First names are used, as is the informal pronoun '*tú*', irrespective of age, gender or other statuses.

Strong undercurrents of tension are frequent because of differences in background and ideology, and sometimes because issues are conflictive. But individual preferences and opinions are well known to all, so conflicts can be averted or joked about, as the situation demands. Much of the joking is sexual but it is seldom denigrating. And women are used to it as a common feature of other gender-mixed contexts. There is some playful flirtation, but serious affairs are discouraged as most activists are married and involved in dense local networks that rapidly carry gossip. All in all, the style of work and interaction is adapted to the cultural and social circumstances so women and men feel relaxed and competent in it.

At association meetings, men tend to use more space than women: they speak longer and louder, interrupt more often, and spread arms, legs, jackets and note paper wider. Women's behaviour is only relatively deferential and circumspect. But the context is political, therefore the men have preference in defining the terms. Countervailing these tendencies, however, is the fact that women know more about *barrio* life, as we saw, and that gives them authority in debating the issues. They do *not* keep quiet. The men concede authority and space to women. They do so because they recognise women's knowledge and because activists are usually radical enough to question all conventions. When asked, they insist that women should have the same rights to speak and act as men. Such statements and/or convictions do not always translate into actual behaviour, but when it comes to *barrio* issues they often do, because women's knowledge of them is legitimate, even according to the traditional gender order.

Political party activists may look down on the informal procedures of the movement. Personally I believe that the grass-roots characteristics of the movement represent its greatest asset. In any case, it is safe to suggest that these grass-roots characteristics, taken together, create a woman-friendly context,[14] this being one of the things that the women themselves stressed when I questioned them about their reasons for joining. However, there are variations according to region and community, as we will see.

Stories about participation

There are certain regularities that emerge in the stories that men and women tell concerning their participation. The regularities are all the more striking, given the variation in all other factors. Some people, both women and men, had clear ideological reasons for being active. They were Christian or communist or had a working-class consciousness, implying that this was a more than sufficient explanation. Some admitted they reached their convictions through working in the association, for others the reasons for first joining were the same reasons for continuing. Whatever the details of their stories, they shared the belief that social injustice was prevalent and that it ought to and could be changed. The need to struggle against injustice overrode all other considerations. It even made established gender ideas pale in comparison, although many men and women confessed to 'contradictions' in their 'mentality' when it came to gender.

For most active women, however, ideological background was irrelevant. Their reasons for joining were social and personal. *No* woman said she was tempted into political activity because she wanted to influence important decisions.[15] The main motive was usually expressed in vague terms as 'doing something for others', 'getting out of the house', 'knowing what is going on', or similar phrases, indicating a 'feminine' (according to the dominant gender order) concern for the well-being of others in combination with a critical attitude towards the confinement of women to the 'house' and their consequent lack of mobility and information.[16]

The influence of someone known to them and active in the movement was a common factor in explanations of how people joined the movement. Their contact was usually described as someone who 'did so much for others without thinking of themselves' and 'who could be trusted always to help you if you needed it', gregarious, 'nice to be with', someone who would 'always stop to greet you in the street' and remember to ask you about your personal problems. An invitation to join might come from this person but often the initiative came from the new recruit herself. This typically took the form of an offer of help. Informants usually explained that owing to their own perception of their 'ignorance' or lack of experience they had needed some persuasion to join.

For men too, personal contacts had influenced their decision to join but they emphasised their own ideological 'evolution' that led them towards the movement. Leaders especially talked in political terms of the need for participatory democracy. Others spoke about the deficiencies of their *barrio*, which they had noticed and had to struggle to correct out of a sense of justice and responsibility. If a *barrio* does not struggle, they said, ordinary politicians will do nothing.

The main difference was not the significance of personal contacts but its characteristics. For both men and women, the helping hand almost always belonged to someone of their own gender.[17] For men it was someone with knowledge and preferably a position, someone who explained the theoretical purposes of the movement. For women it was someone who could convince them that they, too, were valuable. Both men and women needed to overcome their lack of information, but women also confronted a lack of self-assurance. This was felt as an individual problem ('I don't think I am good at that kind of thing') and as gender-specific ('women are not usually good at that kind of thing') or both ('women are not usually good at that kind of thing, and I don't know if I am an exception, and to act as if I were will make me look ridiculous').[18]

Men, then, stressed the problems and the objectives of the movement, sometimes expressed in highly politicised terms. Women commonly denied being involved in politics at all. They wished above all to 'contribute'. Their motives were actually the same as the men's, to solve the problems of their *barrio*. But while the men expressed this thought in political terms, referring to power and their own capacity, the women preferred more humble and moral terms.

Questions about women in the movement

So far I have offered answers to anthropological or outsider questions. The movement itself had questions about women's participation too. But whereas I wondered why so many women do participate, the emphasis from the inside was on non-participation.

Activists wanted to resolve certain gender-related problems for practical reasons, for the good of the movement as a whole. Debates on 'women's issues' were also prompted by the confederation's initiatives. Activists usually assumed that women should participate more in public life, that the neighbourhood movement is a good place to start and that it too would benefit but that most women are 'still' 'limited' to a life centred on the family.

The men in the movement were often critical of both women's and men's non-participation. They thought everyone ought to be more solidary but that most people were lazy or selfish. The criticism applied equally to women and men, but it was often specified that women can no longer claim discrimination or lack of education as an excuse: 'Nowadays everything has changed, so what is stopping them?' The women in the movement were more understanding. They knew from experience that the obstacles were real. But if they had overcome them others should do the same.

One commonly discussed issue was whether separate women's groups were necessary or desirable or whether the goal should be to overcome whatever it is that makes them necessary. Questions of strategy concerned how the movement could be made attractive to women, how to 'get women out of their homes' and what prevented them from joining. Were women's 'traditional roles' keeping them away or was it men's resistance, and if the latter, why do men resist? Debates also addressed ways of improving women's self-esteem and whether the movement addressed specific female needs. One common opinion was that it is wrong to categorise people as men or women, and that it is preferable to identify as 'persons', working in the same associations, with the same activities. After all, the common objective of struggle was a better society for everyone!

The role of women's committees was also an issue: What should they do? Must they be feminist? Or could they be for 'ordinary women' and if so, would they not end up as just clubs for gossip? On the other hand, the presence of a feminist women's committee could scare away other ordinary *barrio* men and women.

Different ways of participating

My generalisations so far have been based largely on data from Madrid and Valencia. Since they are large cities, they can be treated as ideal-typical for the movement, which was born in big cities and focuses on urban issues. But what happens in small and medium-sized places is also relevant. Four examples will illustrate the range of variation in what women do, can do, are allowed to do and want to do in the movement.[19] The gender order differs throughout Spain.[20] Since women need and want different things, the neighbourhood movement comes into their lives in different ways. What the examples taken together show is that the movement can play an emancipatory role in different gender situations and that women in very different circumstances find it useful.

Elda

Elda is a town of some 55,000 inhabitants in south-eastern Spain, in the region of Valencia. The neighbourhood movement started early here and was well established by 1994; all *barrios* had their own association and all except one had their own premises. Co-operation with the city council was close and friendly (too close for some). Both the city council and the movement were dominated by the socialist party, PSOE.[21]

Elda is an industrial town with a proud working-class history. The shoe industry is the single dominant industry here. Elda women claim they have 'always' worked. Most tasks in shoemaking are considered gender-specific, about half being for women, who could thus count on a job. The women of the movement in Elda said they felt different from women from other parts of Spain when they met them at congresses and heard their complaints about discrimination. 'We have evolved beyond all that.' They claimed they were used to having a say because they had always contributed substantially to the family income.

Nevertheless, Elda women complained about husbands who did nothing at home and were unhappy when their wives attended meetings. In most of the associations, there were many active women, but there were some with very few and one with none. Of the eighteen representatives in the federation, only one was a woman. Yet the women's commission of the federation was unsure of its purpose: there were no special women's issues to fight for, they felt, except perhaps to get men to 'help more' at home. Their main concern was unemployment, a recent fact of life in Elda. They underlined that this was a problem for men, too, but they organised a sewing class for women, seeing it as a reliable skill to earn money or save on the family budget. The commission was also vaguely interested in 'clarifying our own ideas on women's issues'. They knew there was a body of feminist theory that might be relevant for them, but did not know how to gain access to it, and seemed unwilling to spend much energy investigating this. Like most movement activists, they were more interested in practical struggles than in theoretical issues.

Linares

Linares is another industrial town, of similar size and not very far from Elda. But it belongs to another region, Andalusia, and it has a very different history. Mining was once the main activity in Linares; now it is the automobile industry. Both have been defined as masculine activities. So unlike Elda, women here have never participated in the labour market to any extent.

The neighbourhood movement was new in the 1990s, and very few women took part in it. A couple of *barrio* associations dated from the 1970s, but the federation was quite recent and, as far as I could tell, it and many of the associations were being pushed into existence by PSOE militants. One young university-educated PSOE woman was trying to organise women's committees. Middle-aged *barrio* women who were long-term activists accepted the initiative because they recognised there was a need, though with scepticism about her motives and ability.

Linares women did not go out much. Visiting each other's homes was acceptable, but the women talked about it as a right conquered in their own life-time. Only recently had it become acceptable for a married woman to have a cup of coffee with a woman friend in a cafeteria. To join an association was construed as the next step on the road towards freedom of movement, and that was where the struggle was in 1994.

Many of the associations had no women at all on the board, and in one association there was organised opposition against the first two women who dared to join the board. In another association, a large group of women had become active, whereupon most of the men quit. Most of the resistance, however, seemed to come from husbands. In such a situation, women can do little association work beyond winning the right to join. On the other hand, hundreds of Linares women demonstrated weekly throughout the winter of 1994, as workers' *wives* when one-quarter of the car industry's workforce was laid off with threats of worse to come. So Linares women took to the streets in their traditional gender role. The distinction between 'street' and 'house' remained intact. Although physically in the street, they remained socially and culturally within the domestic realm. Defending their families was one thing, joining an association for their own sake was another. That could undermine the genderisation of domains, and that was resisted by many women and most men.

But activist women responded. In one association the women staged a play about women who become ill when they are deprived of friendship. One such woman persuades her husband to let her join the neighbourhood association, after which her personality changes and her marriage improves. The husband, impressed, also joins the association. In another case a women's choir had a repertoire of songs about the therapeutic and educational effects of association life on women.

Cordova

Cordova, also in Andalusia, is a city of about 300,000 inhabitants. It is a provincial capital, an administrative and commercial centre for the surrounding agricultural area. It has some industry and attracts tourism because of its rich cultural heritage, notably the famous mosque-cathedral. It is a beautiful but difficult city. Class is a major factor of life. Incomes, educational levels, life-styles and opinions are polarised. In the first democratic local elections, in 1979, Cordova elected a communist mayor, and the communists have dominated city politics ever since.

Cordova is one of the places where the neighbourhood movement has attained most recognition and become integrated into formal city politics. It has remained a mostly male movement. The women said this was because the city and its men were 'still very Moorish'. Only two of the fifty or so associations had women's committees. That does not mean that the women of Cordova were not active – perhaps they were the most radical of all. There was a lively feminist movement, supported by the city council, which had not stayed aloof from *barrio* women.[22] Feminist and other women's groups were organised in a federation-like structure, through which they could obtain financial and organisational support for activities such as congresses, women's film clubs or literacy courses. For the immediate future, they planned a series of workshops on 'sexuality from the perspective of women's pleasure and desires'. The feminist organisers proudly stressed that this brave proposal had come 'from the women themselves'.

Many of the women's groups were *barrio* groups. Their area of action coincided with that of the 'men's association', as they usually called the neighbourhood association, and their purpose was the same, to 'work for the good of the *barrio*'. But they had found it necessary to organise separately from the men. There were tales of women who had tried to work in the 'men's associations' and had resigned because the men did not co-operate, their husbands were suspicious of late evening meetings and neighbours gossiped about their possible sexual motives in being around so many men. In other words, there were actually two neighbourhood associations in many *barrio*s, one for men and one for women, working on similar issues. In some cases they shared the premises, meeting at different times. But the women's groups did not want to be redefined as women's committees of the neighbourhood associations. They feared that would limit their freedom of action and subordinate them to the men.

What these three examples show is that, whatever else women were doing in the movement, they were also working at redefining gender. Minimally, these women had refused to stay 'in the house' in order to join the movement. Implicitly, they wanted more equality in the sense of similarity, since they wanted women and men to work in the same spaces. But usually they postponed this aim to work instead for equality in the sense of justice.

The women of these towns differed in what they identified as most urgent, or most easily attainable, and in what tactics to use. In

Elda, women felt they were already similar to men in the most decisive domain, the labour market. Their implicit theory was Marxian: if there is equality in the economic sphere, other inequalities will disappear. They were therefore confident that, with or without special efforts on their part, women would increasingly enter the movement and men would welcome them, and that husbands would begin helping at home. Unemployment posed the greatest danger to this process.

The women of Linares also wanted to enter men's spaces. Employment was not the means to achieve this given the lack of jobs for women and, increasingly for men too. Most women claimed that women and men were very different deep down, and they wanted to remain 'real women'. However, their 'feminine identity' was not under threat – on the contrary, it was being used as a weapon against them, to keep them 'in the house'. So for them it was important to diminish difference as a way of achieving justice.

In Cordova, too, women felt that decreased gender differences were desirable. They had been working on this for some time, but their experience was rather negative. There was resistance from many quarters, centred on the mixing of unrelated women and men, so they pragmatically opted for separate organisations, though they did not relinquish their concern to abolish rigid definitions of what befits each gender. Equality in the sense of similarity had to give way to equality in the sense of justice.

To use the key analogy of women/house and men/street, while women in Elda felt that men ought to start knocking on the kitchen door, wanting to come in, and the women in Linares knocked their knuckles bloody on the inside of their front doors, wanting to get out, the women in Cordova had opened the front doors, kept the kitchen doors closed until further notice, and built new walls in the public arena in order to be able to use at least parts of it for their own purposes.

A fourth example shows women who are already outside the 'house' calling for other women to come out, and doing it in such a way as to make the walls themselves blur.

Vigo: lace-making or feminism?

Vigo, in the north-western region of Galicia, is approximately the same size as Cordova. Its traditional activities are fishing, canning

industries, shipbuilding and the port. There is also a large automobile factory. There has been much immigration from the
surrounding countryside but links with the land are strong. Most
workers choose to live on the outskirts of the city, where they can
have a small plot of land where the women grow potatoes and
vegetables, keep a few chicken and perhaps a pig.

Galician women are used to making their own decisions, because
their men have often been away for long periods, as fishermen,
sailors or emigrants to America,[23] but they are careful to defer to
their husbands' masculinity. In 1994 most working-class women in
Vigo took no part in political life. They had a heavy load: the
house, the family, the garden plot and the animals, and many also
had jobs outside the household, in the canneries or selling fish or
cleaning the homes of the middle class. Middle-class women
enjoyed many activities and much freedom of movement. The
traditional-minded women of the old part of Vigo were very active
in their neighbourhood association, but refused to occupy formal
positions, claiming: 'We women just argue with each other. A
woman president would try to order everyone around. Things
work much more smoothly if men are in command.'

In 1990 a feminist was elected to the city council. She decided
to make a special effort to 'get women out of their homes', as a
strategic move to empower women. She chose the neighbourhood
movement as her main instrument and summoned the few women
activists, offering special resources to set up women's committees.

As the women paraphrased the councillor, she told them:

> Work for getting women out of the house. Don't be content
> with being just a few of you. Most women of your *barrio*
> probably do not want to be active in the association itself, but
> let them at least know that it exists and if possible understand
> what it is about. Make them come to the premises. One way
> to make them come is to give them things they like.

Her department offered lists of subsidised courses for the committees to choose from. Unsurprisingly, the women chose activities
traditionally defined as female: embroidery, porcelain painting, and
lacework. Some committees also organised literacy courses. The
courses subsidised by the women's department were not open to

men, and this caused some irritation, even though everyone recognised that no man would want to do lacework. Some women protested because they had to sign up as members of the association to take the courses. Some activists also felt hesitant about 'forced' recruitment. But the success of the initiative was enormous and in a few years large numbers of women had joined the movement as the women's networks spread favourable accounts of the programme. By 1994 there were women's committees in practically every *barrio*.

Men felt uncomfortable about this female presence, though they usually expressed this cautiously, talking about how women 'need to learn', how the men were 'trying to help' but with care 'not to meddle', and how the women 'should be grateful for everything we are giving them'. They also joked about women's meetings, as 'a pain in the neck', and referred to the chatter, the lack of any clear decisions, and the women's mistakes that the men then had to help clear up. The men denied wanting to restrict women to traditional roles, but they claimed women needed to learn more before they assumed responsibilities in the association, and so far they preferred lacemaking anyway. In fact, most activities in Vigo continued to be run by men.

Women in the feminist movement or in political parties and trade unions in Vigo were sceptical about these strategies. So were movement activists, men and women, in other federations where the Vigo experiment was discussed. It was generally agreed that many women had been brought out of their homes, and that these women derived great satisfaction from their new activities. It was evident that they were spreading the word, attracting more women to the associations. But it was also felt that they did not understand the aims of the movement. Nor had their lives changed: 'They might as well get together in Church! This changes nothing!', as one sceptic said. In fact, the Vigo programme was sometimes interpreted as one of many attempts to neutralise the movement, diverting its energies away from 'real politics' and undermining its revolutionary potential.

But there was also support for the experiment and for its gradualist tactics. From this perspective it was not considered democratic to tell women what to do nor could people without any experience of life outside the home be expected to take an interest in formal politics or immediately become feminists. The first and crucial step was to get women out of their homes, to meet and to lose their fear of participation. Already many women dared to insist that they wanted to go out when their husbands wanted to stop them. Their self-esteem was growing and they were building networks. Soon they may start discussing *barrio* issues while engaged in their handicraft work. The method may be slow, but change will happen gradually.

My opinion is that both sides were correct, but only partially. The women did come out of their houses and joined the associations, and they did have fun, as they themselves stressed. They enjoyed having a place to go to to do work they liked. It was work they were familiar with, but they were learning more about it, and they were given space and time of their own to do it. They got out of the house with a legitimate excuse, meeting many other women, forming friendships. Most courses organised lunches or dinners and soon groups of women in bars and restaurants were a common feature of *barrio* life in a way they had never been before.

The women themselves told enthusiastic stories of how they used to be bored, but now had 'a place to go to and meet friends.' 'It is easier for women to leave the house if they come back with an object they have made, something for the house, because then the husband will not be so suspicious.' Such statements describe attitudes beyond the traditional pleasure of women's crafts. They speak of small rebellions, small changes, small but new ideas. Too small to satisfy intellectual feminists or radical politicians, but small enough to be viable in the context of *barrio* women's lives, and therefore perhaps more effective in the long run.

The situation in Vigo can be seen as a practical experiment in what Young calls gynocentric feminism, and the debates about it can be seen as local expressions of the tensions between gynocentric and humanist feminism (Young 1990: 73–91), or as a practical dimension of feminist debates on essentialism versus constructivism. In Young's terminology, humanist feminism builds on western Enlightenment values. The fundamental idea is that patriarchal society oppresses women and hinders them from developing their potential as human beings. The goal is a society where gender differences are irrelevant. These ideas are reflected in the so-called progressive discourse on gender in Spain. Gynocentric feminism, on the other hand, defines women's oppression as the devaluation and repression of women's experience by a masculinist culture that exalts violence and individualism. Women should not be seen as passive or weak since they have contributed to civilisation, resisted oppression, enjoyed their bodies and cultivated the values of care and nurture and communication. This position, called 'the feminism of difference' in Spain, is usually criticised as essentialist.

A gynocentric feminist would approve of the Vigo experiment. Here was an ambitious political programme with evident practical results based on the idea that women can change their lives without entering spaces dominated by men. The programme celebrated women's achievements. It liberated women's energies and fuelled their self-confidence. As many women in Vigo said: 'This is what women *like*!' – pronounced with pride, not resignation.

The experiment does maintain dominant gender categorisation and divisions of labour, and thus power. The feminists on the city council hoped that emancipatory messages would percolate somehow and that the women would communicate with each other, as in the consciousness-raising groups of the feminist movement. Most agreed this had not happened. And the feminist agenda remained hidden. Many of the women organising the courses were uncertain about what they were doing and how to distinguish 'what women like' from 'what keeps women in their place'.

Both gynocentric and humanist feminism challenge present power structures, and both have serious shortcomings in the eyes of the other. Therefore, some criterion for comparison is needed. One way might be to identify what the powers that be find most threatening (Young 1990: 89). In Vigo, a woman president of a neighbourhood association was a true threat, especially if she was also a feminist. A woman town councillor with a feminist programme was an even greater threat. Such women, though few, were sneered at by women and men in the anti-feminist camp. Hundreds or even thousands of women, attending handicraft courses, on the other hand, were seen as a somewhat unusual but still harmless phenomenon.

But if these women were doing something new that would lead them to other activities, ideas and values, then the dichotomy between gynocentrism and humanism might be transcended. One could say that the Vigo programme was gynocentric in the short run as a means, and humanist in the long run as a goal.[24] To distinguish between means and ends, or rather, to adapt strategies to circumstances, is necessary, if we consider that gender is a social construct, not an essence. But it is also necessary to recognise that as things stand, women and men in Spain today – and in most parts of the world – do live different lives and experience differently everything from everyday tasks, to relationships to the body, the self and the individual's place in the world. Women are different from men in practice but this is not a necessary condition. It is evidently changing, in Spain, and it is changing towards greater similarity.

Some areas of life, such as the labour market, are being de-gendered to some extent, though in theory more than in practice. Politics is an area that resists; it is still strongly gender-marked in practice and to a lesser extent in ideology. The neighbourhood movement is a political activity that is defined by many as non-political. This has made it possible for women to join, and learn. Many of them come to redefine their idea of politics; others continue denying that they are involved in politics. In either case, the neighbourhood movement makes it possible for women to enter a male activity without having to first solve the contradiction between their 'femininity' and the 'masculinity' of what they want to do. They can let time pass, allowing their practice to slowly undermine the fixity of gender markers.

Conclusion

Gender orders do not change easily or quickly. Issues are seldom clear-cut. The Vigo example demonstrates that the dichotomy of difference and similarity in feminist debates must be transcended. All four examples show that the organisation of gender in many parts of Spain continues to create formidable obstacles for those who wish to see women and men working together to achieve similar goals. The details and the degree of difficulty vary, as will the methods and solutions. While gender hierarchy and the resulting democratic deficit are general facts in Spain, it is also a fact that they are now questioned by growing numbers of urban Spanish women.

The concept of *barrio* is crucial for analyses of everyday life, political institutions and the organisation of gender in Spain. It is a mediator between the culturally central ideas of private and public and their gendered meanings. It is the main context of daily life for a large portion of the Spanish population, and it is a setting where women, more than men, live and work, and where they can act more forcefully and independently than in other public contexts. Because the *barrio* has this significance, the neighbourhood associations can serve as culturally specific instruments for the redefinition of politics in the direction of issues closer to women's concerns and the shaping of democracy towards more direct participation and the creation of woman-friendly contexts for political work. I do not claim that the neighbourhood movement is a feminist panacea. If anything, doing fieldwork in it dampened my earlier optimism. But I do want to claim that it demonstrates some unusual combinations of opportunities for change of and adaptation to social and cultural facts, including the gender order, and that it is producing small but real and viable results for *barrio* women.

The women of the neighbourhood movement are not feminists, or at least they refuse that label. Their political practice is directed towards the immediate environment. It concerns the social and material conditions of the *barrio*, i.e. of the possibilities for the people they care about to obtain what they (variously) define as a good life. But as they adapt to changing times, searching for new forms of activity, they upset the gender order, and they notice that and define the results as good. In this sense they do become feminists, with or without the label. They negotiate entry into new spaces and then claim more space. Their success varies, and they make mistakes, but their actions undermine the key analogy of woman : house :: man : street.

The steps they take may look small, but there are aggregate consequences. The breadth and depth of the changes these women create come from the fact that they are not a vanguard minority. Activist women are a minority in their *barrios*, but they are so-called 'ordinary' women, and represent a majority when it comes to experiences and life styles. What they do is visible and under-standable (though not always acceptable) for most Spaniards. They push and pull at the naturalised definitions of women and men, private and public, possible and impossible, individual and collec-tive, and demonstrate that what seemed solid actually yields. To people not accustomed to see themselves as agents of social change, this is important news.

Notes

1 Obviously such a long list of issues cannot be fully discussed here. In a short piece like this, one must choose between developing just one or two themes well or suggesting a larger number in a more superficial manner. I have chosen the latter course because the neighbourhood movement is so little known that it needs to be presented in broad terms before it can be analysed more carefully. See also note 2.

2 The fieldwork was carried out between March 1994 and March 1995 in six different towns and cities. I also had previous information on the movement. I was an activist in it myself in the 1970s in Madrid, where I was an ordinary housewife, albeit of foreign extraction, for many years before I moved back to Sweden and became an anthropologist. I also used the neighbourhood association as a point of entry in the *barrio* of Valencia where I did fieldwork in 1982–3, so even though that project was not centred on the association, I gained a good understanding of it and have since then remained in contact with it. A monograph based on the 1994–5 fieldwork is in progress.

3 As it would have to after such fundamental changes in other spheres of life. This sketch is offered only as background. A discussion of the possible causal relationships between different facets of these processes would takes us too far from the main purpose of this article. Likewise, I leave open the question of the extent of change in the gender order. It is changing, that is clear, but it is not so clear if the change is affecting deep cultural premises or only their more superficial expressions.

4 As in the rest of Europe, the tendency as a whole is for homes with only one member to become more common. In 1991, they were 13.4 per cent of the total. However, most of these consist of elderly people. One-member households consisting of persons under the age of 25 represent only 1 per cent of all households. And if we look at percentages of the population, 95.2 per cent of all Spaniards reside with kin of one kind or another (Documentación Social, 1995: 144–7).

5 At least this is true for the working class. Middle-class *barrios* vary more, and middle-class people vary in their orientation. In general, middle-class networks have a wider spatial range.

6 These figures were given to me by CAVE (Confederación de Asociaciones de Vecinos del Estado Español), the confederation office. There were also some associations and federations outside this structure.

7 This type of gender order is not specific for Spain, of course. In Southern Europe, generally, the gender orders have been based on complementarity of roles, separation of spheres and a view of gender as a rigid dichotomy. This has been reinforced by the views of the Roman Catholic Church. So feminists in Southern Europe have very often stressed difference, trying to revalorise femininity rather than question its present expressions. See for instance Librería de Mujeres de Milán 1991, and the work of Luce Irigaray. What *is* special about the Spanish situation is that there is a tension between this tradition and the strong stress on Enlightenment values, fomented by the circumstances of the process of democratisation (Thurén 1988 and forthcoming).

8 *Ollas comunes*, literally 'shared pots', are arrangements in which food is prepared communally in order to save on costs. Usually women do not just do the cooking but most of the organising.

9 I speak of activists, not of members in general, for two reasons. First, it is principally as activists that members influence the movement and are

influenced by it. Second, it is as activists that women represent about half of the movement. This can be seen at meetings, demonstrations, and so on. It is more difficult to calculate the proportion of women members. When it comes to registration of members, the movement vacillates between the 'traditional' view that if a man signs up, all persons in his family are automatically members, but the membership counts as one, not several, and the 'modern' or 'progressive' view that membership should be individual. Therefore, membership figures are difficult to interpret.

10 That in turn has to do with the general view of politics as a male sphere, of course, but 'progressive' women who reject that interpretation often stay away from party politics anyway with the argument that existing parties do not understand or bother with women's issues, or, worse, manipulate them. The acrimonious debate on 'double militancy', i.e. whether feminists could/should also be active in political parties, divided the Spanish women's movement into opposed camps during most of the 1980s and is still a sensitive issue.

11 Women tend to organise on the basis of the *barrio*, not only in the neighbourhood movement, but also when they form groups for other purposes (Cf Maquieira 1995: 290).

12 This figure should be contextualised in many ways for which there is no room here. It varies according to kinds of city and region, there is much unregistered work, and so on. One-fifth was the approximate proportion in the Valencian *barrio* where I did fieldwork in 1983. Since then it has become more common for married women to work until they have their first child, and some are going back to work after the children have grown up. On the other hand, unemployment has grown. Statistics now show that about one-third of all adult women are in the labour market. My data from both Valencia and Madrid indicate that women are indeed eager to enter employment if they can, but it is still very difficult and few have regular jobs over long periods. The typical pattern is rather in-and-out of a variety of activities with intervening periods in unemployment or inactivity.

13 This is a common observation in western feminist political studies and also in many other parts of the world. I have met many Spanish women active in parties and labour unions; most of them are proud of the fact that they have learnt new ways. They often dub them 'more efficient'. But women have been socialised to be more sensitive to particular individuals and their particular characteristics, and usually feel more at home with non-hierarchical, non-formal styles of interaction. Cf. note 12.

14 Many feminist analyses of obstacles to women's participation in ordinary western political contexts focus on such things as hierarchy, formality, imbalance in proportions between women and men in a given context, traditional definition of issues, etc. (See, e.g. Astelarra 1990, Bystydzienski 1992, Davis *et al.* 1991, Feijoó and Herzer 1991, Jones and Jonasdóttir 1988, Women's Studies International Forum 1994).

15 Of course, some women might have felt such a thing but deemed it illegitimate to admit it. To want power was not a very acceptable thing

in the movement. But I did hear some men express such feelings. Outside the movement, in political parties, I also met some women who did. So I am inclined to believe that most movement women really were not moved by any wish for power. I would even affirm that they were seldom conscious of the real, albeit limited, power they did exercise.

16 Similar motives for joining associations – of any kind – are quoted in a study on women's organisations in Madrid (Maquieira 1995).

17 An illustration: one woman told me she wanted to become active. Her husband did not oppose the idea, and her children were old enough, she had the time. She also knew some of the activists, and she had a fairly good idea about what the association was. Still, she found it difficult, because there were no other women active in her association. I thought that she did not want to be the only one, and that was part of the truth, but it was not the important part. She thought many women of her *barrio* might become active very soon, if there was only one to start with. What stopped her was rather a circle that needed breaking. She thought a woman always needs the example, the company and helping hand of another woman in order to enter a male space like politics. She would not mind so much being the only woman once inside (and for a short time), but she did not know how to approach the men in order to enter.

18 One type of course that is becoming very popular with women activists are those that aim at raising 'self-esteem'.

19 I do not want to speculate about any causal relationships between different kinds of places (regional culture, economic structure, size of town, etc.) and women's political participation. Such relationships probably exist, but they are difficult to describe correctly and they are not important here. The important thing – and the reason I did fieldwork in various places – is to show, first, that there *are* variations, and, second, that in spite of these variations, there are certain themes that recur throughout the movement. It is in these similarities, in the midst of variation, that we can expect to find the clues to the overall meaning of women's participation in a movement of these character-istics, and thus to make the Spanish experience relevant for women in other countries, especially for feminist strategy building.

20 And of course in different classes, but since the movement is mainly working class, I will not go into that.

21 PSOE = Partido Socialista Obrero Español = Spanish Workers' Socialist Party. It is the largest party of Spain and governed uninterruptedly and usually with comfortable majorities from 1982 to 1996. PSOE activists were seldom seen in the neighbourhood movement before the mid-1980s but their presence is now growing in a way that has many activists worried.

22 In other parts of Spain, there is usually a barrier between feminist groups and women in *barrio* groups. In part, it is a matter of social distance: feminists tend to be middle class and have higher formal education, on the average. It is also a matter of strategy: most feminists prefer to work only with feminist issues, often considering everything

else a waste of time and/or a risk of being manipulated by male interests; women in the neighbourhood movement are mainly interested in *barrio* issues. *Barrio* women are often under the erroneous impression that feminists hate men and despise housewives. Feminists are often under the erroneous impression that *barrio* women do not criticise the hegemonic gender order at all. *Barrio* women are sometimes feminists but think they will be more politically effective if they do not confess that; feminists sometimes think they ought to work with *barrio* women to help them elevate their consciousness, but they fear that this would be paternalistic behaviour and they feel that they have to clarify their own ideas first, before they can teach anything to anyone else. All of these barriers and difficulties seemed somehow irrelevant in Cordova. I am sure they must have been present, but they were not evident, and they did not impede the collaboration I describe.

23 This has sometimes been interpreted as a matriarchy. Most Spanish feminists do not agree, nor do I. My empirical description here constitutes an implicit argument. See Méndez 1988 for more data and explicit anthropological arguments.

24 A recent and very clear argument for the need of transcending this type of dichotomies is Fraser 1996. See also Fraser 1992 for arguments about how the analysis of discursive struggles can illuminate the cultural aspects of political engagement.

Bibliography

Astelarra, J. (ed.) (1990) *Participación Política de las Mujeres,* Madrid: CIS.

Bystydzienski, J.M. (ed.) (1992) *Women Transforming Politics,* Bloomington and Indianapolis: Indiana University Press.

Castells, M. (1986) *La Ciudad y las Masas. Sociología de los Movimientos Sociales Urbanos,* Madrid: Alianza. (*The City and the Grassroots – A Cross-Cultural Theory of Urban Social Movements,* London: Edward Arnold: London, 1983.)

Davis, K., Leijenaar, M. and Oldersma, J. (eds) (1991) *The Gender of Power,* London: Sage.

Documentación Social (1995) *V Informe Sociológico sobre la situación social en España.*

Feijóo, M.C. and Herzer, H.M. (eds) (1991) *Las Mujeres y la Vida de las Ciudades,* Buenos Aires: Grupo Editor Latinoamericano.

Fraser, N. (1992) 'The uses and abuses of French discourse theories for feminist politics', *Theory, Culture and Society,* 9: 51–71.

Fraser, N. (1996) 'Redistribution or recognition? Rethinking gender equity', *Tanner Lectures 1 and 2,* Stanford University.

Jones, K.B. and Jonasdóttir, A.G. (eds) (1988) *The Political Interests of Gender,* London: Sage.

Librería de Mujeres de Milán (1991) *No Creas Tener Derecho,* Madrid:

Horas y horas (*Non credere di avere dei diritti*, Turin: Rosenberg & Sellier, 1987).

Maquieira, V. (1995) 'Asociaciones de mujeres en la Comunidad Autónoma de Madrid', in M. Ortega López (ed.) *Las Mujeres de Madrid como Agentes de Cambio Social*, Madrid: Instituto Universitario de Estudios de la Mujer, Universidad Autónoma de Madrid.

Méndez, L. (1988) *Cousas de Mulleres*, Barcelona: Anthropos.

Molina, E. (1984) *Los otros Madrileños. El Pozo del Tío Raimundo*, Madrid: Avapiés.

Revilla, M. (ed.) (1994) *Movimientos Sociales, Acción e Identidad*, Zona abierta 69, Madrid: Siglo XXI.

Salida 1 (1989) 'Primeros encuentros internacionales sobre movimientos sociales', Madrid: Facmum.

Salida 2 (Tomás Rodríguez-Villasante, ed.) (1990) 'Asociativa y ciudadana. Textos sobre asociacionismo de Madrid', Madrid: Facmum.

Suárez Clua, R. (ed.) (1987) *Espacio Político del Movimiento Vecinal y del Consumerista en la España Actual*, Madrid: Fundación de Investigaciones Marxistas.

Thurén, B. (1988) *Left Hand Left Behind. The Changing Gender System of a Barrio in Valencia, Spain*, Stockholm: Stockholm Studies in Social Anthropology.

—— (forthcoming) *Women, Men and Persons: Managing Gender Meanings in Middle-Class Madrid*.

Women's Studies International Forum. Special issue (1994) 'Images from women in a changing Europe', 2/3.

Young, I.M. (1990) *Throwing Like a Girl and Other Essays in Feminist Philosophy and Social Theory*, Bloomington and Indianapolis: Indiana University Press.

Chapter 9

The 'old red woman' against the 'young blue hooligan'

Gender stereotyping of economic and political processes in post-communist Bulgaria

Siyka Kovatcheva

Ten years on from the events of 1989 and 1990 marking the beginning of a transition from authoritarian rule towards democracy in Bulgaria, the unanimous acceptance that first greeted these changes has faded. Instead, current public interpretations of the restructuring of the country vary from expressions such as: 'Nothing has changed – we still live in the midst of communism' to 'we live in a permanent situation of change – a never-ending circle in which reforms are reforming previous reforms'.[1] Social theories explaining the emergence of post-communist societies acknowledge the complexities of processes which affected all social spheres: legislative, political, economic, cultural (Darendorf 1990; Offe 1991; Lipset 1994; Genov 1998). But change did not happen evenly and the disjunctures that emerged between different areas of social life fomented generalised feelings of uncertainty regarding the transition as a whole.

A gender perspective to social change in post-communist Bulgaria offers an additional and perhaps a deeper insight into the relationship between cultural constructs and economic and political liberalisation. Fifty years ago the ideological constructs of gender egalitarianism served the political task of legitimising the Communist Party's regime and the economic objective of large-scale industrialisation. Similarly, post-communist reforms mobilise traditional stereotypes and new sentiments to facilitate their own course of action. But beyond representations of womanhood connected with national projects, a focus on gender, and more specifically on women's experiences and public constructions of their role in the transition, sheds light on controversial shifts in the social structure of post-communist society.

This chapter examines the principal gender stereotypes mobilised in the transformation of authoritarian structures in Bulgaria, to reveal both continuity and change in the process. The chapter explores these through the analysis of gender issues within the student movement. The student movement played a major role in the transition, pressing for radical political and economic liberalisation. In the process of participating in these momentous changes, young people shaped and reshaped their individual subjectivities and collective identities. The chapter elaborates on a study[2] carried out by the author between 1992 and 1998 of the values articulated in different moments of student participation in the transition. The chapter discusses the dominant gender constructs current within this important group which will provide the future decision-makers and managers of the post-communist social order.

Large-scale surveys indicate that there are continuing differences in the participation of young men and women in contemporary Bulgarian politics. Although there is consensus regarding gender equality in most fields, there are indications that men in particular adhere to a traditional role for women in the context of the family. The individual accounts of young women and men illustrate the complex and often contradictory notions of change and equality that constitute the discourse of student and, more widely, Bulgarian political mobilisation. While young people as a whole expect that the transition to democracy will bring more opportunities for both genders, they have different expectations as to their own self-realisation in the spheres of the economy, the political and the private sphere. A more nuanced analysis of gender attitudes among students is therefore necessary in order to understand their divergent experiences and aspirations during the time of transition.

Gender and age stereotyping during economic and political liberalisation

In the first years following the collapse of the communist regime Bulgarian society witnessed a deep emotional polarisation across all social strata, causing divisions within families and professional groups. Family ties and group solidarities were eroded by the pressure of claims to allegiance either to the 'old' or to the 'new' regime. In an over-politicised reality people's constructions of their experiences gave rise to gender and age stereotyping – a fact which reveals much about the new social order of post-communism. The contradiction between one-party rule with a command economy and multi-party governance with a market-based economy was presented through contrasting images of the 'old red woman' and the 'young blue hooligan'. Both were negative cultural emblems, mutually attributed by competing sides. Thus the 'old red woman' was used as a label to identify defenders of the Bulgarian Socialist (former Communist) Party (BSP) and the 'young blue hooligan' became a symbol for the supporters of the newly formed Union of Democratic Forces (UDF). Both images emerged from the mass demonstrations organised by the main factions of the new political arena. For example, in two of the popular songs from the UDF election campaign in 1991 the Socialist Party was compared with an ageing, no-longer loved woman. In this way, the political controversy was pictured not only through differing colours but also, and more meaningfully, in terms of gender and age.

Opinion polls established a clear-cut age difference between supporters of the two major political actors, that of the UDF being much younger than that of the BSP (Tonchev and Jordanova 1991). A major role in the construction of age and gender political images was played by the media which experienced a boom after tight state controls on the press were lifted and enthusiastically captured the sense of changing scenarios and the high emotional intensity. Pensioners who were among the first to suffer from inflation and the overall economic crisis dominated the meetings of the Socialist Party; images of angry old women banging empty pans were popularised by television and newspaper coverage. But the most vocal critics of the authorities, still represented by the reformed communists, were young people represented by the media through images of male youths at the street blockades. Underlying the portrayal of these two images were particular interpretations of the political and economic changes, shared on both sides of the controversy.

One of the features to emerge from this was the new political space defined as more suited to men, as suggested by the tactics used by the new political parties. Although these parties attempted to work through state institutions, they predominantly used non-institutional channels to exert political pressure. The mass protests – blocking main crossroads, storming the Communist Party's headquarters, the hunger strikes in the 'Towns of Truth'[3] – were very confrontational and were seen as a forceful and hence a typically

male and youthful form of political expression. The Socialist Party
tried to associate itself with a more tolerant image, represented by a
figure who operated within democratic institutions rather than
outside them. The image of an ageing woman used to represent
supporters of the Socialist Party was grounded in the generous
social policy of the communist regime towards underprivileged
social groups – women and the elderly. With the turn toward
democracy, the programmes targeting women as mothers, endow-
ing them with long maternity leaves while keeping their jobs in the
state economy, were perceived as privileges comparable to those of
the hated party '*nomenclatura*'. Thus women came to be seen as
having a vested interest in the preservation of the centrally planned
economy. Current gender stereotypes promoted by party programmes and the media represent women as opposed to liberalisation, prompted by nostalgia for the stability and security of
totalitarianism.

In this way the new political and economic spaces created by the
withdrawal of the state were seen as suitable arenas for the activities
of men and preferably those young enough to be relatively unspoilt
by the communist regime and with the largest reserves of 'natural
energy' to carry out the reforms. Public opinion treated young
women as irrelevant to the new politics – as women they could not
be supporters of the new democratic parties and being young they
could not be full supporters of the 'old' socialist party. Numerous
'facts' supported these assumptions. There were no young women
(under the age of 30) in parliament, neither were they visible in the
youth sections of the political parties. The new opportunities
offered by the market economy were also perceived as irrelevant to
young women. Women comprise a third of the self-employed and
only a fifth of the employers in post-communist Bulgaria (National
Statistical Institute 1997: 49). Furthermore, a comparative study of
women entrepreneurs (Kotzeva and Todorova 1994) found the
Bulgarian group was not only smaller but also older on average
than their Canadian counterparts.

The intermingling of cultural constructs of gender and age is not
an entirely new phenomenon in Bulgarian public life. Its roots can
be traced to pre-industrial society. In the nineteenth century, male
children in farming and craftsmen's families were treated as clan
reproducers and future members while girls were considered to be
only temporary members as they left their father's clan at marriage
(Bobchev 1907). At marriage the young woman received no

inheritance and could only 'take the things she had produced with her own hands, that is, only rags' (Odzakov 1895). While there could be some respect for adult married women as their husbands' informal labour partners, having an important role in the family economy, young women could at best expect to receive care and patronage. The power hierarchy in traditional society is revealed in the following age and gender gradation offered by the sociologist Ivan Khadzijski (1974: 207):

[In the pre-industrial] Bulgarian town it was impossible to see anyone strolling along the streets on a working day – impossible for a boy, even more impossible for a woman, and the most impossible for a girl.

Changes in the social order, starting with the establishment of the one-party regime after the Second World War included the transformation of age and gender relations. The official communist ideology portrayed young people as the builders of a bright future and followed egalitarian principles by showing as many women – for example as tractor-drivers and turners – as men in the state-controlled media. The centrally planned economy needed the female labour force as much as the socialist family needed women's income. In the factories young women were the preferred source of labour because of their lower cost. Bulgarian women worked shoulder to shoulder with men, becoming a basic agent of the 'socialist road' to industrialisation. At the start of communist reforms, in 1951, the number of women working in industry was three and a half times lower than that for men; in 1969 they constituted nearly half of the labour force and more than half of these were young women (Semov 1972: 58). However, in spite of these changes women were concentrated in the lower-paid, less technically developed and lower-status jobs. Similarly, within the pyramid of political power women occupied the lower levels and had little influence on decision making because this was strongly centralised under the one-party regime, which was predominantly male.

Bulgarian women were not fully enfranchised until communism, as late as 1946, in sharp contrast with the political rights granted to men as early as 1879 by the first Constitution of the newly liberated state, when Bulgaria became the fourth country in Europe to introduce 'universal suffrage' (for men only). Under communism the political participation of women was a major factor in the legitimisation of the regime. Women were involved in all forms of political activities – as members of political organisations, as participants in all political campaigns, meetings and demonstrations, marches and delegations. The social sciences in Bulgaria reacted by coining the term 'the triple social role' of women in society to describe women's activities as a mother-wife, worker and political activist (Kjuranov 1982).

Young women were even more involved in representative politics than older women. Nearly all of them became members of the *Komsomol*, the only political youth organisation under state socialism in Bulgaria, which had the highest membership of all the corresponding organisations in the former Soviet block countries. The participation of young people from the age of 14 until the age of 28 was the norm and it was obligatory for those planning to enter into higher education because the so-called '*Komsomol* characteristics' or reference were an essential requirement for acceptance by a university.

While young women represented half of the membership of the *Komsomol*, they were not well represented on its governing bodies – a tendency that reflected the situation of women in the ruling Communist Party. Women *Komsomol* leaders tended to be concentrated in the lower ranks of the organisation whilst the higher offices were dominated by men. Women were in a majority at the lower levels of the organisation, the so-called 'organisational-methodological cadres', and the paid staff of the 'pioneer organisation'. The proportion of women among the higher ranking 'organisational-political cadres' was much lower and they were concentrated in the lower grades and positions, such as regional committees rather than the Central Committee (Kitanov 1981: 47). The recruitment of young women as *Komsomol* officers served the ideological goals of the party rather than being a response to a conscious personal choice or public recognition of women's political potential. In general, the obligatory participation in the 'youth political organisation' reflected the powerlessness of youth in a gerontocratic communist society and this powerlessness was especially marked in the case of young women.

Post-communist Bulgaria attempted to break with the previous ideological tradition. Yet just as authoritarian economic and political practices coexist with liberal mechanisms, so too the 'traditional' and 'modern' cultural models of gender roles and age relationships continue to exist side by side. How is the controversy between the 'old red woman' and the 'young blue hooligan' influencing the current social transformation? How are the complexities of the transformation experienced by the people – men and women, elderly and young – involved in them? In search of answers to these questions this chapter analyses the values and strategies of university students during the first ten years of post-communist reforms in Bulgaria.

The framing of the transition by the student movement in Bulgaria

Student mobilisation occurred at all crucial stages of the transition towards pluralistic politics. The regime change in Bulgaria started on 10 November 1989, as a reshuffle at the top, when Zhivkov, the oldest and longest-serving communist leader in Europe was removed from his post both as General Secretary of the party and as President of the country by a reform-minded group within the party. The old elite planned to carry out the inevitable institutional restructuring according to its own design and interests, keeping the main positions in the political hierarchy under the new conditions of party pluralism. But the collective action of various social groups foiled these plans for limited democratisation. The student movement was prominent among them.

The student 'chains' around the parliament in 1989, the two nation-wide waves of occupations of university buildings in 1990, the road blockades in the winter months of 1997 all promoted radicalisation and the transfer of power from the old to the new political elite. Joining the wider democratic movement in the country, student protests resulted in no less than one change of president (in 1990) and two changes of governments (in 1990 and 1997). The conditions and the resources of the movement (Kovatcheva 1995b) favoured non-violent tactics promoted by the framing contests between the opposing sides.[4]

From the start, student mobilisation involved specific constructs of social reality to support their activism by frame alignment processes. Reality interpretation during the protest wave, which McAdam (1990) conceptualises as 'the phenomenology of social protest', was very important for the loosely structured student movement, as it provided a basis for better co-ordination and a stronger sense of belonging. The Bulgarian student movement showed its activists' ability to define the current social circumstances as unjust and in need of change and pointed to a shift in political opportunities that were favourable for collective action.

Collective protests had powerful symbolic value for students defending their right to political dissent. The new experience of the 'strikes', as the students named the occupations, unthinkable during communism, was for them a search for self-expression and individuality. As Stephan, the leader of the Green Balkans which was a student environmental association in Plovdiv and amongst the first dissident groups in Bulgaria, explained: 'We were tired of being equal with faces as grey as the concrete roads and buildings around us. We wanted to be recognised as still alive, with various faces and thoughts behind them.'

The master frame of students' demands was 'the change of the system' – the complete break with the authoritarian past and the creation of a new liberal society. Young people insisted on a repeal of the constitutional clause designating Bulgaria a socialist country and proclaiming the leading role of the Communist Party (in December 1989), on the resignation of the president of the Socialist Party, on the exposure of irregularities during the first elections, and demanded a greater concern for morality in politics (in June and July 1990). They also demanded the resignation of the socialist government, university autonomy and student representation at all levels of academic governance (in November–December 1990). The leaders of the UDF openly supported the students' protests, declaring that their claims were 'a manifestation of very mature civic thinking' (*Democracia*, 3 July 1990). The Socialist Party elite engaged in disputes with the movement, without directly confronting it. In their speeches the party leaders hinted that the movement was manipulated by the opposition parties. Student tactics were declared 'undemocratic' and accused of creating a needless conflict with an 'unfavourable effect for the life in the country' (*Duma*, 28 June 1990). It was in these framing contests that the fusion of age and gender stereotyping emerged. Protesting students using unruly tactics were defined as hooligans. On their part, the students accused the Socialist Party of being 'old', 'rotten' and 'immoral', incapable of carrying out the radical reforms needed by the country.

While the student movement in Bulgaria did not explicitly use the image of the 'old red woman' in its interpretative processes, they often framed the transition as a 'conflict between generations'. A particular concern of the activists, and one about which they felt most strongly, was the fact that unlike other Eastern European countries such as Hungary, Czechoslovakia or Poland, there had not been any mass revolt against the communist system in Bulgaria. As Dimitar,[5] a member of the first occupational committee at the University of Plovdiv put it:

Only in our country were there no events to show that the old were against communism – such as the Prague Spring in 1968, or the Hungarian revolt in 1956, or the strikes of Solidarity in Poland. There was no open protest, not even the slightest attempt – nothing to wipe the shame from their faces . . . Even now – look who voted for the Socialist Party – all the old people led by fear of the unknown. This fear is their inertia, their incurable habit . . . There should be a long wandering in the wilderness before all those born in slavery have died, as in the Bible, before true democracy can be born afresh.

While accepting this interpretation of the events in 1990, it should be mentioned that when speaking about their own parents, young people were tolerant and sympathetic and did not admit to any bitter family conflicts. The activist cited above even claimed to have convinced all his family to vote for the Union of Democratic Forces.

The first wave of protest continued with varying intensity until the victory of the Union of Democratic Forces in the second general elections in October 1991, followed by the victory of the UDF leader in the direct presidential elections in January of that year. With the transfer of power in such important institutions as the presidency and the government into the hands of new pro-democracy parties completed, student activism became more subdued and turned towards educational issues. Membership of student groups declined, the UDF started to fragment, and the BSP grew in strength, as economic problems became more acute. Several mass demonstrations by pensioners were organised in 1992

and 1993 against the UDF government to protest against both the
meagreness and the system of allocation of state pensions. Now it
was the UDF's turn to accuse the opposition of manipulating
collective action. However, there was no attempt to draw direct
comparisons between the pensioners' campaigns and the earlier
activities of the student movement. With the fragmentation of
political elites, the clear-cut polarisation that had characterised the
interpretations of change weakened, as did the confrontation
between the older and the younger generations.

In early 1997 young people responded to an increasingly
difficult situation through various forms of collective action
throughout the country. This was decisive in that it revealed the
inadequacy of the government to tackle the complexities of the
transition and contributed to the collapse of the socialist government that had been in place since the elections of 1994. The
target of the protest appeared to be the same as during the first
mobilisation – the old elite – but this time the framing of events
was different in a significant way. Although the protest was highly
confrontational, using unruly tactics such as road blockades that
paralysed towns and cities, or storming parliament and demanding
the resignation of the government, there was no contrast drawn
between generations or sexes. Achieving a national consensus for
radical reforms was the new master frame of collective protest after
a decade of fruitless political struggles. Mariana, a young female
student who participated in these events explained: 'We were
jumping[6] not against one party, but against total destruction and
impoverishment, against the irresponsibility and fraud implanted
in one type of politics' (Plovdiv University Newspaper, March
1997: 3).

In their interviews young people warned 'the politicians': 'Don't
paint the interests in Bulgaria in political colours! Professionalism is
without a colour, an attitude above the parties' interests, of concern
for people's destinies' (Mitev 1997).

Instead of mobilising the earlier gendered and age-based forms
of representation, the students now focused on gaining wide public
support, for example pointing to the food and milk brought by old
women from the nearby villages (see for example Plovdiv
University Newspaper, February 1997: 4). The sharp economic
crisis with bread shortages, bank closures and an inflation rate of
300 per cent, was defined as the disintegration of society and a
threat to all social groups. The activists of the movement offered

one very successful framing – the threat of emigration. Popular slogans on street marches and barricades were: 'We are the students, we are the change. We want to live in Bulgaria.' The protests were directed against the disastrous rule of the Socialist Party that forced young people to leave the country, and against the general collapse of society. In this way gender or age oppositions in the movement's framing became irrelevant. Anna, who participated in the 1997 protests explained:

> We all share the same plight. Men and women are equally disadvantaged by low salaries and rising prices. It is true that the old look back with nostalgia to the past while the young look with envy toward the western style of living. But only united efforts will allow people to live normally in this country.

So the public euphoria during the first years of the transition, born from expectations of rapid improvement, brought forth inter-pretations of the change represented by the contrasting images of different ages, genders and colours. Ten years later the sentiments of the mobilisation changed notably: discontent overtook hopes, economic anxieties overtook political concerns while all individuals felt equally threatened by the inability of the state to solve the mounting problems. The old red woman did not regain the lost security and social order of the overturned authoritarian society. But the young blue hooligan was no more successful: society was changing without offering more opportunities for the young, neither professional realisation nor personal self-expression, as living standards were unable to return to their pre-reform level of 1989.

Notions of gender equality among Bulgarian students

Considering survey data from 1992 and 1995 (Kovatcheva 1995b), it seems that students at Bulgarian universities share an acceptance of gender equality, especially when their opinions about gender roles are compared with their opinions regarding other issues identified in the questionnaire. Relations between men and women were among the topics that elicited the highest score with regard to strongly expressed opinions, coming second only to the concern for peace. An interest in politics and confidence in political institutions, for example, elicited answers that were much less clearly defined. Gender relations were also among the issues where there was the greatest extent of unanimity. Consensus was highest on matters of women's rights and the preservation of nature, while opinions were most polarised when it came to evaluating the political leadership and in relation to the issue of whether Bulgaria should join the European Union.

That issues relating to gender roles and to the environment should meet with the highest scores for consensus among students was not accidental. Environmental issues inspired the first mass protests of Bulgarian students under state socialism. An example of this is provided by the march of students from the University of Plovdiv, who carried strings of dead birds around the town in protest at the government's campaign in the summer of 1988 to reduce the population of voles through poisoning, which also killed many wild animals and birds. One consequence of this was the formation of the student organisation 'Green Balkans'. The 1989 protest of young mothers in the town of Rouse claiming the need for clear air for their babies could be considered as the start of an open demonstration of discontent with state policy. After Chernobyl there were growing concerns about the important links between environmental pollution and women's ill health (Petrova 1993: 29).

When student opinions regarding gender roles are examined in more detail, we see the consensus is not unproblematic. Students were most definite in their support of women's professional potential and the need for spouses to share housework. Large majorities in the 1992 and 1995 surveys disagreed with the statement that 'A woman can never make a good surgeon' and accepted the statements that 'Housework is men's responsibility as much as it is women's' and 'It doesn't matter who earns more money in the family'. Nine out of ten students accepted that women's professional abilities were similar to those of men. However, the commitment to gender equality was shattered when it came to considering the importance of the family. Only a fifth of the respondents in both surveys strongly disagreed with the statement that 'Women's fulfilment in life is their home and children'.

Table 9.1 Student attitudes to gender roles, 1992

% agree	1992	1995
Housework is equally the responsibility of men and women	75.0	79.8
It doesn't matter who earns more money in the family	76.3	73.2
Women's main fulfilment in life is through their home and children	41.7	40.8
A woman can never make a good surgeon	12.5	10.1

Survey data suggests that students in post-communist Bulgaria accept the role of women as the equal of men in business but they consider 'the family' as the most significant sphere in women's life. This attitude can be associated with the special place of the family under the authoritarian regime. The home was an anti-political space where people could fully express themselves in a situation in which all public activities were strictly regulated by the Communist Party and its official organisations such as the Youth League (the *Komsomol*) and the Fatherland Front (a mass organisation encompassing all people according to their place of residence).

With the persistence of economic difficulties during the transition, the family acquired a new importance as an institution for pooling resources in the struggle for survival. In this situation the efforts of men and women to maintain family stability in a collapsing social world appear – and not only to students – as a crucial area of fulfilment in life. Old gender stereotypes are mobilised to address this need. Nedka, a woman student specialising in pedagogy explained: 'Men are not equal to women when it comes to endurance, resourcefulness and inventiveness. Only a woman can make something out of nothing. Growing poverty makes this ability even more valuable.'

The survey data indicate that women and men tend to diverge in their opinions regarding gender equality to a much greater extent than on any other subject. Undoubtedly, women show much stronger commitment to gender equality than men. This raises the question as to why egalitarian ideas about women's rights are not so widespread among male students. And then, do women students make any efforts to defend and extend their citizenship rights?

Women's participation in higher education

At present women constitute one-half of all students in Bulgarian universities and higher education institutions and 54 per cent of the labour force with higher education (*Statistical Yearbook* 1995). This statistical equality within the educational system was achieved during communism following a long period of public debate, educational reforms and political changes.

During Bulgaria's early modernisation drive primary education was made obligatory in 1891. However, absenteeism from schools continued until the Second World War when 50 per cent of school-age children in villages and 75 per cent of peasant girls were still not in attendance (Chakarov 1975: 348). Thus in 1940 the rate of illiterate young women was considerably higher than that of illiterate young men and twice as many young men were in higher education than women. Men outnumbered women in secondary education until the middle of the century and women were only allowed into university in 1901. Arguments against women's participation in higher education were based on formal and moral grounds: female secondary education did not meet the standards required by the university and there were concerns about young women and men studying side by side. On the eve of the Second World War the female student population was only one-third of the male university student population. However, by 1965 (after twenty years of communist regime) women actually gained numerical superiority over men in higher education (Semov 1972: 59). Furthermore, women students enjoyed the right to paid maternity leave, child allowances, accessible day care for small children, and the right to free abortion.

During the first five years of democratic reforms in the 1990s, Bulgaria's higher education experienced an unprecedented expansion during which two new universities were founded each year and the subsidiaries of older institutions in smaller towns multiplied. In this period student numbers more than doubled as people took up the opportunities offered in the private universities and the forms of self-paid studies offered by the state universities.

Table 9.2 illustrates the constant increase in the number of newly enrolled students in Bulgaria, particularly in part-time studies (correspondence courses). Women are the principal beneficiaries of the expansion in part-time studies, as they constitute about 70 per cent of students engaged in such courses. Interview data from

Table 9.2 Newly enrolled students in higher education

Students	1990/91	1991/92	1992/93	1993/94	1994/95
Total	31,205	33,388	41,511	44,420	48,422
Regular training	22,254	24,130	26,702	28,702	30,850
Part-time training	8,231	9,130	14,643	16,241	17,572
Female students	14,901	19,923	26,150	27,307	29,782
Female, regular	2,935	13,767	15,608	16,056	17,678
Female, part-time	5,274	6,075	10,399	11,251	12,104

Bulgarian students in 1997 sheds light on the young women's motivation: 'A woman needs more education because she is physically weak and not well suited for manual labour . . .' (Neli). 'Men leave the educational system earlier because they have to work and earn money while it is natural for the parents to support their daughters for longer . . .' (Ivan). 'Women make more efforts and achieve greater success in education because after that they meet more difficulties in the sphere of work – I mean when they search for jobs or want to get a promotion' (Elena).

These 'explanations' of the complete reversal of traditional practice, according to which the male child continued into higher education, nevertheless reveal the continuity of gender stereotyping of women as weak and dependent. There is also a recognition of the discrimination women can expect to face after leaving the university – in the labour market and in their working careers.

The current transition towards a market economy disempowers women students in one important aspect: it makes them more dependent on their parents by concentrating them in the self-paid rather than in the state-funded sectors of higher education (paying fees for higher education is a new practice introduced after the collapse of the communist welfare state). Survey data from 1995 show that while women as a group had the same sources of income as men (parents' support, state stipend, part-time jobs), they were much more likely to rely on their parents and were far less likely to have access to income through part-time work. Women were twice as likely to study in the so-called paid forms of education in contrast with forms that were fully financed by the state. Women students' lack of autonomy was further intensified by the high inflation that accompanied the economic restructuring that also undermined child benefits and student stipends. Furthermore, the lengthily discussed legislation aimed at introducing a system for state loans for education was postponed.

In the post-communist labour market women who are more highly qualified than men constitute the majority of the un-employed (64 per cent in 1993 and 54 per cent in 1998). The prospect of unemployment was a major source of concern for women students, as interview data indicate, and forced them to lower their career aspirations, directing them towards 'more realistic goals'. 'I would like to start an academic career but I don't think there will be any openings. That is why I am taking additional courses in pedagogy as there are still jobs for teachers in my home town' said Svetla, a psychology student at Sofia University and a member of the organising committee of the Independent Student Union. Daniela, who studied law at Plovdiv University and was a member of its Academic Council, declared that she had given up making any plans so as not to be dis-appointed afterwards.

After the first wave of student strikes in 1990, the authorities agreed to student representation (of 33 per cent) at all levels of the university-elected bodies. But by 1997 the students' presence on these bodies was reduced to less than 10 per cent. When con-fronted with this, academic authorities resorted to explanations in terms of student apathy about the problems of higher education at the local level. In fact, the data outlined in Table 9.3 shows strong motivation by young people to participate in university governance in 1995. Between four fifths and two thirds of students expressed approval of student involvement in questions relating to the distribution of state stipends, to educational plans and to faculty promotion.

Women tended to support all forms of student involvement more often than men yet there were fewer women students in the ruling bodies of the universities. This reflected the limited presence of women amongst the leadership of the student organisations.

At the universities included in the research there were two types of student organisations: one formed 'from below' in confrontation with university authorities and the other constituted 'from above', encouraged (in some cases inspired) by university authorities. Organisations of the first type were involved in more violent forms

Table 9.3 Approval* of student participation in forms of university
governance

Forms	Men	Women	Total
Faculty promotion	53.0	70.4	60.8
Educational plans	78.6	84.0	81.5
Scientific plans	36.8	46.2	43.2
Stipend distribution	74.3	83.4	79.0

*Percentages of those approving 'fully' or 'somewhat'.

of activities. At the Agricultural University in Plovdiv both student organisations belonged to this type. They organised occupations of the university buildings at least twice a year from 1990 to 1994. At Plovdiv University student organisations belonged to the second type and were involved in various committees dealing with student issues. Here the occupational committees from the protest waves of 1990 failed to establish an organisation and the first dissident organisation in the town, the Green Balkans, turned their attention to more narrowly defined environmental issues. At the universities in Sofia both types of student organisation were present in each case study and only the Business University 'senate' had representatives from all the associations.

The role of women in these organisations was very limited. There was no organisation defining itself as feminist, nor were there any claims put forward regarding specifically women's interests. Furthermore, there were few women in the ruling bodies of the fifteen organisations included in the research. Women formed the majority of the leadership only in the section of BDM (the heir of the former *Komsomol*) at Plovdiv University in 1992 but by 1994 this organisation had dissolved and in 1995 the new student union which replaced it had no women among its leadership. Women were practically absent from the leadership of the more confrontational organisations. There was not a single woman in the councils of the student organisations at the Agricultural University in 1992 and only in 1995 was a woman leader elected when one of the organisations turned to more moderate activity based on co-operation. Albena, the woman leader of the Alternative, one of the student organisations at the Agricultural University, claimed:

There is a real competition now within the Alternative. So that was how I became the leader. The time of the confrontation with the authorities to show mere strength is over. As is the time when a handful of *Komsomol* leaders could command an organisation of millions. We are an assemblage of personalities and there is real competition. We are individuals and any one can become a leader. The difference between us and the previous leadership is the intellectual level. Then impersonal figures were commanding masses of discontented people. Now we raise initiatives and discuss them with other students, we negotiate with authorities and win through conviction.

Research carried out in 1992 and 1995 indicates that students did not play an effective role in decision making at the university. Ordinary students and activists alike considered that they made little impact on the functioning of higher education and the life of their own institutions. Most decisions were made prior to the assemblies and students were merely invited to vote for them. Everywhere it was rare for an issue to be raised by the students (whether male or female) for inclusion in the agenda of the meetings. Where university authorities encouraged the election of women activists to the Academic Councils and Assemblies it was because they were members of organisations that were considered to be less confrontational and inclined to pursue student interests through more peaceful methods. In the student organisations themselves women were mainly present in the leadership of those that had been founded by and functioned with the consent and often support of the university authorities.

The political participation of women students

The absence of a significant presence of women in the governing bodies of the university system is congruent with women's attitudes and behaviour in the wider world of politics. Following the distinction suggested by Barnes *et al.* (1979) between conventional and unconventional political participation, I will examine the characteristics of women's political behaviour in the context of Bulgarian student politics.

The first and most obvious statement is that women students were not active in the sphere of conventional, institutional politics. At the four universities included in the 1992 and 1995 studies, there were a few women who declared themselves to be members of the Socialist Party while men showed a wider range of party affiliation. Female students rarely admitted an involvement in political party campaigns. This lack of political activity by young women was consistent with their voting behaviour. While young people in general were more likely to vote for the new, anti-communist parties in the first general elections (see Tonchev and Jordanova 1991: 9), young women were less likely to go to the polls than young men. Data from the 1992 and 1995 surveys indicate that a higher percentage of female students were unwilling to vote and were more uncertain of their party choice than male students. Men were twice as likely to vote for the two largest parties as women, but women respondents were just as unlikely to support the smaller parties. On the hotly debated issue of the structure of the post-communist state, women declared they would vote in a referendum to decide on a republican or a monarchical system, but were more undecided about their stance on this issue.

Women students were more disappointed with mainstream politics than men were, they expressed less interest in politics and less confidence in political institutions and political leaders. According to the interviews, women students tended to view politics as a 'dirty business', with parties and their leadership primarily preoccupied with the struggle for power. Milena was an activist from the student union at Sofia University. She explained:

We used to discuss politics a lot at the beginning – in 1989, 1990. At home and when talking with friends, everything seemed so exciting, so thrilling with the new experiences and bright prospects. Now the new politicians have proved that they think only about themselves, about their egoistic interests rather than about the common people. They still come to the university and organise meetings followed by discos but they will do nothing for the students. They are coming only for our support. I didn't even vote in the past election.

Women students were no longer enthusiastic about the multi-party politics of post-communism. Nor did they compensate for this with greater involvement in social activism outside the major political institutions, for example in protest politics.

A brief history of student politics in Bulgaria

Student activism in Bulgaria started soon after the foundation of the first university in Sofia at the end of the nineteenth century. At the time women actively participated in student campaigns. The most prominent student protest in the first half of this century – when the Bulgarian Knjaz was mockingly whistled at in front of the National Theatre on 3 January 1907[7] – provoked a fierce reaction from the government. Among measures such as the closure of the university for a whole year and a tax increase that limited access of working-class and peasant youth to university education, was the banning of women from higher education to prevent them from participating in political protests (Arnaudov 1939). Opposition newspapers at the time commented that the exclusion of women was unfounded, bearing no relationship to women's presence in the protests. In fact at the time male students outnumbered women by ten to one. However, the government's reaction was indicative of the political elite's inclination to interpret civic activity as a consequence of 'the demoralisation at the university', and to associate this loss of morals with particular gender stereotypes.

The communist take-over brought all independent student activity to an abrupt halt. Any initiative that was not authorised by and channelled through the official youth organisation was stigmatised. *Komsomol* officials persecuted attempts to develop autonomous activities even when these were consistent with party policy. This was the case with the demonstration by secondary school pupils in the town of Stara Zagora in support of the state's anti-nuclear campaign. The young participants made the mistake of not organising their protest through the *Komsomol* (Mitev 1988). The dissident activity of the young in Bulgaria generally took the form of youth sub-cultures or campaigns over environmental issues. There were also informal clubs for discussing various problems, ranging from the arts to morality and *'samizdat'*[8] publications. However, the major dissident organisations prevented young people from playing significant roles for fear of 'ruining their future'. Women dissidents were less visible than men and occupied less important positions, a pattern that is also characteristic of such movements in other Eastern European countries (Einhorn 1993).

From the beginning of the transition, young people constituted the majority of those involved in the spontaneous demonstrations. Women students participated in the two nationwide waves of occupations of university buildings in 1990. However, they represented less than a fourth of the members of the occupation committees (Kovatcheva 1995b). Their participation was heavily sexualised as had been the case with women in the sub-cultures during the period of communist rule (Pilkington 1992). For example in 1992 Mladen, the leader of the BDM (the organisation that was heir to the *Komsomol*), claimed to have seen 'girls coming out of the seminar rooms with unbuttoned blouses. Who knows what those staging the occupation did at night in the empty building!'

This observation was confirmed by the data from the second survey five years after the start of the reforms. Fewer women claimed to have participated in student protest (31.7 per cent of women compared with 43.9 per cent of men) and were more likely to disapprove of student tactics, preferring non-violent forms such as petitions.

In 1997, women students joined the mass mobilisation. They participated in the marches and meetings, in the street shows and television discussions. This time the media did not suggest gender-based interpretations of the events. In the only research on this particular campaign known to me (Mitev 1997) gender differences did not emerge as an issue. The principal opposition here was between the corrupt and inefficient party and the students or the young as a whole. One year after the winter strikes and blockades, Tiljo a student from the Union of Independent Students at Plovdiv University, commented:

Table 9.4 Forms of student protest

Forms	Women	Men
Petition	91.9	85.1
Demonstration	91.7	92.4
Occupation	42.8	53.1
Hunger strike	21.4	27.8

*Percentages of those approving 'fully' or 'somewhat'.

The strike and civic disobedience campaign are not the standard way to act and to stabilise the situation in Bulgaria. On the contrary – it is always better to work through negotiations, peaceful means and serious dialogue to tackle problems and take the right solution. But when the politicians prove to be headstrong and worthless, there is no other way left. I consider that the students very seriously influenced the ousting of the BSP government. Just think what would have happened if this government had not fallen. I clearly remember the wrath in the eyes of the protestors.

(Plovdiv University Newspaper, February 1998: 4)

There were some very bright women among those interviewed in my research. None of them believed there was a need to express specifically 'women's interests'. They were preoccupied with their professional development, which they did not see as different from those of men. They relied on the accumulation of knowledge and skills offered by the university to prepare them for the hardships of the labour market. They envisaged the labour market as equally hostile to women and men graduates and saw no useful role for a women's organisation to help in the transition from the university to the labour market. At the same time, the majority of women students were more disillusioned with all forms of organised activity, although this feeling was common among all students and the majority favoured spontaneous campaigns rather than the routinised practice of organisations.

Conclusion

In the course of the transition from authoritarian rule to a democratic society in Bulgaria, cultural contests were consistent with confrontations over political and economic issues. Conservative gender ideologies derived from traditional agricultural society combined with egalitarian ideals promoted during communism and a range of liberal notions about individual enterprise in market-based society. The deconstruction of the values that prevailed among university students reveals that behind their emphatic acceptance of gender equality there are controversial interpretations concerning the nature and meaning of equality. Not only the 'old' university authorities and party leaders, but also male students are less inclined to accept women's full citizenship rights than women themselves. On the other hand women students are not willing to struggle for their rights.

They are less interested in and more disappointed with mainstream politics than men; they are not eager to participate in governing their immediate environment, the university, but have a greater presence in the elected governing bodies than in the student organisations formed during the months of the unruly student protest. This suggests that quotas for women in the power hierarchy should not be dismissed as merely a 'totalitarian state practice'. Rather than wait for self-made 'superwomen' (Corrin 1992), it would be more effective to use such strategies to encourage women's presence in decision-making bodies at the institutions in which they study and work. When women do become involved in organisations or university governance, they favour more peaceful, non-violent forms of intervention than the men. The experiences of women students in Bulgarian universities suggest then that women can make a difference in post-communist politics by influencing the direction of decision making towards greater tolerance and non-violence in conflict resolution.

The analysis of gender stereotypes within the process of Bulgaria's social transformation indicates that cultural constructs are used to promote and facilitate economic and political change. The impassioned political confrontation of the first years of reforms was portrayed as a contest between the old red woman and the young blue hooligan. More subtle forms of gender distinctions, reflecting shifts in public perception later replaced this form of gender and age opposition. Now people are no longer faced with the monolithic authoritarian state and feel free to pursue their own interests. However, in the major restructuring of the social fabric that is taking place, symbolically potent gender images are still used, this time to limit women's activity to the private sphere and leave more space for men in the politics and economy of post-communism.

Sentiments are mobilised by encouraging an anti-communist rejection of the gains that women obtained under communism in the work sphere and the political arena and by promoting both 'memories' from the pre-communist past and idealised Western models. The relationship between cultural visions and economic and political reforms discloses the reformers' inclination to limit and contain the liberalisation of social life. This in turn diminishes the prospects for a successful end to the cherished transition to a market-based economy and to a system of democratic governance.

Notes

1 These opinions were given in interviews conducted by the author with students and faculty at Bulgarian universities in the spring of 1996 when the economic crisis in Bulgaria took a new turn. After six years of reforms introducing market mechanisms people were waiting in long queues to buy bread made of grain imported from war-stuck Yugoslavia.

2 The inquiry in 1992 was supported by the Research Support Scheme of the Central European University (Grant No. 334/93) and a version of the research report was published in Kovatcheva (1995a). The same design was applied in the 1995 study supported by the MacArthur Research and Writing Grant (Kovatcheva 1995b).

3 The Towns of Truth were tent camps built in the squares of large cities where the protestors against the victory of the Socialist Party in the first multi-party elections stayed, claiming that the results had been fabricated. It was common practice for the MPs of the UDF, when coming out of the parliamentary discussions, to go to the nearby tent city to join the protests against the parliament dominated by the socialists.

4 Framing is understood as 'the process of assigning a particular interpretation to an event or condition' (Snow *et al.* 1986). It is part of the symbolic struggle in which both the challengers and their opponents are engaged. The cognitive skills required to provide frame alignment (McAdam 1990) are an essential element of a social movement's efforts to influence social change.

5 Most of the members of the strike committees of the two occupations of university buildings in 1990 were men. In the National Strike Committee there was one woman – the spokesperson. Women were among the supporters, not among the leaders of the occupations.

6 Protesters in the student marches jumped while shouting slogans against the government. Since then 'jumping' has been introduced into public discourse to describe a form of protest.

7 Knjaz was the title of the Bulgarian King before the recognition of the Bulgarian state in 1908. On the occasion of the opening of the new building of the National Theatre students were given invitations to participate in the ceremony which they boycotted as they felt offended by the small numbers of invitations for students. They gathered in front of the building and met the Knjaz's carriage, creating dreadful noise with metal whistles.

8 Unofficial unauthorised publications of original or translated articles and books, informally distributed by hand.

Bibliography

Arnaudov, M. (1939) *A History of Sofia University 'St. Kliment Ohridski' during Its First Half-Century 1888–1938*, Sofia: Royal Press.

Barnes, S., Kaase, M. *et al.* (1979) *Political Action: Mass Participation in Five Western Democracies*, Beverly Hills, CA: Sage.

Bobchev, S. (1907) *The Bulgarian Patriarchal Community – Historical-Legal Essays*, Sofia: State Press.

Chakarov, N. (ed.) (1975) *A History of Education and Educational Ideas in Bulgaria*, Vol. I, Sofia: Public Educational Press.

Corrin, C. (ed.) (1992) *Superwomen and the Double Burden: Women's Experience of Change in Central and Eastern Europe and the Former Soviet Union*, London: Scarlet Press.

Darendorf, R. (1990) *Reflections on the Revolution in Europe*, London: Chatto and Windus.

Einhorn, B. (1993) *Cinderella goes to Market. Citizenship, Gender and Women's Movements in East Central Europe*, London: Verso.

Funk, N. and Mueller, M. (eds) (1993) *Gender Politics and Post-Communism. Reflections from Eastern Europe and the Former Soviet Union*, New York and London: Routledge.

Genov, N. (1998) 'Global trends and national transformation', in P.E. Mitev (ed.) *The Bulgarian Transition. Challenges and Cognition*, Sofia: Bulgarian Sociological Association.

Khadzijski, I. (1974) [1943] *Optimistic Theory about Our People*, Sofia, Bulgarian Writer's Press.

Kitanov, K. (ed.) (1981) *The Komsomol Cadres*, Sofia: People's Youth Press.

Kjuranov, C. (1982) *The Human Communities*, Sofia: Science and Arts.

Kotzeva, T. and Todorova, I. (1994) *The Bulgarian Woman. Traditional Images and Changing Realities*, Pernik: Krakra.

Kovatcheva, S. (1995a) 'Student political culture in transition: the case of Bulgaria', in CYRCE (ed.) *The Puzzle of Integration. European Yearbook on Youth Policy and Research*. Vol. 1, Berlin: Walter de Gruyter.

——— (1995b) 'Learning to value the change. Student participation in the social transformation in Bulgaria', unpublished research report.

Lipset, S.M. (1994) 'The social prerequisites of democracy revisited', *American Sociological Review*, 59, 1: 1–22.

McAdam, D. (1990) 'Political opportunities and framing processes: thoughts on linkages', paper presented at the Workshop on Social Movements, Berlin, July 5–7.

Mitev, P.E. (1988) *Youth and Social Change*, Sofia: People's Youth Press.

——— (1997) 'Bulgaria 97: youth and society', paper presented to the seminar 'Social Integration and Political Activity of Bulgarian Youth', Sofia, 14 March 1997.

National Statistical Institute (1997) *Statistical Reference Book of Republic Bulgaria*, Sofia.

Odzakov, P. (1895) 'Materials about the Common Folk Law: family, heritage and marriage rights', *Juridical Review*, 3: 104; 4: 146–7.

Offe, C. (1991) 'Das Dilemma der Gleichzeitigkeit. Demokratisierung und Marktwirtschaft in Osteuropa', *Merkur*, 279–92.

Petrova, D. (1993) 'The winding road to emancipation in Bulgaria', in N. Funk and M. Mueller (eds) *Gender Politics and Post-Communism. Reflections from Eastern Europe and the Former Soviet Union*, New York and London: Routledge.

Pilkington, H. (1992) 'Whose space is it anyway? Youth, gender and civil society in the Soviet Union', in S. Rai, H. Pilkington and A. Phizacklea (eds) *Women in the Face of Change. The Soviet Union, Eastern Europe and China*, London and New York: Routledge.

Semov, M. (1972) *The Changes in Youth*, Sofia: Centre for Sociological Studies of Youth.

Snow, D., Rochford, E., Worden, S. and Benford, R. (1986) 'Frame alignment processes, micromobilisation and movement participation', *American Sociological Review*, 51.

Tonchev, V. and Jordanova, L. (1991) *Elections 1991. Public Opinion in Bulgaria*, Sofia: LOGIS.

Chapter 10

'The virgin and the state'

Gender and politics in Argentina

Victoria Ana Goddard

In 1978 Sherry Ortner published an article outlining the bold hypothesis of a link between gender constructs and processes of political hierarchisation. More specifically, she suggested that the intensification of hierarchy and political centralisation were accompanied by a growing concern with women's chastity and control over their sexuality. A concern with the purity and the honour of women was associated with the rise of the state, which brought with it an ideology that represented women as being in danger rather than dangerous, pure rather than polluting and that privileged the ideal of women as mothers.

Ortner's argument can be seen as flawed for its sweeping generalisation and simplification of what are extremely complex webs of determination, but it remains inspiring. Her article raises questions which relate to recent debates on the relationship between gender and the political, in particular the construction and reproduction of the nation-state (see especially Yuval-Davis and Anthias 1989; Kandiyoti 1991; Afshar 1996). In the first place, Ortner makes an implicit connection between the spheres of subjectivity, intimacy and sentiment and processes defined as pertaining to the public domain. In the second place, these connections feed into the very constitution of the political and overtly or covertly define and shape it. It follows, then, that actions in the private domain have implications for institutions and practices of the public domain. Ortner's hypothesis suggests that the consolidation of hierarchies will be associated with an emphasis on gender and sexual boundaries. Conversely, when existing hierarchies are challenged we can expect a relaxation or even a reversal of these boundaries.

In this chapter I will argue that the distinction between the public and the private underlies political discourse in important ways that work towards defining the field of politics and the place of actors within it. Women in particular are defined in relation to the ways in which these terms are given content and meaning and how the boundaries between them are understood in specific contexts. The blurring or erosion of the boundaries is potentially subversive and in specific contexts may reflect important changes taking place within a society. Whereas Ortner's point of departure was the hegemonic processes associated with the state, in this chapter the point is made that the inversion or erosion of the boundaries between the public and the private can underwrite both hegemonic and counter-hegemonic discourses.

The chapter considers the deliberate gendering of political discourse and action in two contexts. The first case relates to grass-roots reactions to repression by military regimes in the 1970s in Argentina and Chile. Those who defied the authoritarian regimes resorted to numerous innovative practices in which women played a central role. In addition, the discourses and symbols of these movements were highly gendered and illustrate the transgression and inversion of boundaries. The second example relates to a deliberate attempt to build a new hegemonic position through a rejection and critique of the status quo and of existing hegemonic positions but promoted here as a 'top-down' strategy. The government of Juan Domingo Perón who first ruled Argentina between 1946 and 1955 and the movement that he headed and inspired is frequently taken as a classical example of populism. Populist regimes are associated with moments of tumultuous change and are characterised by a reliance on mass popular support. This chapter will argue that gender played an important symbolic role in securing this support and, furthermore, contributed to a sense of community, participation and inclusion and created expectations of change towards a better society. By considering these two examples the chapter argues that gender discourse constitutes a powerful medium through which changes in power relations can be expressed and achieved.

Gender, order and rebellion

On 22 September 1998 General Augusto Pinochet, leader of the military government of Chile between 1973 and 1982, arrived in London on a private visit that was to unleash a flurry of activity around the globe. On 14 October a magistrates court in Madrid contacted the British Metropolitan Police via Interpol to arrange a provisional warrant for the General's arrest. This was issued two days later. In the meantime, Chilean refugees in Sweden and Switzerland initiated further requests for the arrest of the General. As a result of this, a dictator who had negotiated his way out of responsibility for the repression carried out by his government faced the possibility of trial outside his own country. The Pinochet case extended beyond the limits of Chilean politics and raised broader issues of sovereignty, citizenship and global human rights. It clearly challenged conventional approaches to issues of citizenship anchored as these are within the parameters attached to the notion of the nation-state.

The action taken by the Spanish judiciary was the outcome of a long process of lobbying, investigation and debate concerning whether Spanish legal institutions could legitimately bring to trial several military men involved in the repression of the civilian population of Chile and Argentina. In March 1996 the Spanish prosecutor Carlos Castresana accused several Argentine military men of responsibility for the disappearance of 266 Spanish citizens during the period of military rule. Castresana made it clear at the time that, though focused on the case of Spanish citizens, the Spanish judicial procedures would not make distinctions on the basis of nationality and would therefore encompass all victims, including Argentine citizens. In 1997 the Spanish judge Baltasar Garzón issued a demand for the arrest of the ex-chief of the Argentine Army, Eduardo Emilio Massera who had been a member of the first military junta after the military coup of 1976. The demand for Massera's arrest was one of several, including one for ex-General Leopoldo Galtieri who headed the junta during the Malvinas or Falklands war. The judge had received the statements made by the ex-seaman Adolfo Scilingo, who revealed what he knew about the navy's involvement in dealing with civilians held on suspicion of political opposition. Scilingo also acquainted the judge with the details of the 'flights of terror' as a means of disposal of prisoners as recounted earlier to the Argentine journalist Horacio Verbitsky and made widely available through a book published in 1995. Judge Garzón also heard the testimony of a number of survivors and family of 'disappeared' women and men, including the statements made by Nora Cortinas, one of the founders of the Mothers of Plaza de Mayo.

The procedures initiated by Castresana and Garzón gave rise to a heated legal and political debate in Spain, much as Pinochet's arrest did later in Britain. In Argentina too, opinion was divided, between the official government position and the opposition parties, the human rights organisations and the grass-roots movements representing the families of the victims of the military regime. President Menem of Argentina publicly objected to Garzón's investigation into the disappearance of 600 Spaniards between 1976 and 1983 and expressed his support for the Argentine Armed Forces. Menem's condemnation of Garzón was backed by various attempts by the Argentine government to prevent the investigation from proceeding.

There are clearly precedents that facilitated the development of these procedures, ranging from the Nuremberg trials to the growing concern among certain sectors of the international community to punish those responsible for the gross violation of human rights, as in the trials at The Hague against war criminals in Bosnia. But the specific case of Pinochet, Videla, Massera and other members of the Chilean and Argentine military establishments has a distinct genealogy. Its origins are to be found in the years of authoritarianism, when the grass-roots organisations of the relatives of the disappeared demanded to know the whereabouts of their missing loved ones. They persevered in their demands for information and justice throughout the period of repression and continued to lobby the democratically elected governments. The specific character of the transition to democracy was different in Chile and Argentina. However, in both instances grass-roots organisations have continued to exercise pressure on the government and sought new avenues to publicise their case and achieve their goals, so that they have remained in the public eye at home and in the international arena.

In both countries the repressive military governments that were established in the 1970s restricted the traditional institutions of political mobilisation and opposition, leaving trade unions and political parties very little room for manoeuvre. With the removal of conventional political spaces for legitimate protest and faced with brutally repressive policies, grass-roots citizens' movements assumed a leading role in the opposition to the military governments.

In Chile, following the military intervention against the Allende government, there was a slow but steady increase in non-formalised forms of resistance, such as the hunger strikes initiated in May 1978 by the Association of the Families of Disappeared Prisoners, composed mainly of women. They organised a campaign that culminated in hunger strikes throughout the country and abroad amongst Chilean exiles and their supporters. The protests led by these women forced international organisations such as the United Nations to intervene, demanding information from the government as to the whereabouts of the disappeared (Vitale 1981: 66–7). The imposition of authoritarianism was coupled with the application of radical monetarist policies, which had a dramatic effect on wages, prices, employment, and the provision of services. In response to the deprivation that ensued, initiatives such as the *ollas comunes* or communal kitchens were created to provide food for the poor. Shopping associations and co-operatives were set up to provide cheaper alternatives to the retail sector. Women played a central and sometimes the exclusive role in these initiatives. Thus, opposition to the regime constructed a democratisation process as 'a "process of inclusion" signified by the emergence in Chile of new social and political actors and of a new consciousness and conceptualisation of politics, the political process, and the role of authoritarianism in civil society' (Chuchryk 1994: 65).

In Argentina, the Mothers of Plaza de Mayo were formed in April 1977, following the coup of March 1976. Women from different class and cultural backgrounds rallied together to protest at the disappearance of their children and to obtain information regarding their whereabouts. In spite of repressive measures against them and campaigns intended to ridicule and isolate them, the mothers persevered.[1] In 1979 a group of twenty women signed an official founding document. One of the clauses stipulated that the founders could not join any political party, thus keeping the movement distinct from the formal political organisations. The Mothers, together with the Relatives of the Disappeared and People Detained for Political Reasons, created in 1976, initiated a campaign for the publication of a list of those who had disappeared. Their insistent demands for information shattered the silence that the repressive order had attempted to impose. Other human rights organisations added their voice to the campaigns. The scope of the campaigns widened, eventually including the issue of the Malvinas-Falklands war, and the Mothers extended their range of action, visiting Europe to seek support from political figures there (Feijóo and Gogna 1990).

The transition to democratic government failed to bring with it a satisfactory resolution. In Chile the military government had issued an amnesty law as early as 1978. Pinochet's dominant position seemed unchallenged. Yet in 1988 a referendum intended to confirm support for his government resulted in his defeat. In the light of this Pinochet ensured the continuity of his role in Chilean political life by declaring himself Commander-in-Chief of the army under the elected government that would replace him. His continued influence was an obstacle to the investigation and trial of those responsible for the repression during the years of military rule. A Truth and Reconciliation Commission was set up but was prevented from naming any of the perpetrators of the crimes described.

In Argentina the legal process against members of the military establishment went much further but also encountered obstacles. Here too the military government had declared an amnesty but this was overturned by the civilian government that followed the end of military rule. Investigations into the years of military rule resulted in a report entitled *Never Again*, which carefully documented the testimonies of witnesses, survivors and their relatives. The results encouraged calls for the prosecution of those held responsible for the atrocities but military pressure on the civilian government of Alfonsín resulted in the law of 'Due Obedience' which exonerated junior officers on the grounds that they were fulfilling orders. Top military leaders were tried and some found guilty but again this process was interrupted when a number of army uprisings led the government to issue the law of *Punto Final* or 'Full Stop', which brought the prosecutions to a halt. Later, the government of Carlos Menem, which claimed direct descent from the Justice movement of General Perón, issued a pardon for many of those condemned in the prosecutions that followed the fall of the military. Organisations such as the Mothers and the Relatives of the Disappeared refused to accept any compromise between the military and the civilian government and continued campaigning for information and justice. One of the strategies pursued was precisely to widen the issue beyond the confines of the national government, by appealing to those countries which had historically strong links with Argentina and Chile and which might claim shared citizenship and therefore responsibility for victims of the regimes. However, the Spaniards who agreed to take on these cases have rejected the relevance of nationhood and formal citizenship. In the words of Judge Baltazar Garzón: 'The right to preserve life does not only concern the Government of the individual or groups in question, but the entire international community' (Garzón quoted in *El Periodico*, 26 March 1998).

To what can we attribute the resilience of the Mothers' movement and their capacity to survive state repression in Argentina, Chile and elsewhere?[2] The answer lies at least in part in the very constructions of womanhood and the family that were current and indeed promoted by the authorities. Gogna and Feijóo (1990) point out in relation to the Argentine case that for the military government the family was identified as the principal locus of reproduction of moral values. Mothers fulfilled the role of guarding the family and protecting Christian values, so that ultimately the family was constituted as an institution of social control. Similarly, in Chile Pinochet put forward 'an exaggerated version of the ideology of traditional motherhood in an attempt to depoliticize women' (Chuchryk 1994: 73).

The discourse of motherhood espoused by the military was informed by ideas concerning good mothering that emerged in the nineteenth century. In Argentina these were focused on growing anxieties about rising rates of illegitimacy and of child abandonment in the latter part of the century.[3] Such concerns fomented important shifts away from defining motherhood in terms of mere procreation towards qualitative issues regarding the performance of mothering. Good mothering practices were promoted in theory and practice by secular and medical authorities in their drive to lower infant mortality rates (Guy 1997: 157). A further influence on the content of motherhood were the notions promoted by the Roman Catholic establishment, of motherhood as a sacrifice and mothering as self-abnegation, demanding from women an attitude of passivity and acceptance. However, attitudes shifted and underwent transformations, especially during the 1960s, which witnessed rapid changes in gender and sexual relations and family life, in an albeit distant dialogue with the changes taking place in Europe and the USA. The military repression of all manifestations of behaviour they identified as indicative of 'moral decay' suggests that the 1963 coup was not only prompted by economic and political factors but was also largely aimed at curbing the process of social change taking place in the urban centres of Argentina.[4]

While military ideology constructed the private sphere as a place of retreat from the politicised public arena, state violence simultaneously broke down the barriers, invaded the private space and removed any sense of safety and retreat. The repression of those identified as party militants or trade unionists extended beyond arrest to include murder, disappearance, and the rape of suspects, and of their wives and daughters (Isla 1998). This simultaneous elevation of the family and attack on its integrity and safety provoked an opposition that found expression precisely in the depoliticised family values and the sacred nature of motherhood, as mothers claimed a moral right to the life of their children. Furthermore, the mothers' non-adherence to political parties distanced them further from what might have been defined as 'political' opposition and a 'political' critique. Their demands were personalised, and rather than using the language of political rights, their appeal was couched in the language of family values and the universal value of motherhood. Symbolically they emphasised their link with domesticity and their rejection of violence; the white headscarf became the symbol of their struggle, representing their identity as mothers and their bond with and responsibility towards their children, as well as their commitment to peaceful methods of protest. What these women achieved was the introduction of a new language and a new space of protest in the public arena. What the movement accomplished was no less than an extremely potent inversion of an ideological schema (Feijóo and Gogna 1990).

The performance of this protest and indeed the nature and extent of the military repression that provoked it must be understood in relation to the difficult process of emergence of inclusive democracy in the country and the subsequent extensive politicisation that took place especially during the Peronist regime of the late 1940s and early 1950s. This politicisation of society invoked a markedly gendered model of the political and of the citizen in the process of democratisation.

Democracy in Argentina

The electoral reform of 1912 (Sáenz Peña Law) granted universal male suffrage and represented a concession by the ruling elite to a growing popular rejection of the oligarchic structures that dominated the country since its inception. Indeed, the elections of 1916 brought to government the opposition Radical Party and for the first time important sections of the population achieved political representation, although in the longer term this primarily benefited the middle classes rather than the poorer sectors of the society. But in spite of the significant shift towards wider participation in the political arena, the Conservatives representing the interests of the landed elite still controlled parliament. As Rock points out: 'They had created popular democracy by concession; what they had given they could also take away' (Rock 1993: 149). In fact, in 1930 Yrigoyen's Radical government was deposed by a military coup and the Conservatives were returned to power, where they remained until another military coup in 1943 created the opportunity for the ascendance of General Juan Domingo Perón.

After 1930 the Conservatives attempted to re-establish a political system based on the exclusion of much of the population from political activity. However, changing conditions within the country and abroad, particularly those relating to changes in demand for Argentina's export commodities, made this task increasingly difficult, and perhaps undesirable. Two very important factors here were changes in the agricultural sector that displaced many rural workers, and the expansion of industry. These two processes combined to push the displaced population from the rural hinterlands to the cities. The face of the country was changing dramatically. The 1914 census records 383,000 industrial workers. In 1941 there were 830,000 and in 1946 there were over one million employed in industry (Rock 1993: 195). In conjunction with these changes there was the growth of trade unions representing new sectors of workers.

The 1943 coup reflected and promoted these changes in such a way as to bring about a radical shift in the structure and orientation of the Argentine state, described by one contemporary observer as marking

> the end of a society, an economy and a way of life. With it were buried the Argentina that lived from beef alone, the Argentina of the Enlightened Oligarchy, liberal Argentina, the free trader, and the hopes, the power and the predominance of the landed aristocracy.
>
> (Rennie quoted in Rock 1993: 224)

In a similar vein, Fraser and Navarro consider that the impact of the coup had profound long-term implications, in that 'at its simplest this meant that the country's working classes could never again quite be disregarded' (Fraser and Navarro 1997: 67).

In fact, the new government, especially under the leadership of Perón in the Labour Secretariat, energetically promoted the transformation of Argentine society. Rights were granted to the most marginal of all workers, the rural *peón*; policies aimed at encouraging industrialisation increased urban employment; trade unionism grew to cover ever-wider sectors of workers (Rock 1993: 234). Cheap grain and more urban jobs meant an increase in the standard of living of many. Under Perón the government expanded public spending and strengthened the economic role of the state, and focused on a more egalitarian distribution of income through price controls. In only three years, between 1946 and 1949, real income increased by more than 40 per cent (Torre and De Riz 1993: 249). Interestingly, the real wages of unskilled workers rose more than the wages of skilled workers. Both peaked in 1947 with an index of 124 versus a 1943 baseline in the case of the skilled workers and an index of 137 for unskilled workers (Munck 1987: 133). In particular hourly wages, which affected the more vulnerable sections of the working class, increased dramatically, peaking in 1949. The government introduced the *aguinaldo*, the payment of a thirteenth month as an end-of-year bonus, holiday pay, pension schemes for all, compensation for redundancy or dismissal, health and safety regulations and other measures that greatly improved the conditions of workers. In addition, it fostered a workplace policy of democratic participation through a shop-steward system and a system of internal factory committees. (Munck 1987: 134–5).

As President of the country from 1946 until 1955 Perón introduced redistributive policies which reached much of the population that heretofore had been excluded politically and economically. Through the expanding trade unions, the government incorporated large sectors of the population and benefited from their support. After Perón came to power trade union membership grew dramatically from 877,000 members in 1946 to nearly two million in 1950 (Munck 1987: 133). New legislation brought about radical changes in the work and lives of the working class and the petty bourgeoisie. However, there were limits to industrialisation and to reform, which meant that many poor Argentines were still beyond the reach of government or government-sponsored organisms and did not benefit from the new labour laws. For example, whereas the manufacturing sector had a unionisation rate of 55 per cent by the end of the Peronist period, only 6 per cent of workers in the agrarian sector belonged to a union (Munck 1987: 133).

A crucial complement to the government's policies was the activity of the President's wife, Eva Perón. In particular, through the Fundación Evita Perón, Peronist ideas and practices reached the most marginal, the urban sub-proletariat and the poor of the provinces. Evita's work therefore continued the political mobilisation begun in 1945 and further expanded the reach of the Peronist movement so that new sectors were added to the regime's vast popular following (Torre and De Riz 1993: 253).

Until 1946 the business of charity work was mainly in the hands of the Sociedad de Beneficiencia, headed by a group of upper-class women. Under Perón the Sociedad was closed down on the grounds that the government's policy was to replace charity with 'social justice'. Soon after the closure of the Society, Evita initiated the distribution of clothes and food on a relatively small scale. With time this activity expanded and became the concern of the Fundación Eva Perón. In fact, the Foundation became a crucial protagonist in the redistributive policies of the government and in the construction and dissemination of Peronist ideology. The scale of the operations of the Foundation was equivalent to that of a government ministry and it is estimated that at the end of the Peronist period its assets in cash and goods were valued at over $200 million at the exchange rate of the time (1955). The Foundation employed 14,000 permanent workers, including 6,000 construction workers and 26 priests. It purchased annually for distribution 400,000 pairs of shoes, 500,000 sewing machines and 200,000 cooking pots. As well as distributing clothes, furniture, cooking utensils, toys and food the Foundation also provided scholarships and built homes, hospitals and other welfare establishments (Fraser and Navarro 1997: 118). In addition to its budget from the Ministry of Finance, the Foundation benefited from donations from individuals, organisations and trade unions. Businesses were invited to make contributions and there are clear indications that the invitation was coercive. In 1950 the CGT (General Confederation of Workers) agreed to donate two days of wages for every worker-member. Levies were also imposed on sales of lottery tickets, casinos, cinemas and other leisure activities (Fraser and Navarro 1997: 121).

Industrial growth was an important goal and a pillar of government policy. Most of this growth was focused on light industry producing for the internal market, and especially important were the sectors of food and textiles. These sectors offered new opportunities for women, whose sources of work in crafts and traditional textiles had been eroded throughout the nineteenth and the early part of the twentieth century. Import substitution industrialisation had already brought about an increase in the percentage of women employed in industry during the 1930s. From 1935 to 1939 there was an increase of 27.4 per cent of women working in industry. Most of these were concentrated in the capital city, the province of Buenos Aires and Santa Fe. In the textile sector women represented 61.7 per cent of the workforce in 1939 (Moreau de Justo 1945: 139). Peronist economic policies opened up further opportunities for industrial employment. By 1947, although women only represented 20 per cent of the labour force, they predominated in the textile, tobacco and garments sectors. Women were the principal migrants from the rural areas into the cities and industry offered work to many of them. But overall, the long-term decline in handicrafts and cottage industries had a negative effect on women's economic position and many found themselves isolated in the domestic sphere (Munck 1987: 123).

In any case, by 1943 women already constituted a quarter of the labour force. Furthermore, the composition of the urban centres had changed significantly in terms of gender distribution. Historically, the population of Buenos Aires (and other large urban centres) had been predominantly male, largely due to the mass immigration of European and Middle Eastern men. But as overseas migration decreased dramatically after 1914 and then again after 1930, and as women began to abandon the rural areas in higher numbers than men, the ratio of men to women altered significantly. Whereas the percentage of men in 1869 was equal to 123.7 per cent this had fallen to 94.5 per cent in 1947.[5] Women therefore had become an important economic resource within import substitution industrialisation and moreover they were an important but largely untapped political resource.

The importance of women was recognised in Perón's decision to set up a separate Women's Division within the Secretariat of Labour and in his promise that if elected his government would grant political rights to women of all classes (Carlson 1988: 186). In fact, in 1945 Perón unsuccessfully petitioned the President to grant women the vote by presidential decree since the Supreme Court had already ruled that women's suffrage was not unconstitutional. It is important to note that Perón's request did not take place in a vacuum. The issue of women's suffrage had been hotly debated and fought over by women's groups and feminist organisations.

Women's suffrage

In 1920 a mock election campaign for women was held emulating the Paris experience of 1918 and involving the first outdoor suffrage rally in South America.[6] Some advances were made in gaining women's political rights, though gains were temporary. In 1921, in the western province of San Juan, qualified women were granted the right to vote in municipal elections. In 1927 women were enfranchised for municipal and provincial elections in the province of Santa Fe. This was compatible with the dominant view of women's role in society, as leaders within the family and the community. Thus local politics could involve women because they were primarily concerned with issues of education and health, areas that were associated with women and the private sphere (Carlson 1988: 170). In 1930 Alicia Moreau de Justo founded the Women's Suffrage Committee which gained few supporters, not least because the orientation of the organisation clashed with the growing nationalist sentiments of the time. In the same year the Argentine Association for Women's Suffrage was founded by Carmela Horne de Burmeister with the motto: 'Fatherland, Civic Pride and Humanity'. This group, which had women's suffrage as its only issue, gained greater popularity and by 1934 it claimed 100,000 members and branches in a number of provinces (Carlson 1988: 172).

In 1932 the Chamber of Deputies conducted the first open debate on women's suffrage. A bill was passed on to the Senate who deferred it and it was not debated again until 1938, when it was defeated.[7] Yet feminist and women's organisations remained active and were not altogether unsuccessful. For example, the Union of Argentine Women initiated a successful campaign against President Justo's attempt to cancel the advances for women's status achieved in the Civil Code of 1926. Victoria Ocampo led the campaign,[8] with support from both Horne de Burmeister and Moreau de Justo. However, on the whole feminist groups were restricted in their reach and lacked popular support.

Perón's proposal to President Farrell to issue a decree to give women the vote aroused the anger of feminist leaders who accused him of cynical manoeuvring to gain the support of women in an eventual drive for the Presidency. It was felt by many that Perón and especially Evita were appropriating the issues that had for so long been the focus of struggle for the feminist organisations. In the end, Perón's attempts to appeal to working-class women created an unusual alliance between elite philanthropists and middle-class professional women (Carlson 1988: 187).[9]

Evita played a central role in the Peronist promotion of female suffrage under her husband's presidency. Her speeches emphasised the importance of incorporating women into Argentine society. Women, she argued, had earned the right to vote, through their actions and through the fulfilment of their domestic duties that were also patriotic duties. Work bestowed rights on women: if women had left the home to earn their daily bread, so too should they be given the right to choose their government. In particular, she stressed the participation of women in the demonstrations of 17 October 1945, when popular pressure had forced the release of Perón who was under arrest by his military colleagues, a date that became a landmark in the history and celebration of Peronism. She suggested that their rebellion and their action on that day represented a step towards assuming their own destiny and claimed the vote for women as 'now more than an aspiration, it is now a need that cannot be postponed' (Perón 1996: 248).[10] For Evita, granting women the vote was entirely compatible with and supportive of their familial role. Their incorporation into the public sphere confirmed their place in the family, and reflected their centrality to the well-being of society, as women were the guardians of the moral education of children and the spiritual leaders of the home and the community.

The vote was finally granted to women in September 1947. Thousands of Peronist supporters filled the streets of the capital to celebrate the achievement (Carlson 1988). Soon after this victory Evita founded the Women's Peronist Party, which had a resounding success. Women thus found the means to become full participants in the social and political processes of their country. This was a mass experience, as over 90 per cent of women voted in the 1951 elections. Their vote significantly boosted Perón's position.[11] Women were not only able to choose their representatives, but were themselves appointed to government posts and elected to office as the use of a quota system guaranteed the entry of women into the elected bodies in the 1951 elections. Seven women senators were elected and twenty-four women deputies were chosen from the Peronist party[12] and in 1953 Delia de Parodi became vice-president of the Chamber of Deputies.

The Peronist experience – populism as discourse

As the feminists had feared, the achievement of women's suffrage was appropriated entirely by the regime and became closely associated with Eva Perón. On the eve of the announcement of the law, a delegate from the General Confederation of Workers praised Maria Eva Duarte de Perón as:

> the indomitable leader who, taking up the banner of justice, has been able to triumph over the foolish intellectual aridity of a political system . . . (and) the forces of antipatriotism . . . and leaping into the abyss of misunderstanding has managed to achieve for her sisters . . . what tomorrow the word of the Head of State will seal as a formidable conquest of this liberating revolution.
>
> (*La Prensa* 23 September 1949)

On the day, women's groups filled the Plaza de Mayo, delegates from all over the country were brought to the capital for the occasion. Teachers were granted a holiday so that they could attend the ceremony. Placards bearing the photo of Evita were held high. A stage on the pavement of the Casa Rosada, or government house, was taken over by the Argentine Union of Musicians, who entertained the crowds with a number of popular tunes, including a song entitled 'The Lady of Hope' in honour of Eva Perón. An open truck parked outside the Casa Rosada displayed a young woman, dressed to represent the Republic, and at her side a little girl dressed in the rural style and a little boy dressed as a *gaucho*. When the President and his wife appeared handkerchiefs, flags and placards were waved and the name of Perón and Evita were repeated insistently. After the crowds joined in the National Anthem and a prayer, the act was signed, first by the Minister of the Interior, then by Perón. The decree was then handed to the President's wife, 'as standard-bearer of the Argentine woman'. A group of children presented flowers to Evita, who addressed all the women of the country. The effects of this carefully staged identification of Evita Perón with Law No. 13.010 has endured and was officially confirmed when the fiftieth anniversary of the law was commemorated with the issue of a coin bearing Evita's profile and full name.

In July 1949 Evita presided over the inaugural ceremony of the First National Assembly of the Peronist Feminine Movement. Women delegates from all over the country were told how, for the first time in Argentina, in America or anywhere in the world, the majority or perhaps the totality of women of a nation were represented in a national and democratic assembly with the sole purpose of defining their own destinies. Eva Perón's speech contrasted a past of exploitation, injustice and marginalisation with the present recognition of women's worth. She pointedly laid the merit for these changes at the feet of Coronel (Colonel) Perón, for, she said, it was his analysis of women's condition that inspired her and motivated her efforts to bring about changes in the political and social status of women. With Perón came the dawn of a new value attached to woman, 'who, without renouncing any of the attributes of femininity, transforms her home which until yesterday was the guardian of private conduct, into the supreme judge of public conduct'.[13] Her speech was complex. It outlined not only issues pertaining directly to women such as their political rights, fair wages, etc., but also dealt with the more general precepts of Perón's position, offering a comprehensive exposition of Peronism. This ranged from issues of foreign policy, outlining Perón's 'third position' against 'international capital and extremist materialism', and making her own observations regarding the European experience and what she saw as the failure of both the political right and the left. She was critical of the injustices of oligarchic rule, of capitalism and of liberalism. But she was equally critical of the loss of spiritual direction that prevailed in the world at large. She appealed to women to build the nation but without forsaking solidarity with the women of the world. As women and citizens, women knew that all mothers, women workers and daughters in the world wanted peace.

Although the theme of change was central to her speech, she insisted upon the preservation of feminine qualities and of women's role in the home. For Evita, women's role in the domestic sphere was not a private matter since it related to the very reproduction of

Argentine identity, of morals and of the values at the basis of social life. The moral force of women was reproduced in her own presentation of self. She emphasised her identity as a woman, and a weak woman at that, but claimed she could bring into the world of politics her own, feminine brand of insight and loyalty. She studiously submitted her aims and her achievements to her husband, whom she claimed as the sole source of inspiration for her actions and sentiments. In this as in other aspects of her approach to the 'woman question' she distanced herself from the Argentine feminists. These she saw as well intentioned but misguided by foreign ideas, which led to the masculinisation of women that she opposed vehemently. She unhesitatingly declared that women must submit to the ideas and leadership of a great man, such as Perón. Although she argued for women's full political rights, she saw the role of women in politics as complementary rather than identical to that of men. However, while many aspects of her position would cause distaste amongst feminists, there can be little doubt that it was perfectly compatible with the values and needs of the majority of women at the time.[14]

Eva Perón did not only act as a mediator between women and the President. Her actions in the Labour Secretariat or through the Fundación Eva Perón brought her into close contact with a broad range of people whose needs she addressed personally to a large extent. She saw her role – and by extension that of all women – in politics as one of assistance and care. She was careful to reject any concept of charity, no doubt as a reaction against the charitable activities of upper-class women whom she disdained and who represented a powerful opposition to the government. Her argument was that charity deprived individuals of their sense of self-respect and was therefore counterproductive. Instead, her declared aim was to restore and support the sense of self-worth of the people that had suffered exclusion and humiliation for generations.

She was decidedly anti-bureaucratic in her approach. Even her critics had to accept that she worked extremely long hours and was tireless in her efforts to deal personally with those who came to seek her help. The personal encounter was an important aspect of her brand of politics. Fraser and Navarro quote the Spanish Ambassador to Buenos Aires describing one of the regular afternoon meetings of Eva and her public:

There were groups of workers; union leaders; peasant
women with their children; foreign journalists; a *gaucho*
family with their ponchos, the man with his long and silky
huge black whiskers; there were refugees from behind the
Iron Curtain; people who had come from post-war Europe;
intellectuals and university professors from the Baltic States;
priests and monks; fat, clamorous and sweaty middle-aged
women; young clerks and football players; actors and people
from the circus . . . [And] in the midst of this apparent
chaos, this noisy and confused kermesse Evita listened to
whatever was asked of her, from a simple demand for
increased wages, to an entire industry-wide settlement and
along the way a request for a place for a family to live,
furniture, for a job in a school, food . . . Evita was in-
exhaustible. She kept the momentum of this show running
for hours, often well after nightfall.

(Fraser and Navarro 1997: 123)

Those who were received by her recall the politeness and
gentleness with which they were treated and the blend of
respectfulness and compassion that she showed those who sought
her help. In spite of her well-tailored clothes and (on these
occasions) discreet but expensive jewellery, Evita conveyed a sense
of identity with the poor who visited her. In her speeches and in
her autobiography she stresses time and again the pain she
remembers since her childhood at the awareness of the differences
between the rich and the poor and at the realisation that the rich
were largely responsible for the plight of the poor. She emphasised
her own humble origins, her roots in the people and her permanent identification with them.

Her activities earned her the name of the 'Lady of Hope'. Taylor
suggests that Evita and Perón played complementary roles and
types of power. Evita's leadership was described as spiritual, moral
or religious rather than political (Taylor 1979: 11). This qualitative
difference is certainly emphasised in Evita's own speeches, where
she portrays her husband as the rational, enlightened leader and her
own contribution as emanating from the heart. She explained the
partnership as follows:

In different ways we had both wished to achieve the same
things: he knowing well what he had to do; I, only having a
feeling about what had to be done; he, with his intelligence;
I, ready for everything without knowing anything; he well
educated and I humble; he enormous and I small; he, master,
and I pupil. He the figure, and I the shadow.

(Perón 1996: 55)

Her expressions of devotion and her continuing emphasis on the
superior intellect, strength and capacity of her husband supported
the claims to loyalty of the movement and furthermore expressed
the relations of paternalism and the authoritarian elements of the
Peronist movement and the government.

Evita reached the people through her actions and her words.
Her oratory style was passionate, clear and direct. She unflinchingly
spoke of love: love for the General and love for the people. Fraser
and Navarro suggest that Eva's outspoken appeal to her feelings
was crucial to Peronism. She vividly inspired loyalty and love
toward Perón and, they claim that to many her words 'were the
content of Peronism' (Fraser and Navarro 1997: 112) so that
Evita's emphasis on emotional content contributed to the creation
of a cult of Perón, with Evita as its priestess.[15]

Evita did not merely talk about feelings such as love but she
exalted them. To love she attributed the capacity to transform, to
overcome obstacles and pain. Pain was as important to Evita's public
discourse as love. The pain she was concerned with was that of the
humble, a consequence of social injustice and of the fact that 'Our
wealth was a lie to the children of this land' as the products of
labour fed a privileged few and were marketed abroad. She attacked
the arrogance of the rich who dismissed the crippling effects of
poverty and who thought that the poor lacked the sensitivity of the
educated. She concludes: 'I have seen the humble cry from pain –
but even animals cry from pain! I have also seen them cry out of
gratitude! And from gratitude, from gratitude the rich certainly
don't cry!' (Perón 1996: 128).

Evita addressed those who had had no place in the political life
of the country, those who had been marginalised and excluded. So
she spoke to women who had not been visible. Whereas writers and
poets had praised beautiful and elegant women, she sang the praises

of the 'authentic' woman, the unknown heroine, unrecognised even by her own husband and children. And yet the importance of such a woman could not be overestimated, for Evita claimed that she held the future of the people in her hands. The social responsibility of women was great and so the education of women was particularly important (Perón 1996: 229–30). Similarly, when she spoke to the 'people' she referred to the workers but included the rural poor of the provinces, children and the old, the *descamisados* or shirtless ones who were 'all those who feel themselves to belong to the people' (Perón 1996: 95). Recognising the age-old exclusion of these people she spoke not only of political rights and justice, or of material improvements and equality but also of respect and dignity.

Her delivery and style generated a feeling of immediacy and of a direct connection. When Eva Perón spoke of her political ideas she expressed them as embodied, experienced through emotional and physical pain. She frequently referred to the way in which the awareness of injustice, the sight of the experience of poverty, gnawed at her body, produced a physical pain, wrenched her heart.

At the same time, she was unworried about her own personal displays of wealth. Many, perhaps especially her critics, drew attention to her glamorous style and expensive wardrobe. Self-presentation was crucial. This had to reflect her status, her role, her ambitions and her commitment. As such her clothing and her style shifted throughout her career. After her marriage to Perón, Eva underwent an aesthetic transformation. In particular, as she assumed a highly visible role through the Ministry and the Foundation, she shifted towards a more severe, elegant style, her hair drawn away from the face and held in a tight bun at the back of her head. She wore smart tailored suits and little jewellery. Publicity and wide media coverage were carefully choreographed by the Peronist regime and here too Evita played a crucial role in promoting a convincing and appealing image of the leadership and its message. The records illustrate the careful management that went into adapting her image to suit the occasion. On a demonstration or a football match she might be seen in casual trousers and top, her hair loose around her shoulders, then, dressed in the finest Parisian gown, she would attend an evening event. Beauty and style were cultivated and were integral to her image as the Lady of Hope, as an inspiration to the people. Austerity was not a value that was promoted by or associated with the regime. Just as she felt fully justified to provide the most expensive décor for a young women's hostel sponsored by her Foundation, so too did she feel justified in displaying an astonishing array of gowns, shoes and jewellery. As representative of the *descamisados* and the embodiment of the regime's promise of equality, she was not to be outdone by any middle-class lady or foreign visitor.

Eva's body was not only important as image, representing the aspirations of the regime and its defiance of the oligarchy. It was also at the forefront of her relationship with the people. During the election campaign in the interior of the country it was Evita who reached out to embrace and kiss the people who thronged around the Presidential train, whilst Perón, jovial enough, limited himself to saluting from a safer distance.[16] Some observers make much of a perceived contrast between Perón and his wife. Dujovne Ortiz suggests that Perón experienced distaste at the proximity of the masses and preferred to distance himself from all physical contact, a contact that Eva sought actively (Dujovne Ortiz 1997: 171). Her willingness to ignore dirt, illness or deformity and to embrace the leprous or the syphilitic encouraged a view of her imbued with religious significance, transforming popular perceptions of her secular role (Fraser and Navarro 1997: 127).

The saintly aura attached to Evita was institutionalised within the Peronist movement during her lifetime and confirmed after her death. At the same time, those who opposed Peronism portrayed her in terms of negative sexualisation, frequently referring to her as a whore (Taylor 1979). In more general terms, Dujovne Ortiz refers to the sexualisation of Peronism and the rise of what she refers to as 'political eroticism' in relation to Perón and Evita. She reports an incident that took place in the early years of Perón's government, when a female audience, disappointed by Perón's failure to attend the meeting, reacted angrily to his new wife whom he had sent in his place. They prevented her from speaking. Only later on in the regime would Peronist women identify with Eva and 'make love to Perón through her' (Dujovne Ortiz 1997: 173). On this particular occasion they left the assembly, took to the streets lifting their skirts and shouting that they wanted to bear Perón's son. They assaulted passersby, especially men wearing ties, who were associated with the oligarchy. The women were eventually dispersed with tear gas (Dujovne Ortiz ibid.).

On the other hand, there were insinuations of a lack of sexual drive in both Evita and Perón, and rumours were spread with the intention of devaluing their image and their partnership. Certainly the fact that neither Evita nor Perón produced offspring raised some discomfort amongst their supporters, particularly since it could cast a shadow on Perón's virility. The ambiguities continued even after their respective deaths. The body of Eva Perón, which was embalmed in order both to consolidate her charismatic relation to the people and to emphasise her saintly nature, became the object of obsessive interest for her keepers (Eloy Martinez 1995).[17] Much later, twenty years after his death, debates about Perón's virility or lack thereof were re-ignited when a woman publicly claimed to be his illegitimate daughter.

After 1950 the global economic context ceased to favour Argentine exports. This meant that the revenue of the state shrank and the government's redistribution policies were hampered. Salaries continued to constitute a large percentage of all expenditure, but there were fewer resources available across the board. At this point Evita's energy and appeal were more valuable than ever to the Peronist government. But it was now that her health deteriorated. She continued her work and carried out her public duties until the end of her life, facing what was perhaps her most difficult and bitter battle shortly before her death in 1952, over her unsuccessful bid to become the vice-presidential candidate to Perón's presidential candidacy.[18] At her death the divisions within the country were expressed yet again as some celebrated and others settled into a period of public mourning.

This emotionally charged appeal to the people was certainly an important strand in Perón's brand of populism. No doubt its efficacy also relied on the government's drive to improve the life of the poor and to place them at the centre of the political arena. Perón had at his disposal considerable resources to reorganise Argentine society and offer the poorer sectors of that society a share in the wealth they helped to generate. However there were limits to the resources and to the possibilities of expanding the economy. Because of this Evita's role was central to the aim of achieving enduring support for the regime, a support that would survive the 1955 coup and the numerous military and civilian governments that followed. An indication of her importance in providing a focus and some degree of coherence to the regime is the 'official' input and interest that was invested in the production of the book that was presented as her autobiography. *La Razón de mi Vida* ('My mission in life') spoke in the first person and invoked all the elements of love and passion that Evita deployed during her speeches, yet this very 'personal' text has been recognised as an official product of the regime (Payotti 1994). Similarly, the efforts that went into the preservation of her body after her death testify to the public role that the President's wife played in the political imaginary of the country and the strategy of the Peronist government and the movement it gave birth to.

Evita's anti-bureaucratic, personal style, her passionate oratory, her ability and willingness to express feelings which she believed she shared with the masses of the country, all these brought her close to the people and the people close to the state. Her position was anomalous, as she was powerful but was not a member of government. Her personal history also made her anomalous. She came from a poor background, was illegitimate and she was a woman in the highly masculine world of politics. The anomalous quality of her persona gave pathos and force to her expressions of love and belonging and credibility to her declamations in the name of the people. At the same time, while the Peronist movement and the government reaped the benefits of her appeal, they had to confront the question of women and follow through Perón's early promises to women. This they did successfully and to great advantage to the regime, given that women's votes increased their share of government.

The chanting of '*Evita, Perón: un solo corazón*' (Evita, Perón: a single heart) did not disappear after the 1955 coup. Like the chant, the Peronist movement survived under various guises and in one way or another conditioned the process of political change in the country. A new slogan emerged as the opposition to the cycle of civilian governments and military regimes unfolded throughout the 1960s and 1970s: '*Perón, Evita: la Patria Socialista*' (Perón, Evita: the Socialist Motherland), the rallying cry of the revolutionary brand of Peronism betrayed by Perón[19] on his return from exile to take up the government until his death in 1974. The mass mobilisation that had characterised the early days of Peronism and the kernel of social transformation that many identified in the proposals of the movement and in the speeches and activities of Eva Perón attracted new generations of supporters into the ranks of Peronist ideology and militancy. The political effervescence of which these young militants were a part was subsequently repressed first by the government led by Perón's third wife Isabelita after his death[20] and then culminating in the most brutal and drastic drive to cancel mass mobilisation, pursued by the military governments from 1976 to 1983.

Conclusion

Eva Perón's performance as, simultaneously, leader and wife of the president and embodiment of 'the people' effectively expressed the various contradictory components of the movement. She passionately conveyed a commitment to change whilst defending the conservation of traditions, she expressed the forcefulness of mass mobilisations at the same time that she encouraged through her example devotion and acceptance of the authoritarianism of the movement and the government headed by Perón. This was largely achieved through the idiom of the family and the private domain. She and her husband were childless yet they were the mother and father of the entire country. The language of the domestic sphere, of intimacy and sentiment was therefore appropriate – and highly effective.

For both the government of Perón and for the military regime of the 1970s the family constituted the heart of society and the basis of the moral order. Women as mothers were seen to play a central role in reproducing the values of society and the sense of nationhood that was felt to correspond to these values. However, during periods of acute social change the relationship between the private and public became charged with meaning and the boundaries between them simultaneously confirmed, contested and blurred. For Eva Perón the private sphere worked as a support of the public arena. She stressed the continuities between private and public, expressly in relation to women's roles. It was precisely woman's role in the private sphere that imposed the need for her participation in the public sphere. So while Eva Perón insisted on the preservation of the family and of women's role as mothers and carers, she politicised the private sphere. The private sphere was a microcosm of the nation, it was a component cell and indispensable to its structure and integrity.

For Eva Perón women's participation in the political arena had revolutionary implications. Women could, as some feminists argue today[21] bring specific qualities into the public arena and transform it. The presence of women would promote the values of love, solidarity and peace. Women played a central role in creating the nation through the education of their children, but Evita envisaged that this passionately felt identity need not lead to war and competition, because the worldwide solidarity of women as mothers denounced the human costs of war.

By contrast, during the military regime of the 1970s the intention was to depoliticise the private sphere. The military's perception of an overly politicised public sphere encouraged a view of the family as a refuge from political discourse. Indeed, state repression and the violence of those years encouraged similar views amongst the population, for many of whom the dangers of political participation became all too obvious and onerous. But the extent of the repression was such that it desecrated the family and invalidated its claims to being a refuge and place of safety. The terror hit at the heart of the private sphere, at the most intimate of relationships, experiences and feelings.

What the mothers of Plaza de Mayo did was to recover the morality of the private sphere by challenging the amorality of the public sphere. To do so they confronted the regime with its own contradictions and stressed the values they promoted: the importance of motherhood, the self-sacrifice of women and their subordination to the well-being of their children, risking every-thing in order to stand up for their families.

The gendering of political discourse in Argentina introduced emotional and intimate elements and made visible the role of sentiment in political discourse. Eva Perón articulated a political ideology through means that were inclusive, and in this respect truly populist, so that workers of industry, housewives, the rural poor and indeed sectors of the middle classes were all identified as members of the polity whose needs and rights had to be recognised. The discourse promoted by Peronism reached those that had been excluded and addressed the skewed nature of the Argentine polity as it had developed from the time of its inception in the nineteenth century. As we have seen, many argue that the first Peronist experience changed the profile of the country forever. The people had been granted a place and this would not be relinquished easily, as is testified by the resistance to the military governments that followed. The turbulent years that followed the 1955 coup are a testimony to this resistance, culminating in the most brutal period of repression in the 1970s. In the face of this brutality, only the private sphere, only women and mothers were able to recapture a voice to remind society of its responsibilities.

Notes

1 Women also played a central role in protests against the effects of the economic crisis. In the early 1990s housewives' movements organised protests amongst women in middle-class areas as well as in working-class areas. For a discussion of the broad range of women's responses to military government and the impact of government economic policies, see Feijóo and Gogna (1990).

2 Mothers' movements similar to the Argentine one have emerged in a number of places, under similar circumstances, as for example in El Salvador and Turkey.

3 In 1883 more than 500 children were abandoned at the city orphanage in Buenos Aires. Six years later that number had doubled (Guy 1997: 159).

4 See Feijóo (1998). The defence of morals and of the values of 'western civilisation' was also a feature of the ideology of the subsequent military governments during the 1970s. See Jacobo Timerman, *Prisoner without a Name, Cell without a Number*, for a personal account of his dramatic encounter with the exponents of this ideology.

5 In 1869 the percentage of foreigners was 49.3 per cent whereas in 1947 this percentage had fallen to 27.5 per cent with 31.7 per cent of residents originating in the interior of the country. Perhaps changes in migration patterns are also reflected in the fact that whereas the number of Argentine women is much larger than the number of foreign women amongst the younger age groups of the population of the capital in 1947, they break even and are then overtaken by foreign women in the older age groups (for example in the age group 55 to 59 there were 39,870 foreign women to 32,953 Argentine women in the capital) (Censo General 1947, Tomo I).

6 The platform of the women's organisation was universal suffrage, civil equality for women and men and for children born in and out of marriage, divorce and work legislation, as well as the abolition of capital punishment (Carlson 1988: 161).

7 In 1932 the Brazilian women's suffrage movement led by Bertha Lutz succeeded in obtaining the vote for women after fifteen years of struggle. In Uruguay Paulina Luisi's movement was also successful. Argentina 'seemed to be slipping behind other Latin American countries' (Carlson 1988: 172). Chilean women were granted the vote in 1949.

8 Victoria Ocampo was an aristocrat who assumed a leading role within Argentine arts and literary circles. Carlson (1988) discusses the differences in political orientation between Ocampo, who never espoused the spirit of or commitment to universal rights, and the socialist concerns of Alicia Moreau de Justo.

9 Only Carmela Horne de Burmeister supported Perón's suffrage plan (Carlson 1988: 187). Other women's leaders were concerned that the presidential decree could be reversed with a change of government.

10 The phrase is taken from a speech by Eva Perón on 12 February 1947 and reproduced in E. Perón (1996).

11 Perón's share of the vote increased from 54 per cent in 1946 to 64 per cent in 1951.

12 The socialists and communists had put forward women candidates but they were defeated.

13 'Discurso de Eva Perón en el Acto Inaugural de la Primera Asamblea Nacional del Movimiento Peronista Femenino' 26 de Julio de 1949, Buenos Aires (Instituto Nacional de Historia), page 9.

14 Many feminists were themselves crucially concerned with the family and women's role as educators, in much the same way as Evita.

15 Both her supporters and most of her detractors refer to her by her first name, usually in the diminutive case, emphasising the sense of closeness and immediacy with her person. Her husband was generally referred to by his last name, without the use of a prefix, which also conveys some degree of familiarity but greater distance, authority and respect. In line with this sense of authority he was sometimes referred to as General or General Perón. But it would be rare for any reference to be made in terms of his personal names, Juan Domingo.

16 However, much was made of Perón's physical proximity to the workers by the Peronist apparatus, in particular the occasions when Perón removed his jacket, placing himself on the same footing as the 'descamisados'. His speech was also imbued with sentiment as on 17 October 1945 when he addressed his supporters: 'I want to mix with this sweating mass as a simple citizen, I want to hug it close to my heart as I would my mother' (quoted in Fraser and Navarro 1997: 67).

17 Whether these claims are true or not, it is the case that this hypothesis has become incorporated into the mythology of Eva Perón.

18 Evita was already ill when public support for her candidacy to the vice-presidency caused disquiet amongst the military elite. She was forced to renounce her candidacy in a radio broadcast, following a dramatic and emotionally intense public rally on 22 August 1951 during which the crowds urged her to embrace the candidacy.

19 The internal differences were apparent well before Perón's return, though they were tragically expressed when gunfire was opened on the crowd that eagerly awaited the returning General after his exile in Spain. Shortly before his death, on 1 May 1974 during the traditional Labour Day celebrations Perón responded to chanting from the crowds accusing the youth of being 'mercenaries paid by foreigners' (Torre and De Riz 1993: 320).

20 Ironically Isabel Perón unlike Eva, *was* nominated as her husband's vice-president, taking over the government at his death. Her government was characterised not only by the repression of dissenting factions within the Peronist movement but also by measures and legislation which were not sympathetic to women. As Feijóo and Gogna point out: 'There is little need to point out that having a woman in this office (of President) did not guarantee *per se* implementation of policies to improve women's situation . . . the Peronist movement, in spite of all it had achieved for women in previous periods (1946–55), took what to say the least, can only be called an ambiguous stance on women's issues during the 1973–76 period.

Some of the measures taken did reflect their concern for the situation of women in the popular sectors . . . ' (1990: 81).
21 See in particular S. Ruddick (1989) 'Maternal thinking', in *Feminist Studies*, 6/2: 342–67.

Research for this chapter was supported by the University of London and Goldsmiths' College.

Bibliography

Afshar, H. (ed.) (1996) *Women and Politics in the Third World*, London: Routledge.

Calvera, L. (1990) *Mujeres y Feminismo en la Argentina*, Grupo Editor Latinoamericano.

Carlson, M. (1988) *Feminismo! The Women's Movement in Argentina from its Beginnings to Eva Perón*, Chicago: Academy.

Chuchryk, P. (1994) 'From dictatorship to democracy: the women's movement in Chile', in J. Jaquette (ed.) *The Women's Movement in Latin America. Participation and Democracy*, second edition, Boulder, Colorado: Westview Press.

Dujovne Ortiz, A. (1997) *Eva Perón. A Biography*, London: Warner Books.

Eloy Martinez, T. (1995) *Santa Evita*, Barcelona: Seix Barral.

Feijóo, M.C. (1998) 'Democratic participation and women in Argentina', in J.S. Jaquette and S.L. Wolchik (eds) *Women and Democracy. Latin America and Central and Eastern Europe*, Baltimore and London: The Johns Hopkins University Press.

Feijóo, M.C. and Gogna, M. (1990) 'Women in the transition to democracy', in E. Jelin (ed.) *Women and Social Change in Latin America*, London: Zed.

Feijóo, M.C. and Nari, M.M.A. (1994) 'Women and democracy in Argentina', in J. Jaquette (ed.) *The Women's Movement in Latin America. Participation and Democracy*, second edition, Boulder, Colorado: Westview Press.

Fraser, N. and Navarro, M. (1997) *Evita. The Real Lives of Eva Perón*, London: Andre Deutsch.

Guy, D. (1997) 'Mothers alive and dead', in D. Balderston and D. Guy (eds) *Sex and Sexuality in Latin America*, New York and London: NY University Press.

Isla, A. (1998) 'Terror, memory and responsibility in Argentina', *Critique of Anthropology*, Vol. 18(2): 134–56.

Kandiyoti, D. (1991) 'Identity and its discontents: women and the nation', *Millenium: Journal of International Studies* 20(3): 429–43.

Laclau, E. (1987) 'Ideology', in E.P. Archetti, P. Cammack and B. Roberts (eds) *Sociology of 'Developing Societies' Latin America*, London: Macmillan.

Moreau de Justo, A. (1945) *La Mujer en la Democracia*, Buenos Aires: El Ateneo.

Munck, R. (1987) *Argentina from Anarchism to Peronism. Workers, Unions and Politics, 1855–1985* (with R. Falcon and B. Galitelli), London: Zed.

Ortner, S. (1978) 'The Virgin and the State', *Feminist Studies*, 4(3): 20–34.

Payotti, A. (1994) ' "La Razón de mi Vida" de Eva Perón. Autobiografía y politica', in H. Achugar (ed.) *En otras Palabras, otras Historias*, Montevideo: Universidad de la Republica, FHCE.

Perón, E. (1996) *La Razón de mi Vida y otros Escritos*, Buenos Aires: Planeta Editores.

Rock, D. (1993) 'Argentina, 1930–1946', in L. Bethell (ed.) *Argentina since Independence*, Cambridge: Cambridge University Press.

Roxborough, I. (1987) 'Populism and class conflict', in E.P. Archetti, P. Cammack and B. Roberts (eds) *Sociology of 'Developing Societies' Latin America*, London: Macmillan.

Taylor, J.M. (1979) *Evita Perón: the Myths of a Woman*, Oxford: Basil Blackwell.

Torre, J.C. and De Riz, L. (1993) 'Argentina since 1946', in L. Bethell (ed.) *Argentina since Independence*, Cambridge: Cambridge University Press.

Verbitsky, H. (1995) *El Vuelo*, Barcelona: Seix Barral.

Vitale, L. (1981) *Historia y Sociología de la Mujer Latinoamericana*, Barcelona: Editorial Fontamara.

Yuval-Davis, N. and F. Anthias (eds) (1989) *Woman-Nation-State*, Basingstoke: Macmillan.

Chapter 11

Writing the usual love story

The fashioning of conjugal and national subjects in Turkey

Nükhet Sirman[1]

The social sciences have recently turned their attention to the construction of identity in and through discourses that fashion communities, often naturalised as primordial (Anderson 1983). Anthropologists too have slowly begun to turn their attention to the study of written texts produced by different societies (Messick 1993). A recent edited volume raises a number of issues with regard to the ways in which various types of written texts can be made the object of anthropological analysis (Archetti 1994).[2]

The aim of this chapter is to use novels as text in order to show the way in which women take up subject positions in and through these discourses and the extent to which these positions may or may not subvert the original intent of the discourse. The novels analysed in this chapter were written by the first renowned woman novelist of Turkey, Halide Edip Adıvar. I shall argue that, taken as a whole, the literary work produced by Adıvar generates a new discourse on women by taking up, interrogating and redefining the limits of the existing discourses on women. The main issue at stake in these novels is the production of conjugal subjects.

Feminine, and, to a certain extent masculine, subjectivity is redefined through these novels by positioning men and women as the subjects of love to see whether and how love can become the grounding on which strong and stable conjugal ties might be produced.

These novels were written in a context when questions of marriage and the production of the modern family were a major societal concern. Since the 1870s, the issue of reform was taken up in the Ottoman Empire through numerous discourses articulating critiques of forms of governance, and together have had the effect of producing in discourse a realm of the social as distinct from the political.[3] These discourses took various forms, including traditional satires and tales, newspaper articles, and were also at the forefront of a new, modern literature that began to be produced.[4]

In this chapter I shall analyse three of the novels written by Halide Edip in an effort to show how the writing of the novel itself can be read as a painful search for the proper subject of the conjugal family. Recent work has shown how, through narrative, readers construct identities by taking up subject positions suggested by the plot.[5] This process is one of active negotiation where the subject considers various story lines and tries to make sense of self and of events, of experience and of cultural histories. Constructing the self becomes a process through which other collectivities such as family, ethnicity and nation are also constructed in relation to one another. And in spite of the fact that these identities are multiple and changing, the stories and the social life which, to use a neologism coined by Somers and Gibson, are thereby 'storied', navigate within the limits set up by previous stories and histories available within a finite repertoire of social, cultural and public narratives (Somers and Gibson 1994). I shall focus on the writing rather than the reading of the novel and show the process through which the plot allows some subject positions, while excluding others. Looking at Halide Edip's successive novels, I shall try to show which subject positions are made possible and which, to use Butler's terminology, are turned into 'excluded' or 'repudiated sites' that are 'refused the possibility of cultural articulation' (Butler 1993: 8).

In a search of the construction of feminine subjectivity in Republican Turkey, I concentrate on realist romances for four reasons. First, they are about the person who as hero or heroine of a love story becomes the subject who enters into negotiations with history, society and culture (or with the present and with meaning) in whatever guise these emerge in situations suggested by the plot. Hence they work through problems of sentiments and especially desire, those aspects of the self that need to be analysed in a study of subjectivities (Jackson 1993). Second, love stories, although not exclusively written or consumed by women, allow greater scope for the constitution of female subjectivities, compared say to the heroic tale, the adventure story or the mystery tale. The romance is often set within the intimate sphere of daily life and thus provides the reader with a set of possible modalities for interpersonal relationships. Third, the love story is also a traditional narrative genre that allows the reader to trace the process of transformation and reworking of old forms according to new sensibilities. Finally, the construction of the subject in love stories also constitutes the social collectivity as a particular, possible collectivity that inscribes a set of values around which it is constructed. These values are often in contradiction and it is this that produces the energy that propels the story forward. In the process, the values are redefined, negotiated, managed and grounded arriving momentarily however, at a resolution.

The love stories that I choose to analyse were written as realist novels by Halide Edip Adıvar (b. 1882), the first modern Turkish novelist. Halide Edip was a prolific writer who tried a wide range of literary genres, ranging from newspaper columns, to short stories, memoirs, travel logs, as well as novels from about 1908 until her death in 1964. Most of these texts deal with the social, cultural and philosophical issues raised by the rapid transformation of the Ottoman Empire into the Turkish nation-state. At present, Halide Edip is an important figure in the panoply of famous Turks produced by the hegemonic nationalist discourse in Turkey. She is cast as a model for the modern Turkish woman, the first to embark upon a public career. She is depicted in popular film and dramatic documentary as a more or less passive witness of the heroism of a nation in the making and of its almost mythical leaders. As such she is transformed into the educated, enlightened woman who is ready to sacrifice herself for the good of her nation.[6]

But in the novels and short stories written about the Turkish War of Independence (1919–22) (in which she participated as a French and English-speaking corporal charged with translating for the nationalist command in Ankara and later, with the documentation of Greek atrocities in western Turkey), she took on responsibilities that were much more than a passive recording of events. Her memoirs of the war, published in England in 1928 under the title *The Turkish Ordeal*, attribute these atrocities to the war itself. She sees war as the product of western aggression against the Ottoman Empire. War in her view is a relentless will to power, the product of excess masculinity.[7] She describes vividly the dramas, hopes and suffering of the Anatolian peasantry, including their desires, and their longing for those at the front. Her own sentiments and moods are also described, interrogated and judged by a narrator who, as in a trance, is not sure about 'the reality of the self who is doing the writing'. The national cause is the only reality, which she says eclipses all others, including her sense of self. She thus makes strategic use of the many genres of western literature, including stream of consciousness, to which she was exposed as a student at the American College for Girls in Istanbul before the war, in order to explore the nature of the relationship between the individual and the collectivity. In all these pieces what is interrogated above all is the nature of the writing, the thinking and the national subject.

Before the war, she was known for her nationalist and feminist activism, writing in Istanbul dailies on issues of women's education and the negative consequences of polygamy. She was also among the founders of a women's club, the Society for the Advancement of Women and of the Turkish Hearths (founded in 1911) which provided a cultural script for Turkish nationalism. Later, in 1924, she and her second husband opposed Mustafa Kemal's author-itarian policies and left the country on a self-imposed exile until Atatürk's death in 1938. They were also known (and discredited) as supporters of an American mandate during the troubled days preceding the occupation of Istanbul by the Allied forces in March, 1920, which launched the process of national resistance led by Mustafa Kemal Atatürk. He and other nationalists, among whom were members of the Ottoman parliament, army officers and intellectuals (including Halide Edip and her husband Adnan Adıvar), left what they saw as a corrupt city to join, unify and lead the dispersed resistance movements in Anatolia.

Halide Edip wrote twenty-one novels between 1909 and 1964. In spite of the fact that she tries new ways to talk about collectivity in all her novels and addresses different problems associated with it, it is always love that makes the narrative. She herself off-handedly talks of the centrality of love in her understanding of the novel in her memoirs when depicting one of them, *Yeni Turan*, as a book 'which has the usual love story, [but] . . . not much pretension to art' (1926: 332).[8] In fact, as I shall try to show, hers are never simply 'usual love stor[ies]' at all. Love makes the narrative in these novels in the sense that it provides the dramatic tension around the issue of union, the impossibility of which is predicated on a moral formula: one's duty towards family, friend, companion or nation is greater than personal desire. Sacrifice for these values defines a moral code, compliance with which entails recognition and respect from self and other. The domestication of love becomes another way of speaking about a just social order, one based on love rather than repression and authority.

The twist in Halide Edip's novels lies in the way she constructs her heroines. They are an inversion of the heroines of the modern Turkish novel that appeared in tandem with Turkish modernisation after the 1870s. These novels, realist renderings of traditional love stories, based their plot around the impossibility of the union of two lovers as a result of social and/or psychological obstacles (Moran 1983). Two basic female figures appear in these novels: those of the *femme fatale* and the innocent victim. It is either the unjust social order constructed around tradition itself or the unbridled passion of the *femme fatale* (frequently used as an allegory of false modernism) that causes the plight of these often voiceless heroines (Moran 1983; Kandiyoti 1988). Thus male authors use these heroines to critique both the traditional social order and the new forms of adopting western patterns of life and consumption (Mardin 1974; Kandiyoti 1988). These novels work out the subjectivity of the male-headed nuclear family and the forms of intimacy imagined by modern men. They serve as male discourses of liberation from the authority of the ruler/father (Sirman, in press) and the fears that accompany such liberation (Parla 1993).

In these modern novels, as in the traditional love stories, love derives its authority by appealing to supra-societal power. In traditional tales this authority is ultimately God since love of another leads to love of the ultimate. In the modern versions, the naturalness of emotions is substituted for the divine, thereby naturalising society as well as the family, and through sentiment, the subject him/herself. In both cases, moreover, the authority of love legitimises and extols the virtues of sacrifice of personal desire for loyalty to a collectivity larger than the person and the family. These virtues are deemed necessary for both men and women. But while innocence deprives women of any agency in attaining these goals, it turns them into the means through which men can transcend their own masculinity, understood here as the brute force of the sword that symbolises the ruler/father (Erol 1992).

Halide Edip, by contrast, combines the innocent victim and the *femme fatale* in the same person and thereby problematises the identity of woman. In her early novels,[9] written before the war, the problem is resolved by the realisation that what looks like one is really the other. The problem posed by the female heroine is really a problem for the male gaze. This is signaled in the novels through the narrative device of describing the heroine through the male voice. The novels are often written in the third person, but it is the male hero's thoughts and actions that are given priority, and events that he could not witness are often described through letters.

Indeed in *Handan*, the near absence of dialogue, the social presentation of self, are striking. The plot moves forward through internal dialogue expressed in letters. These are first written by the the hero and his male friends, and it is only towards the end of the novel that the reader gets a glimpse of the heroine's voice, still, however, through her letters. This literary device has the effect of turning the female voice into the product of the narrative. Moreover, some of the letters written by the heroine are never sent (in Handan's words, they are 'destined to the dustbin' (110) and at the end of the novel, her thoughts are narrated under the title of 'Handan's sentiments' (156)).[10] Thus, a distinction is made by the author between thoughts and sentiments that can be articulated and those that cannot. These thoughts and sentiments that cannot become social and hence are excluded belong only to Handan, the heroine, while her male counterpart has no trouble in sharing his sentiments that defy the norm with his male friend. Through such narrative strategies, Edip can depict an outer reality compared to a different inner self, thus problematising the feminine and raising the issue of the difference between identity, a temporary unification of contradiction that is basically social, and subjectivity, the inner process through which such contradictions have to be continually resolved.

In all of Halide Edip's early novels, the hero first hears about the heroine indirectly through others. What is more, he does not like what he hears. She seems to contradict some norm: either of femininity through excess of physical prowess, or of morality by transgressing the code of honour and modesty as it applies to women. When he meets and gets to know the woman, he cannot help but fall in love with her, overwhelmed by her courage and sincerity. Appearances are indeed deceptive, especially for women. For although these heroines do transgress some societal code, it is the code that is ultimately wrong according to another, superior code: the quest for self-knowledge and for the truth of the self. But the social moral code is too strong, or human (especially male) fallibility too unavoidable[11] and drama ensues. The resolution resides in situating the self in collectivities that are constructed in opposition to the one in which the heroine finds herself: the true Ottoman order in contrast to that created by its western-struck elite, nation as opposed to empire, companionate marriage in contrast to the traditional polygamous and extended Ottoman family, the tolerance and humanism of the traditional Ottoman quarter as opposed to the oppression of the centralised authoritarian state, the nationally conscious youth in contrast to the parasitic post-independence bourgeoisie. Reference to two different moral codes is a device also used by the earlier novels where it is used to subvert the legitimacy of the existing social and political order. But there is also a difference in the way Halide Edip makes use of this well-known formula: it is not just the social order but also its subjects that need to change.[12]

In effect, in the novels she writes before the establishment of the Turkish Republic in 1923, her heroines first appear to be *femmes fatales* but end up being victims: they die or are doomed to an unhappy marriage. The old order destroys them. By contrast, the new order accords her heroines the possibility of marriage and happiness as well as of self-actualisation through education and work. But many of these novels read as programmatic statements, devoid of passion, especially compared to the more dramatic earlier novels. In the following, I shall first concentrate on *Handan*, one of Halide Edip's early novels, to show that the happy endings of the later novels are the result of a painful process of negotiation that women as subjects have to enter into in order to gain respect, stability and happiness. This process of negotiation requires the female subject to edit out her passion, which then becomes a spectre haunting the writer and her heroines, as well as the reader.

Handan, written in 1912 at the height of the Balkan War, tells the story of the eponymous heroine through the letters that others write about her. The main narrator is Refik Cemal, her cousin's husband, a sensitive politically involved young man who starts the story by announcing to his friend exiled in Paris his marriage to Neriman, one of the quarters' 'English' (i.e. well-educated and wealthy) girls. But the marriage turns out to be a double one: on the one hand to Neriman who acts as a foil to Handan and on the other to Handan, the cousin she grew up with and is very strongly attached to. The reader follows the life story of Handan narrated by Refik Cemal and Neriman. At the age of 16 Handan takes lessons in philosophy, mathematics and sociology and develops a close friendship with her tutor. He falls in love with her and asks her to marry him but she refuses him on the grounds that he only wants her as a comrade in his political struggle. He loves her mind and not herself. The revolutionary tutor is arrested soon after and commits suicide in his prison cell upon his realisation that his cause had no meaning without Handan. She then marries an older Ottoman bureaucrat who makes her feel like a woman.[13] But all he is interested in is her sexuality. He begins having affairs with other women once he is assigned to a mission in Europe and he finally leaves her. Handan spends most of her time in England in the home of her cousin, who follows her husband there when he is forced to leave Istanbul for political reasons. They set up a ménage à trois, Neriman providing wifely care and Handan platonic intellectual stimulation. Handan becomes ill when her husband leaves her and in a reversal of roles Refik Cemal takes care of her. He is already in love with her and she too falls in love with him and, suffering from a temporary loss of memory, she returns his kiss. When she regains her memory she recognises her own betrayal of her cousin, her best friend with whom she had shared everything, and dies.

Handan's illness can best be described as the embodiment of pain. Refik Cemal describes it to his friend as the 'rushing of blood to the brain' (117), while doctors diagnose it as meningitis. Handan's pain stems from her inability to realise the conjugal love she desires. In her unsent letters to her husband she makes clear that she is suffering because of her understanding of love as total union of mind, body and soul, a definition she claims as a product of her own will.[14] Her husband has in the meantime decided on a separation and leaves for France with a mistress, Handan's former chambermaid, because he is disturbed and estranged by her independence and strong personality which he sees as expressions of superiority and haughtiness. He is Edip's first description of excess masculinity, all materiality, and no soul. He is only capable of sexual desire, and it is the recognition that her marriage was based only on this that drives Handan to lose her memory. Her struggle (signaled by a high fever) with her own mind that led her to think her husband was more than he was, leads Handan to lose her faculty of thought and remain pure heart or sentiment. But loss of thought also results in the loss of memory and therefore identity. She is now innocent and childlike. Therefore, her love for Refik Cemal in the absence of the past, and therefore of identity, cannot produce happiness. It cannot be cognisant of family, duty, loyalty and collectivity.

Halide Edip's heroines, like Handan, are not pretty, but they are passionate. This makes them irresistible, but also places them at the centre of a drama that imbues them with an air of extreme sadness though also of dignity. This drama is the result of the fact that these women are the subjects of desire, the object of which is knowledge as well as sexuality. This makes them like men. Both pose a problem for Halide Edip: serenity, stability and continuity, in short the family, are rendered impossible under these circumstances. In fact, Handan cannot have children: she has to play with Neriman's son. But it is also desire that inscribes her as a free spirit and makes her the object as well as the subject of intense desire. Refik Cemal begins to be bored with his life with the complacent Neriman until Handan joins them. So simple domesticity and complete subjugation and devotion on the part of women cannot make for a stable family either. Only total communion can achieve this. But total communion can only be between total human beings, mind as well as body, or in short, the communion of souls.

The novel plays with the opposition of mind and body by interposing a third term, the soul, to resolve the opposition. Handan discovers the importance of sexuality in the process of seeking knowledge. She rejects the proposal that will make her refuse her sexuality only to be thrown into a relationship that constructs her as nothing but a sexual being. This is equally unacceptable since it reverts to the view that equates women with sexuality.[15] Refik Cemal is the only man with whom a complete and fulfilling union can be contemplated because in his person are combined both feminine and masculine qualities: compassion and intellect, affection and politics, action and serenity. But the happy union of mind and body is an unrealisable dream. Something essential is lacking, something she calls soul. This has to be sought actively by the desiring subject who thereby becomes the heroine of a narrative of quest. Learning and reason are the tools that will help the heroine in this quest that is concluded when both body and mind are transcended. Unlike the body and the mind, the soul is neither material nor immaterial but both, a totalising way of speaking about the whole person.

This leads us back to the formula used by the traditional love tales in Turkish culture where the love that a man and a woman feel for each other leads them to the realisation of the love of God which can only be reached through the love of beauty which is unity (*vahdet*). So Halide Edip mobilises the concept of love described by traditional Sufi orders to resolve the question of earthly love.[16] And the same love is also extended to the nation which, expressed in Handan's words, is imagined as a unity of souls:

> I shall love people with unsurpassed sacrifice and compassion, and give them my soul until the last drop. I shall travel all over this dark and unfortunate land and let flow into the soul of my country's people all the goodness that beautiful and great souls have before me bequeathed to humanity.
>
> (41)

This is contrasted to the masculine nationalism of the Young Turks, intent only on domination, a point she later develops in her critique of Mustafa Kemal Atatürk. It is also a nationalism that rather than only seeking the sovereignty of the nation as unique and distinct from others is geared towards a unified and harmonious humanity. The enlightened, tolerant Islam practised by her grandmother and other modest inhabitants of Istanbul provides her with the cultural and moral matrix on which her version of a modern social order rests. It is only by being true to this culturally specific self, the soul that provides the inner spring for real love, that not only Turks but all of humanity will, according to Edip, be really free.

It is in her novel *The Clown and His Daughter*, published in 1936, that Halide Edip has the chance to look into the nature of this utopia.[17] Many critics describe this novel as her most mature, representing the apex of her writing career (Enginün 1986). The novel is set in a small neighbourhood of Istanbul during the reign of the absolutist sultan Abdülhamit II (1877–1908).[18] The neighbourhood is more than a context, it is, in fact, the main protagonist. What are being narrated are the complex relations of competition as well as solidarity that exist within the close-knit community of the neighbourhood (*mahalle*). This is the world of what can be called the 'big house' where every individual acquires his or her identity from the house to which he or she belongs (Sirman 1998). The house is structured by a hierarchy based on kinship, age and gender and ruled by the oldest male, the father. Hierarchy between the houses is established through social status, the primary element of which is defined through the relation of the head of the household to the palace. Thus in the neighbourhood people of different social classes co-exist, comprising a moral as well as a social universe (Dubetsky 1971; Mardin 1989).

The romance that propels the story in *The Clown and His Daughter* in fact occupies a rather marginal part of the novel compared to Halide Edip's previous works. It describes the slow growth and maturation of a strong attachment between the daughter of a shadow puppeteer who is known for the beauty of her voice and her deep piety and her piano teacher, an Italian priest. The priest decides to convert to Islam and marries this young woman whom every one recognises as being wiser and more mature than most. But the priest is not the only man in the novel who is lauded for having both feminine and masculine traits. Like Refik Cemal in *Handan*, the shadow puppeteer too knows of love and compassion, as his nickname kız Tevkif (girl Tevfik) indicates. The characters in the novel are almost epic characters who in general have few personal or moral dilemmas but are rather faithful renderings of the status and collectivity they represent. The love story is an allegory that serves to represent the right combination of East and West that the author deems necessary in order to reach true happiness. The novel as a whole, however, reads as a representation of a social imaginary, that of a bygone, 'traditional' social order as imagined ex-post facto.[19] Halide Edip is reflecting about the past in 1936 through the lens of her experience of having watched the creation of a modern social life and order, about many aspects of which she is furiously critical. These aspects are detailed in her later, and often less enthralling novels such as *Tatarcık* (1939), which traces the life choices that young university graduates face in a society which declares itself new and different.[20] Recep, the son of the wise hero and heroine of the previous novel, is among them and it he who makes the best choice: to modernise and civilise the small Black Sea village in which he and his modern bride-to-be decide to settle.[21] The fact that he is the son of the heroes of the previous novel thus indicates the genealogy through which such proper morals can be attained. But in *The Clown and His Daughter* and in the later novels, the subjects are already fixed and it is social identities rather than the process through which subjectivities are produced that are the main issue.

Before this closure, however, Halide Edip published two more novels that deal with subjectivity, love and the collectivity, *Kalp Ağrisi* (1924) and its sequel, *Zeyno'nun Oğlu* (1926–7), after which she confined herself to writing her memoirs, touring the United States, India and Pakistan, and writing essays on the nature of the relationship between East and West. These novels constitute an interesting bridge between the earlier dramas which interrogate the nature of love and the possibility of conjugality as a basis for marriage and the later ones, when love is no longer an issue, and instead the excesses of the *nouveau riche* and a fast-growing but rootless middle-class are explored through a much more peda-gogical discourse. It is in fact in these two novels that the problem of love posed by Handan is finally resolved. Zeyno, a 1920s version of Handan, falls madly in love with Hasan, an army officer and a veteran of the War of Independence. Hasan responds in kind, but neither of them is absolutely sure about the other's intentions, nor the meaning of their own sentiments. In the meantime, Zeyno's best friend also falls in love with Hasan who for a while plays along with her. When she learns about Hasan's relations with Zeyno, the girl tries to commit suicide. In good sacrificial spirit Zeyno con-vinces Hasan that he must marry her friend, Azize, which he does. Azize becomes dreadfully ill after her suicide attempt but neverthe-less goes on to conceive a child in spite of the dangers that this involves. She dies in childbirth in Austria, where in the meantime Hasan has become involved with another woman, this time with a liberated western woman, Dora. Zeyno remains alone with her heartache (the meaning of the Turkish title).

Zeyno and her heartache are explored in this novel by position-ing the protagonist between the liberated western woman, Dora, and Azize, her superficial local imitation, one of the objects of satire in the new Republic intent on defining modern but national gender identities. Where Azize is frivolous and childlike in her determination to get the man she wants, Dora is intellectually accomplished, mature and ready to give him up in the face of moral obligation. Zeyno, by contrast, cannot consider love without marriage, nor marriage without the union of souls. She is thus unable to act unless it is to mistrust her desire and give it up. Dora is the one who finally domesticates Hasan and it is Azize who gives him a child. Contrary to what occurs in her previous novels, *Kalp Ağrisi* starts directly with the female protagonists' voice, thus indicating the possibility of the realisation of female agency under the new Republican regime.[22] Internal dialogues belonging to both protagonists gradually expose a difference between man and woman in their analysis of the meaning of love. While Hasan is more impetuous and less analytical, Zeyno is compelled to deconstruct her sentiments by placing them in the triad of nature (physical passion), mind, and soul. This difference, fixed at the end of the novel, contrasts sharply with the first scene when Hasan and Zeyno meet at a picnic with friends. They immediately engage in a contest of wits, which then is continued in the field of sports. They race, but the athletic soldier is not able to outdo the woman. The problem of excess femininity displayed by Handan is no longer an issue. Men and women are physically and mentally equal. Instead, difference has to do with sentiment, with the value men and women attach to love, and it is the lack of soul in male love that finally makes both lose. But this is the truth that the heroine has to learn through much pain in the course of the novel. Gender difference then becomes the product of the text and of female reflexivity and agency.

The sequel, *Zeyno'nun Oğlu*, continues the elaboration of these differences. Zeyno is now married to a much older man, also an army officer like Hasan.[23] But it is not passion that has led to this marriage, although love is not absent. It is the feeling of security, understanding and maturity that she finds in Muhsin that finally makes Zeyno believe that she can forget Hasan and the delusions of the flesh that he represents. The novel is now set in Diyarbakır, in south-eastern Turkey, at a time when a number of Kurdish rebellions are in preparation. Rather than dealing with a Kurdish issue as such, the book is about the relations among civil servants in a remote government post. Compared to the earlier novel, there are many more social issues broached here and the problem of setting a good model for the new generation of young Republicans is paramount. Hasan discovers he has a son by a Kurdish woman with whom he had had a brief affair and through Zeyno's careful guidance he is brought to recognise his love both for his son and for Zeyno and to appreciate the value of this sentiment. This is his story,[24] a story through which he gains wisdom and maturity by having to accept life as it is: he will not be able to marry Zeyno, whose own appreciation of her husband has also matured, but he will have to marry the mother of his son. Excess masculinity is finally brought to heel in the face of life itself.

But there is an important twist to *Zeyno'nun Oğlu*. The title of the novel means Zeyno's son, and the Zeyno in question is the Kurdish woman Hasan ends up marrying as the mother of his son. Handan is finally exorcised as the Kurdish Zeyno, an uneducated woman whose devotion to her son and his father is a product of her motherly instinct rather than her mind. Sexuality is thus cast out and given to nature while modern Zeyno proceeds to set the example of the new proper femininity through restraint, reflexivity, duty and compassion.

The transformations that love has to go through to create a stable marriage are now complete. Furthermore, the transformative power of love is clearly gendered. There are two words for love in Turkish: *aşk*, passionate love and *sevgi*, the deep attachment between intimate persons such as friends, parents and also between the individual and the nation, citizen and state and among citizens themselves that creates the fraternity described by Anderson in his analysis of nationalism (1983). The difference between these two terms is best explained by Mualla Eyüboğlu in an oral history interview. She asks: 'What is *aşk*? Just peanuts! Your heart goes thumpety thump when you see a pair of gray trousers. But *sevgi* is really what lasts a life time. It is, in short, respect'.[25] According to Halide Edip's version, *aşk*, when transformed into *sevgi*, has the power to curb both femininity and masculinity to create the subjects of companionate marriage.

In the end Halide Edip calls on women to domesticate their desire through a mystical unity with a higher totality: love of God and/or the nation and companionate conjugality. The communion of souls is the bedrock on which collectivities such as the family and the nation can be made stable and lasting. But it is women themselves who have to actively perform this communion by seeking knowledge through self-contemplation. It is the two Zeyno novels which best express the pain involved in transforming Handan into Tatarcık. Doris Sommer (1990) has argued that 'Passion' and 'Polis' mutually construct one another in what she describes as the Latin American foundational fictions. In Halide Edip's narratives it is women who construct both passion and polis through the construction of true companionate marriage. The modern Turkish woman is a subject with a specific agency, a socially competent individual who, as a result of her education, is able to cultivate her mind, but who also, through love, learns to sacrifice self and desire for the care and guidance of others in the family and in the nation. It was perhaps this unity of self-assertion and compassion which appeared as a paradox to Turkish academics who attempted to explain women's position in modern Turkish society through the phrase 'emancipated but not liberated' (Kandiyoti 1987; Toprak 1990).[26]

One of the issues that anthropologists need to address is how to link the world of the text and the world of reality (Archetti 1994). The reappearance of characters in Halide Edip's novels provides a key to my reading of these texts. Each of the novels places the protagonists within a situation in which he or she is faced with a serious moral and social problem. The problem is often the same: how to create a politics of life for an individual that would lead to the construction of positive social relations between self and collectivity. The difference lies with the social context, itself a function of the passing of time. Thus, the dilemma at the turn of the century is the problem of creating companionate marriage through love in a society where progressive individuals denounce the tyranny of subordination, of powerful men as heads of large households. Halide Edip herself is at that time facing the daunting prospect of a polygamous household when her husband, a professor of mathematics much older than herself, announces his intention of taking a second wife. She decides to divorce him and later marries a doctor she meets on the boat to Alexandria.[27] Later, the war novels face the individual with the choice of leaving self and interest behind and joining the national will. Finally, the novels written after the establishment of the Republic deal with the problems of constructing a new society in a situation where traditions have been de-legitimised and each individual faces the issue of choice as an immediate and pressing personal dilemma.

These novels then set out the material personal processes the individual must navigate through to be able to become subjects able to fill the positions created by a rapidly changing social order. As argued by Hall, the process of constituting identities and subjectivities is a complicated one:

> I use 'identity' to refer to the meeting point, the point of *suture*, between on the one hand discourses and practices which attempt to 'interpellate', speak to us or hail us into place as the social subjects of particular discourses, and on the other hand, the processes which produce subjectivities, which constructs us as subjects which can be 'spoken'.
> (1996: 5–6, emphasis and quotation marks in the original)

I would therefore like to read Halide Edip's novels as providing instances of practices through which subjectivities are created.

They take as given those discourses that attempt to provide new subject positions for a 'modern' Turkish society. They then take these subject positions and place them in various situations, creating chains of cause and effect constitutive of the narrative. In other words, the novels represent ways of 'suturing the subject into structures of meaning' (Hall ibid.), painful processes that are undertaken by the subject herself. This attempt at simulating practice through the novel is perhaps what blurs the distinction between discourse and practice that Hall makes above. The novel, as almost-practice, allows the reader to experience the pain and suffering of the protagonists, thus becoming one of the (relatively safe) sites for the creation of both subject positions and subjectivities, as well as attributing meaning to lived experience.

Conclusion

The meaning of modernity is the basic question that most of the written texts of the early years of the Republic attempted to provide an answer to. I would like to read Halide Edip's novels as engaging the same question. The novels, I argue, provide us with quite a powerful map of the social imaginary constitutive of modernity in Turkey. The term 'imaginary' is used by Castoriadis (1987) to indicate a domain of signification that is necessary for the production of all meaning within a particular society. It is a central signification that provides the meaning of the world, the basic orientation of a society, somewhat akin to what anthropologists used to call 'world view'. But the imaginary is a much more dynamic concept in the sense that it describes a single but central aspect of the complex process through which meaning is produced and the world made sense of. The range of the various permutations and combinations of meanings that can be produced on the basis of this imaginary are enormous, but always circumscribed by practice, and constantly changing. It is possible to argue that for many of those post-colonial countries that created modernism through nationalism, modernity is itself a basic ingredient of the social imaginary. Halide Edip's novels are part and parcel of the process through which this new social imaginary was produced in Turkey.

The issue of the family has been a central focus of the new social imaginary in Turkey. Modernity in Turkey is conceived as being made up of a collectivity of nuclear families within which reign peace and serenity.[28] Relations between husband and wife, parents and children are supposed to be regulated according to love (*sevgi*), rather than the obedient respect of traditional Ottoman society. In fact, it is the construction of this imagined Ottoman world of the family, itself the product of numerous narratives, which serves as the basis for the production, through juxtaposition, of the new imaginary. According to this imaginary, the Ottoman family was the locus of strife and subordination, especially for women who were subjected to the double inhumanity of polygamy and repudiation. The modern Republic, by contrast, recognised women's rights within the family and made them (not so equal) members of the family.[29] The existence of the past in imaginary form serves to attribute to the present the task of signifying modernity. Halide Edip's novels trace the passing from traditional to modern in marriage and gender relations according to the basic structure of this imaginary. They moreover provide the modern subject with flesh, blood, sentiment and pain. Zeyno finally succeeds where Handan and all the other Ottoman heroines dismally fail.

And yet Handan remains a problem despite the fact that even Halide Edip dismisses her in her memoirs as being too sentimental. A hero or heroine in later novels remembers her, a woman on the street resembles her. All the later heroines have a bit of Handan in them, her eyes, her intellect, her taste in clothes. She becomes a spectre that women in modern Turkey have to remember to forget, to borrow the phrase used by Ernest Renan in relation to nationalism. Each of the heroines in the novels following *Handan* seem to start with one of Handan's problems solved, thus editing out piece by piece the painful process of the creation of new subjectivities.

I have argued that Handan represents what Butler calls the constitutive outside, the marginalised subject outside the domain of the representable which in Hall's words 'then returns to trouble and unsettles the foreclosures we now call "identities"' (1996: 15). Handan suffers from having excess desire which her mind is unable to curb. She is unable to reach a resolution of her problem, except through loss of self and memory or death. Through her death she takes her place among those Butler calls the abject, 'those who do not enjoy the status of subject, but whose living under the sign of "unlivable" and "uninhabitable" is required to circumscribe the domain of the subject' (1993: 3). While Butler elaborates her approach to the materiality of the body in the production of heterosexuality, I have extended her usage to include the sublimation of sexual desire for the collectivity, another definition of 'sex'. The consecutive reading of these novels shows the process through which abjection takes place. The desire which is recognised as being internal to the modern woman is slowly exteriorised, first because of social norms (as in *Handan*) and later because of excess masculinity (in the case of Hasan). While Zeyno suffers at the end of the first volume, the exteriorisation is complete in the sequel in the form of Kurdish Zeyno, the peasant woman who can now serve as the constitutive outside of modern Turkish female subjectivity.

But the death of Handan haunts the new women. Even Lale, the positive example of modern femininity in *Tatarcık,* is startled to see a woman who resembles Handan. Handan belies Halide Edip's efforts to construct the peasant woman as the modern Turkish woman's other. It is not Kurdish Zeyno but Handan, the woman who could not give up her desire and live, who, as constitutive outside is 'after all, "inside" the subject as its own founding repudiation' (Butler, ibid.). She is that which serves to remind modern Turkish women that sexuality, passion and desire, unless domesticated through love, cannot produce the woman-subject of the modern Turkish nation.

Notes

1 Associate Professor of Anthropology, Boğaziçi University. I owe the inspiration for this paper to Ayşe Saktanber who has shown me how powerful, constructive tools and destructive weapons narratives can be. I would therefore like to thank her once and for all. I would also like to thank Dicle Koğacıoğlu and Nazan Üstündağ for sharing my passion for Halide Edip's novels, for encouraging me to go on and for being my best critics and friends.

2 I would like to thank Hülya Demirdirek and Eduardo Archetti for making this volume available to me.

3 See Mardin (1966) for a classical analysis of Ottoman society as a patrimonial state, and the nationalist discourses that emerged with it as a response to what Anderson terms 'official nationalism'. Also see Sirman (1998) for an analysis of the house as a political rather than a familial domain in traditional Turkish society.

4 Especially in the early novels and plays, existing family arrangements were the main focus of attention. See Mardin (1974) and Parla (1993) and Sirman (in press) for different analyses of these novels in the context of modernisation, political change and nationalist discourses.

5 See Bruner 1986, Sommers and Gibson 1994 and Jackson 1993.

6 The War of Liberation in fact functions today in Turkey as a foundational myth which explains and validates relations between the collectivity and the individual as one of sacrifice on the part of the latter for the former. Peasant women are depicted here as making up the silent columns of ox-drawn carriages carrying ammunition to the front.

7 War, according to Edip, is the logical extension of masculinity, both as subjectivity and as practice. For Halide Edip the desire to dominate, or 'the will to power' is masculine in essence and in effect defines masculinity. Both the West, in its aggression towards Turkey, and Mustafa Kemal, in his relentless will to destroy his opponents, exhibit this trait.

8 In the book in question Edip depicts a political and national utopia where women have the vote and work outside the home, a society in which work and simplicity are the highest ideals, as she thinks they ought to be in a liberal and democratic political regime. She is among the few truly liberal nationalists of the period and puts the right of the individuals above all else. Although the 'common good' is also a troubled ideal, Edip cannot imagine a truly good society that would not guarantee freedom for the individual.

9 These include especially, *Seviye Talip* (1910*), Handan* (1912*) Yeni Turan* (1912), *Mev'ud Hüküm* (1917) and *Son Eseri* (1919). During the war, she wrote two novels, *Ateşten Gömlek* (1922) and *Vurun Kahpeye* (1923) where the heroines become the epic characters of the patriotic novel.

10 All quotations from the novels are my translations from the Turkish original.

11 The hero often becomes jealous, or capitulates to gossip and thus brings about the destruction of the heroine as well as any hope for his own happiness. In her later novels such as *Kalp Ağrısı* (1924), the tragic flaw in men is clearly defined as excess masculinity.

12 This difference can be summarised by using Chatterjee's distinction between the problematic and the thematic, where the first is a definition of what is wrong with the status quo and the latter provides the justificatory structures that enable the critique to be made and an alternative elaborated (Chatterjee 1986).

13 This is the figure of the oppressive father/ruler of the earlier novels authored by men.

14 Handan describes her need for her husband as the result of her love for him: 'This (her love) did not happen all by itself' she says in one of the letters she discards, 'I wanted it to be so and I made it so' (102).

15 Halide Edip is here opposing the use of female sexuality by male novelists to distinguish between good and bad, victim and demon. Her memoirs indicate that the main influence on her at this time is Emile Zola and his use of realism to study human nature and the conditions under which anyone can become victim or victimiser. Thus, she sees sexuality as part of human nature, both male and female, and tries to

work out how best it can be domesticated by both men and women to suit the needs of modern society.

16 Halide Edip's memoirs show the extent to which she was influenced by the quiet and serene world of the traditional Istanbul quarter where her grandmother and her nanny lived. Rather than following the teachings of a particular Sufi order, she borrows a spiritual notion of the person inherent in these views and tries to make it the grounding of a humanistic, secular morality. It is only on the basis of such a construct that rationality and spirituality, West and East can be in harmony in the modern world.

17 This book, like the memoirs, was written first in English and subsequently published as *Sinekli Bakkal* (1936).

18 This is the sultan who was dethroned by the Young Turks in 1908 in what was then known as the 'Turkish Revolution for liberty' *(hürriyet inkilabı)*.

19 In an oral history project undertaken by the Social and Economic Foundation in Istanbul, one respondent, architect Mehmet Fazıl Aysu who had been charged with the building of a large sports and conference complex in Istanbul in the 1940s, describes the house and *mahalle* of his youth in terms of a stable and just order in which everyone knew who their superiors were. Respect and hierarchy are the key terms of this rather striking rendering of what can be called the imaginary of the traditional. I would like to thank Orhan Silier of the foundation for allowing me to make use of these records.

20 Tatarcık is the nickname of the heroine, Lale. Even her name is a modern, Republican name, meaning tulip. She is well educated, a good swimmer and from the beginning of the novel has already made up her mind about the meaning of modernity: hard work for the good of the collectivity.

21 This choice is offered in contradistinction to those of other young men who are drawn by the (false) glitter of Istanbul life. This resolution comes at a time when the Ministry of Education launched its 'Village Institutes' project that would undertake the modernisation of Turkey starting from villages. Young villagers would be trained in teacher training schools situated in a few villages in the countryside and would then become enlightened teachers/modernisers in other villages, thus avoiding the false modernity of the big city. For a description of the sentiments of one such village teacher, see Makal (1954).

22 This is in accordance with the goals of the young Turkish Republic which by 1924 had written a new Constitution declaring the equality of all its citizens regardless of race, creed, sex and colour.

23 The marriage had taken place in the first novel while Hasan and his wife were in Austria. Hasan had heard of it through the letters Zeyno wrote to his wife, or from her entries in a journal.

24 Although Zeyno, like Handan, does not have children and although this causes her enormous pain, she fulfills her desire by adopting Hasan's daughter from his marriage to her friend. Childlessness is not the stuff of drama any more as it was for Handan.

25 This interview carried out by Semra Somersan was undertaken as part of the oral history project of the Social and Economic History Foundation referred to earlier in footnote 19. The aim of the project was to collect the life stories of masons and architects, the builders of the nation. Mualla Eyüboğlu is an architect who is known for various grand-scale projects, including the restoration of Topkapı Palace. She was also one of the teachers at the first teacher training college established in the village of Hasanoğlan near Ankara under the aegis of the Village Institutes project

26 Emancipation in this phrase refers to the legal equality that women were granted after the Republican reforms in the first half of the 1920s. The persistence of the force of socio-cultural traditions accounts for the fact that real liberation cannot be easily realised. While Toprak sees Islamic traditions that define women as subordinate to men as constituting the main source of these traditions, Kandiyoti identifies the practices of gender segregation in producing dependent female consciousness and sexuality. Edip, by contrast, complicates matters by implicating women themselves in the production of gendered subjects in the process of major social transformation.

27 This is Adnan Adıvar, medical doctor and student of the philosophy of science with whom she spends the rest of her life. Her two sons are from her first marriage.

28 Alan Duben (1982) has criticised interpretations made by Turkish social scientists of statistical data regarding household size and composition for different sections of urban Turkey. He argues that the high incidence of families of small size among rural migrants to large cities is underplayed by attributing undue attention to the presence within the household of the parental generation of the main conjugal unit, while the relatively larger size of old urban families, and the multiplicity of ties of dependency that exist between kin who are residentially separate, are ignored in many analyses which start from the basic premise that urban is modern and modern, nuclear, and thus often equated with family size.

29 The Turkish Civil Code still states that the husband is the head of the family and that the wife is his helper and advisor. The present government has now placed a new bill before parliament according to which husband and wife are defined as partners.

Bibliography

Adıvar, H.E. (1979) *Handan*, Istanbul: Atlas, 10th edition (first published in 1912).

—— (1993) *Kalp Ağrisi*, Istanbul: Remzi Kitabevi, 7th edition (first published in 1924).

—— (1996) *Zeyno'nun Oğlu*, Istanbul: Remzi Kitabevi, 7th edition (first published in 1924).

—— (1926) *Memoirs of Halidé Edib*, London: John Murray.

———— (1996) *Sinekli Bakkal*, Istanbul: Atlas, 46th edition (first published in 1936).

———— (1943) *Tatarcık*, Istanbul: Muallim Ahmet Halit Yayinevi, 5th edition (first published in 1939).

Anderson, B. (1983) *Imagined Communities*, London: Verso.

Archetti, E. (ed.) (1994) *Exploring the Written. Anthropology and the Multiplicity of Writing*, Oslo: Scandinavian University Press.

Bruner, J. (1991) 'The narrative construction of reality', *Critical Inquiry*, Autumn: 1–21.

Butler, J. (1993) *Bodies that Matter. On the Discursive Limits of 'Sex'*, London and New York: Routledge.

Castoriadis, C. (1987) *The Imaginary Institution of Society*, Cambridge: Polity Press.

Chatterjee, P. (1986) *Nationalist Thought and the Colonial World. A Derivative Discourse?*, London: Zed Press.

Duben, A. (1983) 'The significance of family and kinship in urban Turkey', in Ç. Kağıtçıbaşı (ed.) *Sex Roles, Family and Community in Turkey*, Indiana: Indiana University Press.

Dubetsky, A. (1971) 'Class and community in urban Turkey,' in Van Nieuwenhuijze (ed.) *Commoners, Climbers and Notables*, Leiden: Brill.

Enginün, I. (1986) *Halide Edip Adıvar*, Ankara: Kültür ve Turizm Bakanligi yayınları.

Erol, S. (1992) 'Güntekin's *Çalikuşu*, a search for personal and national identity', *Turkish Studies Association Bulletin*: 65–82.

Hall, S. (1996) 'Introduction: Who needs cultural identity?' in S. Hall and P. Du Gay (eds) *Questions of Cultural Identity*, London: Sage.

Jackson, S. (1993) '"Even sociologists fall in love": an exploration in the sociology of emotions', *Sociology* 27, 2: 201–20.

Kandiyoti, D. (1987) 'Emancipated but unliberated? Reflections on the Turkish case', *Feminist Studies* 13, 2: 317–38.

———— (1988) 'Slave girls, temptresses, and comrades: images of women in the Turkish novel', *Feminist Studies*, Spring: 35–50.

Makal, M. (1954) *A Village in Anatolia*, London: Vallentine Mitchell (first published as *Bizim Köy*, Istanbul: Varlık yayınları, 1950).

Mardin, Ş. (1966) *The Genesis of Young Ottoman Thought*, Princeton: Princeton University Press.

———— (1989) *Religion and Social Change in Modern Turkey. The Case of Bediüzzaman Said-i Nursi*, Albany, NY: State University of New York Press.

———— (1974) 'Superwesternization in urban life in the Ottoman Empire in the last quarter of the nineteenth century', in P. Benedict and E. Tümertekin (eds) *Turkey: Geographical and Social Perspectives*, Leiden: Brill.

———— (1996) *The Genesis of Young Ottoman Thought*, Princeton: Princeton University Press.

Messick, B. (1993) *The Calligraphic State. Textual Domination and History in a Muslim Society*, Berkeley, CA.: University of California Press.

Moran, B. (1983) *Türk Romanına Eleştirel Bir Bakış*, Istanbul: Iletişim, Vol. 1.

Parla, J. (1993) *Babalar ve Oğullar, Tanzimat Romanının Epistemolojik Temelleri*, Istanbul: Iletişim, 2nd edition.

Sirman, N. (in press) 'Gender construction and nationalist discourse: dethroning the father in the early Turkish novel', in F. Acar and A. Güneş-Ayata (eds) *Gender and Identity Construction*, Leiden: Brill.

—— (1998) 'Nous vivons pour notre honneur', *Hommes et Migrations*, mars–avril 1212: 53–61.

Somers, M.R. and Gibson, G.D. (1994) 'Reclaiming the epistemological "other": narrative and the social constitution of identity', in Calhoun, C. (ed.) *Social Theory and the Politics of Identity*, Cambridge, Mass: Blackwell.

Sommer, D. (1990) 'Love and country in Latin America: an allegorical speculation', *Cultural Critique*, Fall: 109–28.

Toprak, B. (1990) 'Emancipated but unliberated women in Turkey: The impact of Islam', in F. Özbay (ed.) *Women, Family and Social Change in Turkey*, Bangkok: UNESCO.

Index